Guillaume de Machaut

THE COMPLETE POETRY & MUSIC

VOLUME 9

THE MOTETS

The Middle English Texts Series is designed for classroom use. Its goal is to make available to teachers, scholars, and students texts that occupy an important place in the literary and cultural canon but have not been readily available in student editions. The series does not include those authors, such as Chaucer, Langland, or Malory, whose English works are normally in print in good student editions. The focus is, instead, upon Middle English literature adjacent to those authors that teachers need in compiling the syllabuses they wish to teach. The editions maintain the linguistic integrity of the original work but within the parameters of modern reading conventions. The texts are printed in the modern alphabet and follow the practices of modern capitalization, word formation, and punctuation. Manuscript abbreviations are silently expanded, and u/v and j/i spellings are regularized according to modern orthography. Yogh (ȝ) is transcribed as g, gh, y, or s, according to the sound in Modern English spelling to which it corresponds; thorn (þ) and eth (ð) are transcribed as th. Distinction between the second person pronoun and the definite article is made by spelling the one thee and the other the, and final -e that receives full syllabic value is accented (e.g., charité). Hard words, difficult phrases, and unusual idioms are glossed either in the right margin or at the foot of the page. Explanatory and textual notes appear at the end of the text, often along with a glossary. The editions include short introductions on the history of the work, its merits and points of topical interest, and brief working bibliographies.

Medieval Institute Publications is a program of
The Medieval Institute, College of Arts and Sciences

WESTERN MICHIGAN UNIVERSITY

Guillaume de Machaut

THE COMPLETE POETRY & MUSIC

R. Barton Palmer and Yolanda Plumley
General Editors

VOLUME 9: THE MOTETS

Edited by Jacques Boogaart,
translated by R. Barton Palmer and Jacques Boogaart,
with art historical commentary by Domenic Leo

TEAMS • Middle English Text Series • University of Rochester

MEDIEVAL INSTITUTE PUBLICATIONS
Western Michigan University
Kalamazoo

Copyright © 2018 by the Board of Trustees of Western Michigan University

Manufactured in the United States of America

**Library of Congress Cataloguing-in-Publication Data
are available from the Library of Congress.**

ISBN (paperback) 9781580442879
ISBN (hardback) 9781580443029

Printed and bound by CPI Group (UK) Ltd, Croydon, CR0 4YY

Guillaume de Machaut

THE COMPLETE POETRY & MUSIC

R. Barton Palmer and Yolanda Plumley
General Editors

GUILLAUME DE MACHAUT: THE COMPLETE POETRY & MUSIC

Contents

❧ ACKNOWLEDGMENTS

A project of this scope would have been impossible without institutional support and, even more import-ant, substantial assistance from colleagues. Barton Palmer and Yolanda Plumley, the co-editors of Guillaume de Machaut: The Complete Poetry and Music, have been exceptionally fortunate in this regard. Key parts of the editing process have been supported by a generous grant from the Leverhulme Trust, for which Plumley has been the principal investigator (as part of a larger project entitled The Works of Guillaume de Machaut: Music, Image, and Text in the Middle Ages (see http://machaut.exeter.ac.uk), while Palmer's participation, including released time from teaching and travel expenses, has been supported by the Calhoun Lemon Endowment and the College of Art, Architecture, and the Humanities at Clemson University, whose dean, Rick Goodstein, deserves special thanks. The digitizing of previously published material, as well as the preparation of both front and back matter for certain of the volumes, has been handled with dispatch, energy, and expertise by TEAMS: Teaching Association for Medieval Studies and the Middle English Text Series (METS), working in concert with Medieval Institute Publications (MIP). Their work is supported by a continuing grant from the NEH, and we are most appreciative of what that funding has made available to us. We are grateful as well for the wise counsel and enthusiastic support we have received from Russell A. Peck, general editor of METS, and Martha M. Johnson-Olin, the assistant editor. Staff editors at METS have worked tirelessly and patiently on the several demanding tasks associated with the project; we owe a substantial debt to those editors, past and present: Leah Haught, Katie Van Wert, Alison Harper and Laura Whitebell.

The staff at MIP and the press' editorial board have been helpful, patient, and flexible, especially in meeting the needs of an edition devoted to both verse and music, whose representation on the page is so very different. Special thanks go to Tyler Cloherty, Kathy Bond Borie and Tom Krol. Warm thanks go to all those who have helped with the various aspects of the present volume, especially to Eddie Vetter, Eric Jas, and Bernhard Ridderbos for their critical remarks and corrections, to Lawrence Earp for his wise advice, and of course to the other members of the editorial team who have meticulously checked texts and scores: Yolanda Plumley, R. Barton Palmer, Anne Stone, Uri Smilansky, and Tamsyn Mahoney-Steel. Our collaboration with the Orlando Consort, which is presently recording the complete polyphonic songs and selected motets by Machaut from our edition with Hyperion Records, has been an invaluable help to test our editorial ideas in practice. We thank the Consort for their critical and stimulating remarks that have greatly contributed to make our edition "performer-friendly."

❦ Preface

Guillaume de Machaut is the sole medieval poet and composer whose impressive oeuvre has, miraculously, been preserved in what we presume to be its entirety. Although editions of his poetry and music have appeared from the nineteenth century onward, this is the first time the poet-composer's entire output is edited by a cross-disciplinary team of experts in an integrated editorial campaign that embraces all the literary and musical works, as well as the art- historical commentary on the accompanying miniatures found in the medieval manuscripts.

This volume is devoted to the master's oldest achievements in the field of polyphony, the 23 motets. These form the largest surviving corpus of such works by a single composer from this period. Earlier editions appeared in 1929 and 1956. Our edition is based on one of the most authoritative sources, manuscript *Paris, Bibliothèque nationale de France, fonds français 1584*. It aims to serve both scholars and performers, ranging from professionals to newcomers to Machaut's work.

Performers are presented with a clear and easily readable score, with full English translations of the French and Latin texts. A mini-guide for the pronunciation of Middle French is provided at the end of the introduction. Suggestions for "musica ficta" (accidentals) are indicated in the score, with details provided of what is specified in the various sources; guidance is thus provided to performers, who can also choose different solutions according to the different manuscript versions or to their own tastes. Technical information and details of manuscript variants are given in the commentary to each piece at the end of the volume. In order not to overload with information we have refrained from providing a glossary for all the musical technical terms. The most specific terms are explained in the Introduction, particularly in the chapter on editorial policy. Most of the terminology for medieval music can be readily found online (for instance, see: <http://the-orb.arlima.net/encyclop/culture/music/orbgloss.htm>). For further reference the reader is advised to consult *The New Grove Dictionary of Music and Musicians*.

Scholars are here offered a score in which the structure of the motets and the formal ideas of the composer are laid out as clearly as is possible when "translating" this music of very different notational conception into modern notation. The Introduction synthesizes existing knowledge about the motets with new insights. Detailed commentaries, including tenor sources, analytical information, variants for each piece, and relevant bibliography are found at the end of the volume. An interpretation of the miniature that illustrates the motets in the base manuscript, by art-historian Domenic Leo and Jacques Boogaart, follows the Introduction.

Most of the manuscript originals that contain these works can be freely consulted on the website <gallica.bnf.fr> of the Bibliothèque nationale de France, which possesses five of the complete-works manuscripts; all can be viewed in excellent digital color images. A magnificent facsimile edition with an extensive introduction and commentary by various specialists is now available for the only complete-works manuscript not in Paris, the Ferrell-Vogüé manuscript, which is in private ownership (see Bibliography). This codex can also be viewed on the website of the Digital Image Archive of Medieval Music (DIAMM): <http://www.diamm.ac.uk>.

Additional information concerning the present edition project, including alternative versions for certain works, a complete bibliography, together with updates, supplementary materials, and resources, can be found on the website of The Works of Guillaume de Machaut: Music, Image, Text in the Middle Ages, at: <http://machaut.exeter.ac.uk>.

INTRODUCTION

Thanks to his outstanding poetic and musical craftsmanship, Guillaume de Machaut rose to great fame during his long life (c.1300–1377). In Gilles Li Muisis' *Méditations*, written around 1350, he heads the rank of French poet-musicians, mentioned even before his contemporaries Philippe de Vitry and Jehan de Le Mote:

Or sont vivant biaus dis faisant	Today makers of beautiful tales are living
Qui ne s'en vont mie taisant,	Who in no way keep silent,
C'est de Machau le boin Willaume,	There is the good Guillaume de Machaut,
Si fait redolent si que baume.	His works are fragrant like balsam.[1]

Eustache Deschamps, poet and pupil of Machaut, attested to his master's celebrity with the nobility abroad when he delivered a copy and read parts of Machaut's latest creation, *Le Livre dou Voir Dit* at the court of Flanders.[2] And at Machaut's death Deschamps paid his respects to the master in a set of two ballades with a common refrain calling all to mourn *La mort Machaut, le noble rhetorique* (the death of Machaut, the noble rhetorician);[3] the texts were set to music as a *ballade double* by the composer F. Andrieu.[4] The first ballade lauds his courtliness and his songs:

Onques d'amours ne parla en folie,	He never spoke foolishly about love,
Ains a esté en tous ses dis courtois,	Rather he has been courtly in all his tales,
Aussi a moult pleu sa chanterie	And also his songs have much pleased
Aux grans seigneurs, a Dames	Great lords, ladies, and burghers.
[et bourgois.	

---

[1] Gilles li Muisis, *Poésies*, pp. 88–89. Unless otherwise indicated, translations are mine.

[2] Deschamps relates in ballade-form how he transmitted a copy of *Le Livre dou Voir Dit* to Count Louis de Male of Flanders and was asked to recite passages from it, to the great pleasure and admiration of all the present lords (Ballade 127 in *Œuvres*, I, pp. 248–49). The date of this event is uncertain; both 1369 and 1375 have been proposed. For a recent discussion and further references see Coleman, "The Text Recontextualized," pp. 233–48, about the dates, especially note 12.

[3] Ballades 123 and 124 in *Œuvres*, I, pp. 243–46. About this *ballade double*, see Leach, *Machaut: Secretary*, pp. 306–12 and Plumley, *Art of Grafted Song*, p. 416. In yet another ballade (no. 447, *Œuvres*, III, pp. 259–60), Deschamps praises Machaut as "Plus qu'Ovide vray remede d'amours" ("More than Ovid a true cure in love").

[4] In manuscript *Chantilly 564*, fol. 52r, with a number of textual variants; ed. in Ludwig, *Machaut Werke*, I, pp. 49–51 and *Polyphonic Music of the Fourteenth Century*, XIX, pp. 114–16. In the musical setting the texts are declaimed simultaneously.

The second ballade addresses Machaut in person, praising him as the *fleur des fleurs de toute melodie* (flower of flowers of all melody), and as the *mondains dieus d'armonie* (earthly god of harmony) whose death is to be deplored by all *faiseurs* (makers, composers) of poetry and music.

Both authors confirm Machaut's renown as a poet and composer, in France and abroad.[5] Manuscripts devoted to his works remained for a long time a sought-after luxury commodity, as shown by the peregrinations of the surviving books to courts in France, Aragon, Flanders and, possibly, England.[6] For some decades after his death his songs were remembered and cited in other chansons, in France as well as in its neighboring countries. However, although Machaut's name as a composer lingered in music-theoretical writings, his music gradually faded into obscurity. His poetic renown and influence lasted longer, until well into the fifteenth century. King René d'Anjou was one of the last to honor him, as both poet and composer, in his *Livre du Cœur d'amours épris* (1457), where he evoked Machaut's imaginary tomb amidst those of five other famous poets in the cemetery of unhappy lovers, at the *Ospital d'Amours*.[7] It was "[...] made wholly of fine silver and all around were inscriptions in blue, green and violet enamel, and incised were well-notated chansons, also virelais, serventoys, lays and motets, made and composed in various ways [...]."[8] On its epitaph Machaut is speaking in person, as the lover from *Le Livre dou Voir Dit*: "Guillaume de Machault, that was my name. I was born in Champagne and acquired great fame for being enflamed by loving thoughts for the love of one [lady], in truth, so much so that never in my life was I happy unless I could see her [...]."[9]

After a long period of oblivion Machaut's name resurfaced in the late eighteenth and early nineteenth centuries, primarily as a composer.[10] At the beginning of the twentieth century his musical compositions became accessible in an accurate edition (starting with the motets and chansons) thanks to the work of Friedrich Ludwig; since then they have enjoyed an ever-increasing popularity. In the mid-twentieth century Ludwig's work (completed posthumously by Heinrich Besseler with the lays and the Mass) was succeeded by Leo Schrade's less meticulous but more accessible complete edition. Machaut's poetical works, although for the greater part also made available in careful editions from the early twentieth century on, have taken longer to become appreciated; only in the last few decades have their subtle design and original ideas been more fully discovered. Now, after a century of scholarly discussions and burgeoning analytical insights, not least with regard to the complex interaction between Machaut's poetic and musical art, a fresh edition of his complete poetical and musical works seems well justified.

LIFE OF THE AUTHOR

Notwithstanding Machaut's renown in his own day, little is known for certain about his life. A few dry facts about his social career can be gleaned from ecclesiastical documents; more personal and intimate details are provided

---

[5] About Machaut's (posthumous) reputation in France and its surrounding countries, and his "afterlife" in the works of other, especially Italian, composers, see Earp, *Guillaume de Machaut*, pp. 53–69; Leach, *Machaut: Secretary*, pp. 301–25; Plumley, *Art of Grafted Song*, pp. 416–22; and Earp, "Introductory Study" to the *Ferrell-Vogüé Machaut Manuscript*, pp. 40–43.

[6] About the vicissitudes of the manuscripts see especially Earp, *Guillaume de Machaut*, pp. 77–97, and id., "Introductory Study" to the *Ferrell-Vogüé Machaut Manuscript*, I, pp. 28–80.

[7] René d'Anjou, *Le Livre du Cœur d'amour épris*, p. 258 (the translations are my own). The six tombs of poets are, in order, those of Ovid, Machaut, Boccaccio, Jean de Meun, Petrarch, and Alain Chartier.

[8] "[...] elle fust d'argent fin toute faicte, et a l'entour escripte d'esmail bleu, vert et violet, et ensise a chanczons bien notees, a virelaiz aussi, a servantoys, a laiz et a motetz, en diverses faczons faictes et composees [...]."

[9] "Guillaume de Machault, ainsy avoye nom. / Né en Champaigne fuz, et si euz grant renom / D'estre fort embrazé du penser amoureux / Pour l'amour d'une, voir, dont pas ne fuz eureux / Ma vie seulement tant que la peüsse voir [...]." On this passage see especially Cerquiglini, "*Un engin si soutil*," pp. 239–43.

[10] For an overview of nineteenth-century historiographic studies, see Earp, *Guillaume de Machaut*, pp. 195 ff. and 277 ff.; id., "Machaut's Music in the Early Nineteenth Century."

by the author himself, scattered throughout his narrative works, but the problem with this type of information is that we cannot know where factual data ends and poetic fiction begins.[11]

Machaut was born around 1300 in the region of Champagne, in Reims or its near vicinity, possibly in the village of Machault. Although he would in the future rub shoulders with the highest nobility, he typically portrayed himself in his narrative poetry as a humble clerk. Various sources — though none by Machaut himself — refer to him as *magister* or *maistre*. The erudition displayed in his works suggests that, after an early education, quite probably at the cathedral school in Reims, Machaut had indeed pursued studies at a university, most likely in Paris. Whether he obtained the title of master of arts or left earlier, as often happened, is not known; the title *magister* may also simply be a testimony to the respect he had earned.[12] In Paris he must have come into contact with such outstanding music-theorists as Philippe de Vitry and Johannes de Muris. Machaut's music shows clear traces of Vitry's influence and is entirely in line with De Muris' theoretical treatises, in which he is the only composer to be mentioned by name, as one of several *cantores* (singers, professional musicians) who take notational liberties.[13] Although he may also have followed courses in theology, Machaut apparently never took higher orders than that of subdeacon.[14]

While in his early twenties (perhaps even earlier) Machaut entered the service of the most illustrious noble from the neighboring Ardennes region: John (Jehan), count of Luxembourg and king of Bohemia, who was a steadfast friend and ally of the French royal house.[15] During his long years of service, Machaut climbed up through various administrative posts, as almoner, notary, and finally as the king's personal secretary. One of his obligations may have been to read for his lord;[16] in this way Machaut could have acquired the fabulous literary knowledge betrayed by the countless quotations in his works. John's prodigality (admittedly at the cost of his grumbling Bohemian subjects), his bravery on the battlefield, and his courtly refinement made him the epitome of a noble ruler in this time of decline of the aristocracy and its chivalrous ideals; until the end of his life Machaut continued to write in the most laudatory terms about John of Luxembourg. According to his own reports he traveled widely in the king of Bohemia's company during John's frequent military campaigns in northeastern Europe and Italy. From about 1331, however, it is not clear whether he continued to follow the king in this adventurous lifestyle or settled into a more independent and sedentary existence; perhaps by then he already had entered the service of John's daughter Bonne. Officially, Machaut remained in royal service until John's famously heroic death on the battlefield of Crécy in 1346. About the king's blindness, his misadventures,

[11] For a critical view of the value of such data, see Leach, *Machaut: Secretary*, pp. 26–33. Gradually more glimpses into reality appear in the narrative works, beginning with the introduction to the *Jugement dou Roy de Navarre*, an evocation of the horrors of the Black Death. One of Machaut's last works, *La Prise d'Alixandre*, is a historical chronicle. The *Voir Dit* is particularly rich in personal detail, although the extent of its veracity remains an unresolved issue. For the documentation on Machaut's life see Earp, *Guillaume de Machaut*, pp. 3–51, Bowers, "Machaut and His Canonry of Reims," and Leach, *Machaut: Secretary*, pp. 9–25.

[12] About education at the medieval university, see Schwinges, "Student Education, Student Life"; about the importance of Paris with respect to music, see North, "The Quadrivium," pp. 343–44. A depiction of Machaut as a *magister artium* teaching a small circle of students is shown in a miniature in manuscript *F* (Paris, BnF, fr. 22545), fol. 40r; it illustrates the opening sentence of *Remede de Fortune*: "Cils qui vuet aucun art aprendre / A .xii. choses doit entendre" ("He who wishes to learn any art / has to take heed of twelve things"); an almost identical miniature appears at the opening of the *Dit de l'Alerion* at fol. 75v.

[13] See De Muris' *Ars practica mensurabilis cantus*, p. 25. Since this treatise was copied until well into the sixteenth century, Machaut's name as a composer survived with it.

[14] See Bowers, "Guillaume de Machaut and His Canonry of Reims," p. 6.

[15] He is also known as Jehan l'Aveugle since in his later years he was struck with blindness. According to Machaut's *Prise d'Alixandre* (l. 785) he had served John for more than 30 years, but other documents point to a shorter period. Earp suggests that John may have paid for Machaut's study, which would explain the thirty-year period; see Earp, *Guillaume de Machaut*, p. 12. About John's own, his son Charles', and his daughter Bonne's patronage, see especially Wilkins, "A Pattern of Patronage."

[16] Reading apparently belonged to the tasks of a secretary; the *Jugement dou Roy de Behaingne* refers to an unnamed clerk (but presumably Machaut himself) who reads for the king the *Battle of Troy* (ll. 1474–75: "Et ot .i. clerc que nommer ne saroie / Qui li lisoit la bataille de Troie."). See also Earp, *Guillaume de Machaut*, p. 9.

and his last years, including this glorious final battle, Machaut is strangely silent (John's death is recounted by Machaut's younger contemporary, Froissart, in his *Chroniques*).[17]

During his time as secretary to John of Luxembourg, Machaut wrote several *dits* (narrative poems), the most popular being the *Jugement dou Roy de Behaingne*, in which the king figures as the arbiter of a love debate.[18] He also produced a considerable number of lyrical poems and musical compositions; among these were surely some monophonic lays and chansons, and the majority of the motets, which probably represent his earliest polyphonic exploits.

From papal documents it appears that, due to John of Luxembourg's intercession with the pope, Machaut received various ecclesiastical benefices in expectancy, two of which were eventually realized, a canonicate in Reims and one in Saint-Quentin, which carried no obligation of residency. These benefices secured him a regular income, but at the same time he continued to enjoy the protection of the high nobility.

According to his own statement, after John's death Machaut served the king's daughter Bonne, who was married to the future king of France, John II the Good (Jehan le Bon). He seems to have been very attached to her, as various of his writings attest; unfortunately Bonne's premature death from the plague in 1349 put an untimely end to this patronage. What his service to her involved is not known: Machaut may have been associated with the couple's court at Vincennes in Normandy, of which John, as the dauphin, was duke. Lawrence Earp suggests that many virelais and lays may have been written for this court, as well as a number of the new-style polyphonic ballades and rondeaux.[19] The earliest complete-works codex to survive contains a series of 34 outstanding illuminations for the *Remede de Fortune*, Machaut's first pseudo-autobiographical love story, which also features seven exemplary musical compositions. Bonne probably commissioned this manuscript; it is tantalizing to speculate that she might be embodied in the adored lady in the *Remede*.[20] The work with which the codex ends, the subtle and tender rondeau-motet *Trop plus est bele que biauté / Biauté paree de valour / Je ne sui mie certeins d'avoir amie, mais je sui loiaus amis* (M20), seems to have been dedicated to her: the triplum text emphasizes the words "bonne" and "bonté" and the work is a promise of faithful love-service, ending on a double "Amen."[21]

In the eventful years after Bonne's death, Machaut won the protection of her son-in-law Charles of Navarre, who figures as the king and arbiter in his second great debate poem, the *Jugement dou Roy de Navarre*.[22] Unfortunately, this prince became a tenacious opponent of Bonne's consort John II, who in 1350 was crowned as king of France and whose right to the throne Charles disputed. Exasperated after a number of rebellious acts, King John finally had Charles imprisoned; on this occasion Machaut wrote for Charles a consoling narrative poem in the style of a *Miroir des princes* (an ethical guide for princes), *Le Confort d'Ami*. Sometime in the 1350s, however, he distanced himself from the by now apparently inopportune Navarrese protection.

Later patrons were three sons of Bonne and John II: the future King Charles V, who even visited Machaut in his house, and his brothers Philip the Bold (Philippe le Hardi) and John of Berry (Jehan de Berry). For this last prince Machaut composed his *Dit de la Fonteinne Amoureuse*. All three possessed manuscripts with Machaut's

---

[17] Froissart, *Chroniques, Premier livre*, pp. 578–80. Froissart was nine or ten years old at the time of the battle of Crécy, so he must have obtained his information from accounts by others. It is unknown why Machaut kept silent on John's heroic death while relating in full detail the ignominious murder of his other chivalrous hero, Pierre de Lusignan, in his *Prise d'Alixandre*.

[18] Edited in Volume 1, *The Debate Poems*, of the present complete works edition.

[19] Earp, "Genre in the Fourteenth-Century French Chanson," pp. 123–41.

[20] See Wimsatt and Kibler, eds, *Jugement Behaigne & Remede*, pp. 34–35.

[21] However, it was probably not written as a "memorial benediction" at the occasion of her death in 1349 — as was once suggested but later retracted by Earp — since the customary rhetorical references to death are completely lacking in the texts of the motet. See Earp, *Guillaume de Machaut*, p. 25 and id., "Introductory Study," p. 31n17.

[22] This *dit* was probably originally written at the instigation of Bonne of Luxembourg, but at her death re-dedicated to Charles of Navarre.

poetical and musical works (in the case of the bibliophile king Charles V, this is not securely documented but highly likely).[23]

At the end of the 1350s at the latest,[24] but possibly earlier, Machaut settled definitively in Reims, living with his brother Jehan in a spacious house near the cathedral.[25] His last three motets reflect the dark political situation around 1358–1360 when, during King John II's captivity in England, France was in political turmoil and Reims was besieged by the English. During the 1360s, Machaut wrote his most adventurous literary works, the (pseudo- autobiographical) *Livre dou Voir Dit*, which features eight musical compositions, and — as a unique genre in his œuvre — the chronicle *La Prise d'Alixandre*. In the domain of music he composed a number of grand polyphonic chansons and his famous *Messe de Nostre Dame* (perhaps destined for his brother's and his own commemoration).[26] From about 1350 until the end of his life, he took care to have his works copied into beautiful manuscripts at the command of his noble patrons and, around 1370, he provided his œuvre with a prologue in which he formulated his artistic creed. Conspicuous in the *Prologue* is an emphasis on the role of music in his conception of artistic creativity.[27] Machaut died in April 1377 and was buried in Reims cathedral, side by side with his brother.

ARTISTIC ACHIEVEMENT: THE MOTETS

Machaut's musical œuvre is by far the best-preserved collection of works by a single composer from the late Middle Ages. In the majority of the six extant complete-works manuscripts the musical compositions follow the literary works and are classified according to genre.[28] The successive codices present a growing œuvre that in its most extended form comprises c. 143 compositions.[29] It consists of 19 lays, 23 motets, a six-movement Mass and a textless hocket, 42 ballades, 22 rondeaus, 33 virelais, a chanson royal, and a complainte. All the customary musical genres of Machaut's time are represented, with the addition of a few generically unique compositions. The works range from monody to four-part settings, from very short to impressively long,[30] and from apparent simplicity to great complexity and subtlety. Machaut seems to have exercised strict control over the copying of his compositions, which may have impeded their wider diffusion.[31] A few of his songs and one

---

[23] It seems that Charles V possessed at some time the early manuscript *C* (probably written at his mother Bonne of Luxembourg's command), although it is not listed in the later inventories of the royal library; see Earp, "Introductory Study," p. 31n20. Two manuscripts, *Vg* and *E*, were in the possession of John of Berry (for some time only as regards *Vg*; he gave it to Gaston de Foix before the end of 1388), and contain only works by Machaut, although *E* was not an authorially controlled copy like the other complete works-codices; see Earp, "Introductory Study," Chapter 2. In addition to manuscript *Tremoïlle*, of which now only a fragment survives but which once contained works by Machaut and other composers, the library of Philip the Bold and Marguerite of Flanders probably held a manuscript similar to *E* but in two volumes; see De Winter, *Bibliothèque de Philippe le Hardi*, pp. 124 and 156–57, and Earp, *Guillaume de Machaut*, pp. 94 and 102. For a description of the manuscripts, see note 28 and the Editorial Policy, below.

[24] See Bowers, "Machaut's Canonry of Reims."

[25] See Brejon de la Vergnée, "Note sur la maison."

[26] For a summary of the discussions on this subject see Leach, *Machaut: Secretary*, pp. 274–79.

[27] For an analysis of the prologue see Cerquiglini, "*Un engin si soutil*," pp. 15–21 and Leach, *Machaut: Secretary*, pp. 87–103.

[28] These manuscripts, with their sigla, are in chronological order: *C* (Paris, BnF, fr. 1586), *Vg* (private ownership of James E. and Elizabeth J. Ferrell), *B* (Paris, BnF, fr. 1585), *A* (Paris, BnF, fr. 1584), *F-G* (Paris, BnF, fr. 22545-22546), and *E* (Paris, BnF, fr. 9221). Further detail is given under Editorial Policy. For a complete survey of all the manuscripts containing works by Machaut, see Earp, *Guillaume de Machaut*, pp. 77–128.

[29] A few works exclusively found in *E* have doubtful attributions, hence c. 143 musical works.

[30] The performance of a lay may take twenty minutes; a full performance of the Complainte from the *Remede de Fortune* (36 stanzas) might last more than an hour.

[31] In the *Voir Dit* Machaut writes to his beloved that he is not accustomed to let a composition circulate before he has heard it himself. (*Voir Dit*, Lettre 33, ed. Leech-Wilkinson and Palmer, pp. 430–31; ed. Imbs and Cerquiglini, pp. 558–59).

motet nevertheless became very popular and are found in many sources, though usually without the author's name. As Earp rightly states: "Without the large complete-works manuscripts of Machaut, we could guess little of his importance as a musician."[32]

Evidence of Machaut's musical activities and renown comes from literary praises (see above), from the rare ascriptions of works to his hand,[33] from borrowings and imitations in later songs, and from the appearance of his name in two musicians' motets, *Apollinis eclipsatur / Zodiacum signis / In omnem terram* and *Musicalis sciencia / Sciencie laudabili / Tenor*. Here he is listed in the illustrious company of, respectively, twelve and twenty composers, among whom figure Johannes de Muris and Philippe de Vitry (in both motets). Although the second work is a critique of certain musical practices,[34] Machaut's presence nevertheless attests to the respect he had won. The lists even suggest that the named composers formed a circle of musician-friends who gathered to perform and listen to each other's motets, probably in Paris. Friendly meetings of "*litterati* and those who look for the refinement of skills" (presumably competent singers and poet-composers) as the scene for the performance of motets were already described by Johannes de Grocheio around 1300 (or earlier) and might be considered as a clerical counterpart of the so-called *puys*, the public poetical contests that were held in various towns.[35] Since John of Luxembourg possessed a palace in Paris and was on excellent terms with the French royal family — a friendship that often brought him to Paris for ceremonies of state or for informal encounters — there must have been ample opportunities for his secretary to pay a visit to this center of musical science and to meet there other poets and composers.

Machaut's reputation with his colleagues must have rested in the first place on his own achievements in the genre of the polytextual motet;[36] this was the musico-theoretical forum *par excellence*. During the fourteenth century the motet had increasingly developed into a learned game with the sounding numbers of music, which themselves traditionally reflected the proportions of the ordered cosmos. It thus became the ideal vehicle for discussions of lofty subjects, often in cryptic Latin, and for music-theoretical speculations; eventually it was regarded as the most suitable musical genre to adorn ceremonies of state and religion. Presumably, the motet was thus the first and most important polyphonic form for a young aspiring composer to learn and explore. In theoretical treatises about mensuration motets are often cited as examples.[37] Traces of imitation, exchange, and emulation between musicians are often found in the surviving compositions.[38] Philippe de Vitry's motets in particular seem to have appealed to Machaut, stimulating him to try to surpass the older master or to elaborate

---

[32] Earp, *Guillaume de Machaut*, p. 64.

[33] His name is attached to four works only: B18 *De petit po*, B34 *Quant Theseus*, M8 *Qui es promesses / Ha, Fortune / Et non est qui adjuvat* and R20 *Douce dame*. In the lost source Strasbourg BM M.222 C.22 three widely diffused songs were wrongly attributed to Machaut while the three that he did compose remained unascribed, suggesting that, although his precise achievements were not known, his name at least had acquired enough renown to ascribe those popular songs to him.

[34] It concerns the splitting of words by the technique of hocketing. See Zayaruznaya, "Hockets," pp. 461–501.

[35] Rohloff, *Die Quellenhandschriften*, pp. 144–45, Grocheio, *Ars musice*, ed. Mews, pp. 84–85, Page, "Johannes de Grocheio," p. 36. The meaning of the term *litteratus* is a debated issue but suggests at least a certain amount of culturedness. Plumley cites evidence that motets were sung at meetings of the goldsmiths' guild in Paris; see Plumley, *Art of Grafted Song*, p. 178. It seems likely that Machaut also took part in the contests of the poetic *puys*, such as those that were held in various cities, Paris among them; see Plumley, *Art of Grafted Song*, p. 212, p. 367. See also Huot, "Reading across Genres," for an interesting reference in Froissart's *Joli buisson de Jonece* to the singing of one of Machaut's motets at a festive occasion. Earp, however, thinks that in this case a polyphonic chanson was meant by the term (Earp, *Guillaume de Machaut*, p. 54).

[36] See Howlett, "*Apollinis eclipsatur*," pp. 152–59.

[37] For instance, Machaut's M8 is cited in one version of the famous treatise *Ars nova* for its use of imperfect tempus with minor prolation.

[38] See Leech-Wilkinson, "Related Motets" and Kügle, *The Manuscript Ivrea*, pp. 119–50. References to other composers' songs are, however, also found in many chansons.

certain compositional ideas in his own works; a number of the earlier motets show traces of Vitry's influence but even Machaut's late works attest to the impact of the older composer's achievements.[39]

Machaut's 23 motets comprise about a quarter of the surviving fourteenth-century motet repertory. Six Latin works were apparently written for various ceremonial occasions; the other seventeen, in French or French and Latin, are devoted to subjects of courtly love. The composition of the motets took place in two different periods of Machaut's life. The majority were probably composed during his early career, probably including his student period, between c. 1320 and at latest c. 1356 (but in all likelihood much closer to the earlier date);[40] considerably later followed the three grand four-voice Latin works, M21–23. The earlier twenty motets show signs of having been composed in several sets, marked by similarity of techniques and experimentation. The late motets are also stylistically related; their despairing texts suggest that they were composed around 1358–1360, when France's political situation was at its nadir.

In the oldest manuscript (C, c. 1350–1356), its nineteen motets already feature in the order they retain in all the later manuscripts except in the posthumous E,[41] a sign that Machaut had devised at an early stage how these works should be arranged as a corpus. In the later manuscripts the last three motets were simply added to that earlier corpus. Traces of an ordering system will be considered further below, after a discussion of the general structure, the subject matter, and the possible relationships between texts and music of Machaut's motets.

STRUCTURE

In the musicological literature Machaut's motets initially suffered from a rather negative judgment: compared with other Ars nova-motets and with his own songs they were considered to bring nothing new or surprising.[42] In studies of the last decades, however, literary scholars have uncovered the richness of ideas they contain, and in their slipstream the negative view has changed for the better also with regard to the music. Recent analyses of the motets' musical content have revealed far more subtlety and originality than had been recognized in the past. Machaut himself proclaimed his determination to create things as yet unheard and new (estranges et nouviaus) in several places in his works, already in the fairly early Dit de l'Alerion (ll. 1583–1604), but especially in the Voir Dit:

> J'ay fait le chant sur Le grant desir que j'ai de vous veoir, ainsi comme vous le m'aviez commandé. Et l'ai fait ainsi comme un rés d'Alemaigne. Et vraiement il me samble moult estranges et moult nouviaus, si le vous envoierai le plus tost que je porrai. (Livre du Voir Dit, ed. Imbs & Cerquiglini, Lettre IV, p. 128.)

> I have composed the music for "The Great Desire I Have to See You," just as you have requested me, and I have done so in the German form. And truly it seems foreign and novel, so I will send it to you as quickly as I am able. (Trans. Palmer, Livre dou Voir Dit, pp. 77–79.)[43]

Novelty is not so much to be sought in the overall structure of the motets, which indeed follows the formal concepts developed by composers before him, as rather in the detail of the elaboration. Nowadays theorists

---

[39] See especially Leech-Wilkinson, Compositional Techniques for an extensive analysis of all Vitry's and Machaut's four-voice motets; also Boogaart, "Encompassing," pp. 51–86. M5 and 10 in particular show clear traces of the impact of Vitry's compositions, but also M12 and 17 (the two mixed language motets, which may be the oldest works in the corpus) betray some influence.

[40] The dating depends on the completion of the earliest manuscript in which they appear, C, which is assumed to have been written somewhere between c. 1350–1356. Only for M18 is there a secure date (1324 or 1325). M21–23 are so different in style from the majority of the motets that a time lag of only a few years seems highly unlikely.

[41] The original corpus probably comprised twenty motets, M4 presumably having been omitted by mistake at a certain stage of rebinding of C; see Earp, "Scribal Practice," pp. 140–42.

[42] See e.g., the judgments in Besseler, "Studien zur Musik des Mittelalters" II, Sanders, "The Medieval Motet" and Günther, "The 14th-Century Motet."

[43] A new edition and translation of Le Livre dou Voir Dit by Barton Palmer will appear as Volume 4 of the present complete works edition.

and musicians alike are discovering Machaut's motets to be exciting pieces, not least in their subtle interaction of text and music.[44]

Since its origins in the early thirteenth century the French medieval motet was traditionally composed departing from a borrowed melody, with its text, which served as the foundation voice, the *tenor*. In most works this borrowed melody is a short melismatic fragment from Gregorian chant, usually from an antiphon or responsory, rhythmicized in large values and repeated several times. During the thirteenth century a restricted number of such melismas served as the basis for many motets or rather, motet-families, since both the melodies and the texts of the upper voices could vary from one piece to another. Machaut's contributions to the genre similarly are mostly based on chant fragments, but, like his fellow composers, he only rarely used a chant known from another work (M13 and 17 are the only examples).[45] In three works he took the complete melody of a secular song, thereby continuing another thirteenth-century tradition, which, however, otherwise had little follow-up in the fourteenth.

In contrast to the thirteenth-century motet, where voices or texts could be changed, added, or subtracted, but in line with fourteenth-century practice, Machaut seems to have considered his motets as finished and rounded compositions: the variants in the manuscripts are minimal and can mostly be explained as scribal mistakes or misunderstandings; no voices or texts are ever changed, added, or discarded.

The choice of the melisma that was to serve as the tenor depended on the pre-defined subject matter of the work, as the treatise on motet composition by Egidius de Murino makes clear.[46] Thus, for each motet Machaut had to find a suitable chant fragment to illustrate his chosen subject, featuring both the right word or words and a melody that permitted the composition of a rounded polyphonic work, that is, one offering possibilities for musical development, cadences, and a satisfying closure. Moreover, it should preferably possess a characteristic contour suited to give expression to the subject. Machaut must have known the chant repertoire thoroughly to make the apt choices we find in his works.[47] Most but not all of his tenors have been identified; of the known ones it is amazing how well not only the words but even their original liturgical and biblical contexts suit the subject discussed in the upper voice texts, and how at the same time the melody forms the nucleus of an exciting piece of music.

The series of pitches of the tenor, known as the *color*, was usually chosen so that their number can be divided into equal parts.[48] The next step was to rhythmicize these parts to form repeating patterns of notes and rests, known as the *taleae*. Thus prepared, the tenor provided the basic outline of the motet; in some works a *contratenor* with the same ambitus and type of motion accompanies the tenor. The durational values of tenor and contratenor usually are longae and breves, sometimes maximae, longae, and breves (with the mensuration of modus and maximodus).[49] The tenor can be repeated with the same values (*integer valor*) or in values a degree smaller than the initial ones (replacing longa by brevis, brevis by semibrevis), in so-called *diminution*, which

---

[44] Ground-breaking studies are the combined analyses of M15 by Brownlee and Bent, "Machaut's Motet 15" and "Deception, Exegesis."

[45] Closest to the thirteenth-century repertoire is the tenor of M13, *Ruina*, from the motet *Presidentes / Super cathedram / Ruina*, which is transmitted in the *Roman de Fauvel* but might well be a much older work. Vitry's motet *Vos quid admiramini / Gratissima / Gaude gloriosa / Contratenor* is based on the same antiphon as M17 (although Machaut transposed the melisma up a fifth). Machaut's M8 and 21 are based on the same chant, but with a larger fragment in M21.

[46] "Primo accipe tenorem alicuius antiphone vel responsorii vel alterius cantus de antiphonario; et debent verba concordare cum materia de qua vis facere motetum." ("First take a tenor from some antiphon or responsory or another chant from the antiphonal; and the words must concord with the [subject] matter about which you want to make the motet." Text from MS Sevilla, Biblioteca Colombina, 5-2-25, fol. 60r.)

[47] In a few instances the tenor melodies were slightly modified for musical purposes.

[48] The few exceptions all feature a special talea construction (M3, 6 and 22); see the commentaries.

[49] Mensuration determines the relationship between the different durational values: perfect or imperfect maximodus determines whether a maxima contains two or three longae, perfect or imperfect modus whether a longa contains three or two breves, perfect or imperfect tempus the same with respect to brevis and semibrevis, and major or minor prolatio with respect to semibrevis and minima. All possible combinations are found in the motets. See further under Editorial Policy.

causes a speeding-up of the basic motion; the mensuration of modus is then reduced to tempus, maximodus to modus. In some motets, to create more variety, two colores taken together are divided by three taleae (expressed in a formula: 2C=3T), with the result that the two identical melodies become entirely divergent in rhythm (used in M4, 7, 9; M14 has the reverse procedure, 3C=2T); this procedure can be also repeated in diminution (M4, M7). Related structures are found in M19 (in which 2C=5T) and M22 (where a structure of 2C=3T is followed by a partial repeat of the first color and talea).

Upon this slow-moving foundation two upper voices were composed, *motetus* (or *duplum*) and *triplum*. The motetus is the middle voice, moving in durational values mostly a degree smaller than the tenor's and declaiming a relatively short poem. The triplum is the upper voice, moving fastest and declaiming a much longer text, predominantly with a restricted number of small rhythmic formulas, with the mensuration of tempus and prolatio. This hierarchic stratification of motion and texts became standard from the end of the thirteenth century and continued in the fourteenth.

During the motet's development in the fourteenth century the upper voices increasingly tended to reflect the rhythmic configuration of the tenor. Their phrases also were constructed into repeating patterns, albeit less strict than the tenor's: identical rhythms are concentrated in the larger note values and in the so-called hockets (*hoquetus*, a technique of quick exchange of short notes and rests between the upper voices) and usually increase in frequency both towards the end of the talea and towards the end of the entire piece, especially in motets featuring a diminution section. Normally these phrases end with a rest. Their length mostly corresponds with that of the tenor taleae, but with a little overlap, to avoid simultaneous points of silence and to ensure continuous motion. In several motets melodic repetition within the phrases, or a melodic refrain at their ending (e.g., in M7, 8, and 17), enhances the sensation of repetition and variation.

Construction in such "iso-rhythmical" patterns increased during the fourteenth century and culminated in the fifteenth with Dufay's grand motets.[50] Of Machaut's works two are almost pan-isorhythmic (i.e., isorhythmic in all the voices), namely M13 and 15, while M4 comes close to it. Upper voice isorhythm can, however, also take on a more independent character and even change the perception of the tenor's repetitive form. Several motets show formal experiments in this direction; in the simplest case it is effectuated by coupling two tenor taleae into one larger "super-talea" as a result of isorhythmic figures in the upper voices. However, M6, for instance, has a much more complex structure in which the phrases of motetus and triplum, not the tenor taleae, ultimately define the form of the motet. In the three chanson-motets, regular phrases of the upper voices, marked by repeating rhythmic formulas, operate independently of the more irregular sections of the tenor's melodic form.

Machaut's motets explore all the possibilities the Ars nova theorists had uncovered by their systematization of rhythmic and notational experiments at the beginning of the fourteenth century. In several works Machaut tried his hand at complex syncopations;[51] in others he experimented with the ambiguities of the notational system and with the paradoxes in the conception and measuring of time it afforded. It is clear that Machaut thoroughly understood the entire potential and even the paradoxes of the notational system; his explorations betray remarkable insight into contemporary music theory.

Machaut seems to have had an unusually linear conception of counterpoint.[52] Although the quick triplum parts mostly form a regular, consonant counterpoint with the tenor notes, elaborated as a mosaic of Machaut's

---

[50] The term "isorhythm" for this phenomenon was invented early in the twentieth century; Friedrich Ludwig was the first to use it. For a critical discussion of the term and qualifications for its use, see Bent, "Isorhythm" in *New Grove* and ead., "What is isorhythm?" For an explanation of isorhythm as a mnemonic device, see Busse-Berger, *Medieval Music and the Art of Memory*, pp. 210–51.

[51] Syncopations in the sense defined by Johannes de Muris: "The syncope is the division of any figure in separate parts which complement each other (litt.: are reduced one to another) when the perfections are numbered." ("Unde sincopa est divisio circumquaque figure per partes separatas, que numerando perfectiones ad invicem reducuntur"; Johannes de Muris, *Ars practica*, p. 65.)

[52] See Leech-Wilkinson, *Compositional Techniques*, p. 116 and note 26. For analyses of Machaut's counterpoint and compositional procedure in his four-voice motets see especially this work; for analyses of the counterpoint in three- and four-voice motets see the various studies by Helmuth Kühn, Sarah Fuller, and Jared Hartt listed in the bibliography.

typical fixed melodic motifs, the slower-moving motetus parts generally have a far more independent and capricious character. In principle the melodic range of the motetus lies between triplum and tenor, but many unexpected upward or downward leaps make it rise above the triplum or sink below the tenor, and it is often this voice that steers the counterpoint into the surprising and biting dissonant clashes that are so characteristic of Machaut's music.

SUBJECT MATTER AND BORROWINGS

Machaut's six Latin motets were composed for different ceremonial or political occasions and thus reflect events from the real world. Two are festive works, composed for ceremonies in the churches where Machaut held a canonicate; M18 lauds Bishop Guillaume de Trie at his enthronement in the cathedral of Notre Dame in Reims; M19 sings the praises of Saint Quintinus, for an unknown occasion in the collegiate church of Saint-Quentin.[53] In particular the last three motets, M21–23, echo in their texts France's miseries as a consequence of political strife, warfare, and recurrence of the plague around the years 1358–1360. M21 and 23 were probably written for ceremonies in the cathedral of Reims and are pleas for heavenly support. M22 is an exhortation, probably addressed to the Dauphin Charles to act as a political leader. The earlier M9 might be a political work as well; it is supposed to attack in allegorical and biblical terms an inimical lord, probably King Edward III of England, who would then be personified as Lucifer himself.[54]

The majority of Machaut's motets, the seventeen works in French or mixed French and Latin, evoke a refined courtly civilization. They continue the amorous poetics of the trouvère tradition, although Machaut shaped his texts according to the more intellectual approach of the Ars nova motet. Each motet treats a different problem from among the various obstacles which an *I* encounters in the learning process of an ennobling love: a peregrination during which the lover continuously aspires to, but never achieves, fulfillment, and remains loyally waiting for grace in an ever-receding future.[55] The rondeau text of M20's tenor best expresses the problematic courtly ideal: "Je ne sui mie certeins d'avoir amie, mais je sui loyaus amis" ("I'm not at all certain I have a sweetheart, but a loyal lover is what I am"). The upper voices always refer to the tenor word(s) but approach the central problem each from a different angle, complementing or opposing each other's argument and ending with a pointed conclusion.

In subject matter Machaut's motets thus diverge from most of those of his fellow composers; from early on, he seems to have been fascinated with composing speculations on the paradoxes of courtly love in this dialectical form *par excellence*. His poems exhibit an erudition he may have acquired in his function as secretary/reader of John of Luxembourg. Both in the French and the Latin texts, quotations, paraphrases, or even transformations of lyrics from the past — often fragments and snippets from thirteenth-century trouvère songs fitting the chosen subject — betray Machaut's literateness.[56] Also a good number of classical texts like the *Roman de la Rose*, the *Ovide moralisé*, Boethius' *De consolatione philosophiae* and Alain de Lille's *De planctu naturae*, as well as epic romances, have left their traces.[57]

---

[53] Robertson suggests this was the inauguration of the new choir stalls in 1342, but it may of course also have been written at an unknown date for the saint's feast day (31 October) to be sung at some point during the office. See also Fiala, "La collégiale royale," pp. 195–205.

[54] See Markstrom, "Machaut and the Wild Beast" and Boogaart, "Encompassing," pp. 5–11. King Edward first paid homage for his French fiefs to King Philip VI of France in 1329 but later, in 1338, claimed the French throne for himself; this might set a date for the motet. A very different interpretation is proposed in Robertson, *Machaut and Reims*, pp. 137–51.

[55] The development of Machaut's conception of love in his *dits* is discussed in Kelly, *Machaut and the Medieval Apprenticeship*.

[56] Generally these borrowings are, however, not cited together with their original melody as with the tenors. In only a few motets, e.g., M7 and M17, melodic quotations can be found or suspected.

[57] See De Boer, *Ovide moralisé*, pp. 28–43 and Imbs-Cerquiglini, *Livre du Voir Dit*, pp. 16–20. Boethius and Alain de Lille also must have belonged to the authors Machaut had studied; see the Introduction to Hoepffner's edition of the narrative works, especially to *Remede de Fortune* in vol. II; also Huot, "Patience in Adversity" and Boogaart, "Encompassing," pp. 41–50. For a possible quotation from a *chanson de geste*, see the commentary to M2.

The semantic foundation of the motet, on the other hand, is formed by the liturgical, biblical, and exegetical contexts of the tenors, a field with which Machaut appears to have been equally familiar (it suggests he may indeed have studied theology for some time). In his motets the two domains, spiritual and secular, come to an intriguing confrontation and fusion, which obviously leaves room for, and has given rise to, many diverging modern interpretations. Whether one interprets Machaut's amorous motets as reflections on courtly love to which the liturgical tenor provides a transcendent critique, as allegories concealing spiritual exhortations, or, in contrast, as lofty speculations on the role of love in world harmony, magnified by the tenor's spiritual underpinning, it is clear that they are utterly profound works.[58]

All these borrowings and references highlight the motet's intellectual credentials. To fathom the deeper meaning of the work, the performer or listener must first recognize the liturgical and secular quotations in tenor and upper voices, understand their provenance and original contexts, and the reason they were chosen and combined; finally, apprehend how they function and what they mean in their new, musically complex, context. In each motet Machaut set himself and his performers a new challenge, both in subject matter and in compositional technique. Only a select group of experts can have had the literary and musical culture needed to unravel such webs of references. It follows that a motet was — and still is — as much a work for careful consideration and reflection as it is a composition for repeated performance.[59] Understanding these works involves gradually discovering how all of their elements interact to reflect the many facets of a complex idea and how that idea is achieved in a captivating harmony of verbal and musical sounds.[60]

TEXT AND MUSIC: FORMAL RELATIONSHIPS

In contrast to most of Machaut's other musicalized texts, those of the motets, with one exception, are nowhere transmitted as autonomous poems without their music.[61] The reason may well be that the essential quality of motet texts lies in their direct confrontation and complementarity. The only way to coordinate the simultaneous declamation of two texts differing in length and rhyme sounds is by a precise rhythmicization, and thus in a musical setting. Texts and music are inextricably connected in a complex counterpoint of words, rhythms, and melodies, and must be interpreted together and in their interaction to make full sense. Interrelationships between text and music concern both their formal appearance and their content.

Compared to Machaut's other lyric poems the formal variety of the motet texts is striking; no two motets have exactly the same text form, although some types of rhyme and stanza occur more than once (the rhyme schemes are given in the commentary of each motet).[62] Monorhyme is used as an emphatic sound effect in M8, 19, and 20. Paired rhymes are the most common, some with only two rhyme sounds, others with continuously

---

[58] See e.g., Brownlee, "Machaut's Motet 15"; id., "Polyphonie et intertextualité"; id., " La polyphonie textuelle" and id., "Fire, Duration"; Huot, "Patience in Adversity"; ead., *Allegorical Play*; Robertson, *Machaut and Reims*; Boogaart, "Encompassing." Robertson is the most staunch defender of an allegorical-spiritual interpretation; for a critique see Boogaart, "Review of Robertson, *Machaut and Reims*." See also the lucid remarks in Poirion, *Le poète et le prince*, pp. 536–37.

[59] See especially Bent, "The Late-Medieval Motet."

[60] See the interesting remarks on the experience of sound in motets in Dillon, *The Sense of Sound*, especially the Prologue.

[61] The exceptions are the upper voice texts of M8, which are preserved in a peripheral source, and even there with an indication that originally they were musicalized texts. The triplum text bears the indication "Tresble Guillaume de Marchant." Vitry's motet texts, on the other hand, are indeed found without their music and may have been considered as independent literary works, although several manuscripts, especially the earlier ones, also label them as voice parts. On the transmission of Vitry's texts in humanist circles, see Wathey, "The Motets of Philippe de Vitry"; on the exceptional status of their transmission, see especially p. 127: "[…] the texts of motets from the early fourteenth century have almost no independent literary circulation — with the sole exception of the texts of motets that have since come to be associated with Vitry's name. This pattern persists well into the following century, and is broken only when newly composed liturgical poetry begins to appear in polyphonic settings."

[62] For a study of versification in fourteenth-century motets, with many examples from Machaut's works, see Clarkson, "On the Nature of Medieval Song."

changing rhymes. A long series of four-line stanzas of which the fourth line is a short *vers coupé* (scheme aaaB), is characteristic in the plaintive triplum texts of M3, M7, M9, and M16; a similar stanza type but with six or eight lines occurs in M18, 21, 22, and 23. Five-line stanzas are found in M17 and M18 (diminution section). Longer stanzas are rarer and occur mainly in the triplum parts, e.g., in M14 with four seven-line stanzas, M13 with four eight-liners, M2 with three ten-liners, M1 with three eleven-liners, and, the longest, M15 with two stanzas of nineteen lines. Stanzaic texts often end with an irregular or incomplete last stanza. Nine motetus texts consist of just one long strophe with an irregular rhyme scheme, in majority with only two rhyme sounds.

Usually, stanzaic structures correspond, at least partly, with the talea divisions as reflected in the upper voice phrases; the few notable exceptions are the triplum parts of M2, 3, and 5, and the motetus parts of M19 and M22, where textual and musical forms operate more or less independently.[63] Only two works, M1 and 18, show an exemplary correspondence of textual and musical form: together with the diminution of the talea, the stanzaic form is also reduced, so that textual and musical forms are entirely matching. In two other works with diminution the undiminished talea contains two stanzas, the diminished talea one (M7 and 21); in yet another division type three taleae contain one stanza each, while the fourth stanza is divided over the three diminished taleae (the triplum parts of M10 and 23). In several works the correspondence between stanza and talea becomes looser towards the end.

Decasyllabic, octosyllabic and heptasyllabic meters prevail in the triplum texts, octosyllabic and heptasyllabic ones in the motetus. Very short lines (of two or three syllables) are rarer; the play with verbal rhythm and rhyme-sound which such lines invite, and which are often found in lays and virelais, seems less important in the motets than the meaning and confrontation of the texts, although the first motet contains a nice instance in its hockets. Disturbances in patterns of regular declamation can serve as an expressive device.[64] The frequency of certain words often points to the subject of a specific work (e.g., the emphasis on *mors* or *mort* in M3 or on *desir* and *espoir* in M4), and also the placement of related words in the various voices can bring about meaningful connections; coincidence of the same word in both texts is rare and always meaningful.

TEXT AND MUSIC: RELATIONSHIPS IN CONTENT

In older literature on late-medieval music, discussion of text-music relationships in motets in general focussed exclusively on their formal and numerical-symbolic aspects.[65] For instance, the five taleae of M19, a motet praising Saint Quintinus, clearly alluded to the name of the saint (Quintus = fifth).[66] More recent studies have revealed, however, that composers in this period, just like those of the following centuries, often endeavored to transmit the meaning of the text in the musical setting.[67] Machaut — expert poet and composer that he was — devised many ways to enhance the message of his texts by musical means. The following discussion explores in turn a range of approaches, from direct to indirect effects, from moments that can be immediately heard and felt, to notational and mensural problems that demand a mental effort and knowledge of music theory

---

[63] For a complete inventory see Reichert, "Das Verhältnis."

[64] See especially Earp, "Declamation as Expression."

[65] A representative judgment on text-music relationships in medieval music in general is given by Stevens, *Words and Music*, p. 409: "When words and music come together they have to agree, certainly, but this agreement is primarily a matter of parallel 'harmonics,' agreements of phrase and structure, of balance and 'number,' so that in song the mind and ear may be 'doubly charmed by a double melody.' Such a view does not exclude from the effects of music emotional experiences of great power [...]; indeed it is often invoked to explain them. It does, however, seem to exclude — or at least, patently and consistently neglects — the close and detailed expressive relations between words and music which we find in the songs of later periods. For this reason a theory of expressive sound closely related to subject-matter, a theory apparently derived from antique rhetoric, has only a limited place in the medieval experience of music. It remains marginal and never finds a comfortable place in the Great Synthesis."

[66] See Günther, "Sinnbezüge," p. 267. This fundamental article proposes a fivefold classification of text-music relationships, from concrete imitation of natural sounds to form-symbolism; however, the conclusion points out that examples are found mostly in refrain forms and canons, not in masses and motets.

[67] See for text-music relationships in motets especially the seminal studies of Bent, "Deception, Exegesis," "Polyphony of Text and Music," and "Words and Music in Machaut's Motet 9."

and practice to make their purport understood. The boundaries between direct and indirect effects, however, are often fluid.

1. Direct effects often have the character of a surprise. Exclamations like *Hé*, *Helas* or *Hareu* which, when spoken, would have an immediate impact on the listener, are rarely if at all emphasized by the music of the motets. There are, however, a number of aural effects that do make themselves immediately felt, although the performer or listener needs the text to understand their specific meaning. Several motets have a striking opening to alert the listener. A rhythmic example is M2's opening with notes broken up by rests in tenor and motetus, which evoke the lover's sighs, the subject of the work. Surprises in counterpoint occur more often. Right at the beginning of M11, an unusual imperfect consonance of major third and major sixth produces an effect of intense longing for resolution, in accordance with the beseeching texts. M18, which addresses a bishop at his enthronement, begins with an unconventional triadic melody in both upper voices, sung in contrary motion (low to high in the triplum, conversely in the motetus).[68]

A contrasting aural device is the absence of sound, by means of a series of rests. It can, very literally, express the silence of a timid lover, as in M2 and M5 (the triplum parts of both motets start with nine brevis rests). It may also evoke the silence of death, as in M3 where regularly recurring simultaneous rests in the upper voices — otherwise extremely rare — interrupt the flow of the music.[69]

Extremes of register equally belong to this category of direct effects. A very eloquent example is M16: its motetus constantly sings in close duet with either the tenor or the triplum, leaping from low to high and back, and causing many dissonances, as if to make the listener feel how an unhappy lady's heart is rent asunder, the subject of the work. The low setting of this motet symbolizes her depressed state of mind; examples of such low tessitura in combination with a text expressing sadness are also found in the next motet in the series, M17, and in some chansons.[70]

A special sound effect, but whose exact performance unfortunately remains uncertain, is the *plica* (the "fold");[71] it occurs as a plicated longa or brevis. In earlier polyphony it was used to divide a note into two, the main note and an ornamental passing-note which fills in the interval to the next pitch, most often of a third. In Machaut's motets and Mass the plica can, however, appear in combination with much larger intervals or, on the contrary, occur before a repeated note or a rest. Machaut used this ornament rather sparingly; where there is a profusion of plicae, as in M2, 5, and 17 — all three have plaintive texts — it seems indeed they are meant as expressive accents. It is difficult, however, to pin down the plica as a means to highlight a single word since it also occurs on conjunctions like *et*, *or* or *quant*; more likely, the plica served to call attention to an entire verse or sentence.

2. Imitations or suggestions of physical movement also form part of Machaut's arsenal of musical rendition of textual ideas. The tenor of M9, *Fera pessima* (A most evil beast), combines an iconic and an aural representation of movement (Fig. 1). In its texts two evil beasts represent the tenor's *Fera pessima*: the serpent and the scorpion.

The obsessive tenor melody, with its constantly repeated four notes F-G-a-b♭, was well chosen to evoke the fascinating effect of a writhing serpent. Machaut composed a talea rhythm that is suggestive of the scorpion's stinging from behind: each tenor talea ends with a syncopated brevis, which at the end of the entire piece

---

[68] The triad is repeated at the corresponding place in the second color (talea III), now descending in the triplum and ascending in the motetus; it suggests that the triad motif carried a specific significance.

[69] Rests were already used in this way in a cluster of thirteenth-century motets on the tenor *Mors* and with the theme of death.

[70] For instance, B12, *Pour ce que tous mes chans* or R18, *Puis qu'en oubli*. A related device is the long-term exchange of register; in some motets (notably M12 and 15) triplum and motetus change register for about half the length of the motet, which again finds an explanation in the texts. However, since this has no direct impact on the listener but would puzzle only the performers, it rather belongs to the category of ideas expressed by a problem. See Zayaruznaya, "She Has a Wheel."

[71] Its origin lies in the Gregorian liquescent neumes *epiphonus* (ascending) or *cephalicus* (descending), used mostly with the liquid consonants *l*, *m*, *n*, and *r* but also in some other cases. See Hiley, "Plica" in *New Grove* and Haines, "Lambertus' Epiglotus." For suggestions about its performance, see below under Editorial Policy: Plica.

Fig. 1. *A*, fol. 423r, detail. The tenor of M9.
Bibliothèque nationale de France, with permission.

sounds alone, as if coming too late. It influences also the upper voices, since both triplum and motetus phrases end or begin with an isolated textless semibrevis. The two beasts, evoked by the hypnotizing melody and the continuous rhythmic "stings," are both pictorial on the page and audible for the listener.

In M3 the gloomy subject of death and dying for love is evoked in the utterly slow movement of the tenor in maximae and longae, interrupted by simultaneous rests. Other such slow tenors in very large values similarly occur in motets in which the theme of approaching death is prominent in the texts (M7, 13, and 21).

In many pieces syncopations produce an unsettling effect. In M10, built on the melisma *Obediens usque ad mortem*, the tenor part is continuously in syncopation until its very last note, moving in perfect modus or tempus against the imperfect mensuration of the upper voices; thus, however difficult, the singer must try to remain "obedient until death." Syncopations often also evoke Fortune's destabilizing movements and surprises.

3. Text-painting, as just discussed in relation to the tenor of M9, is rare in Machaut's music, but his use of words and terms that have a meaning in both poetry and music comes close to it. As is apparent from his poetry, Machaut was fond of double meanings and ambiguities.

Terms for musical signs can sometimes have a poetic equivalent. *Suspirium* was the name for a breathing sign in the old organum; notated as a stroke it evolved into the rest sign (the quarter rest is still called a *soupir* in French). Both the tenor *Suspiro* and the motetus *De souspirant cuer* of M2 illustrate through their interruptions by rests a natural sound, the sigh, as seen above in the category of direct expressive effects; at the same time the words also allude to the *suspirium*. "Ligature" rarely occurs as a word in poetry but there is one example, in M17; according to the Latin motetus text, the universe is held together by a *ligatura uniforma*, a uniform bond. It is illustrated by the uniform ligature that connects each phrase-end of the motetus end with the beginning of the next; only at the transition to the last talea does the ligature disappear and the bond breaks. This break spells a disaster, which becomes manifest in the dissonant ending of this motet.

A number of poetic words lend themselves eminently to musical rendition. "Perfection" and "imperfection" are key notions in courtly love poetry, meaning "fulfillment" or the contrary; they are also the primary concepts of mensuration. In the motetus text of M1 the subject of perfect love is announced by the repeated word *parfaite(ment)*; exceptionally, the motet's mensuration is entirely perfect, bearing out the same message: perfection is thus the key notion in this work. The word *parfaite* occurs also in M7, whose texts express a desperate but vain longing for fulfillment in love; here the mensuration is imperfect overall. Another word bearing out the same idea of perfection is the word *fin* or *finement*, but this can at the same time have the meaning of "end"; this ambiguity is played on in both M1 and M11. The poetic meaning of *mesure* and *desmesure* is that of self-control or the lack of it and (im)moderation, while in music they refer to mensuration. Fortune's being *sans mesure* in M8 is expressed by isorhythmic passages in syncopation. The importance of the concept of *desmesure* in M4 and 7 is illustrated in the tenors of both works, which are impossible to read in a consistent mensuration. *Durer* or *duree* ("to endure, to remain in existence") is another such word. In M4 the words are combined: the lover's immeasurable (*desmesuree*) desire impedes him to have *duree*; transgressions in mensuration occur in this motet more than in any other. At the same time there is a similarity in sound between *durer* with *dur* or *durement* (in the sense of "hard"); at the words *durement endurer le m'estuet* (yet I must endure this in a "hard" way, i.e., firmly) a dissonant clash between cc and c♯ occurs.

Dur in this sense is a term from solmization, pointing to the use of the "hard" (*durum*) hexachord.[72] This category of poetical words that are also meaningful in solmization is particularly rich: *dous* (sweet, soft), *muer* (change), *amollir* (to soften), *faus* (false), *faintement* (feigned), *adversaire* (adversary), and *autre* (other) all belong to it. As musical terms these refer to the hard or soft (*molle*) hexachords, to mutations or to *musica ficta*, the notes that lie outside the regular hexachords; often, though not always, they find an equivalent in the music. In M1 the lover's initial joy must change (*muer*) into sorrow by his endless waiting for *mercy*; precisely in the passage where the change is mentioned in the text the tenor melody mutates from the *molle* to the *durum* hexachord. And M11, whose texts feature a continuous opposition of *dur* and *dous*, contains many passages of strong contrapuntal tension, contrasting with moments of perfect harmony. In M14 the lover is accused of singing "feigned" joyous songs; at the moment he confesses that in reality they are sad, the 'feigned' f-mi (f♯) changes unexpectedly into the natural f-fa (b. 16–23).

4. Notational and contrapuntal problems often reflect the central preoccupation of the text. Machaut was extremely clever in using the ambiguities of the notational system to trick his performers, and he also loved to steer his counterpoint into a clash or a dissonant impasse, one that is often almost impossible to solve.

Clear examples of confusing notations are found in M2, M5, M6, and M21: in all these works the perfect or imperfect mensuration suggested by the notation (Machaut used no mensuration signs) turns out to be the wrong one;[73] since the composer could easily have used a clearer notation the performer is deliberately misled. A comparison of these problems with those described in the texts leads to an interpretation of the work and its specific challenge. For example, the conclusion of M5's motetus, that, while the imperfect lover is rewarded, the perfect lover is not, finds a parallel in the problematical mensuration, which plays with the relativity of both perfection and imperfection.

Clashes that explicitly reflect the texts include the dissonant endings that occur in four motets (M4, 10, 15, 17). In M4 the upper voices end earlier than the tenor, but must hold out until the tenor has finished (*jusqu'au morir*, until death). The same happens in M10, where according to their text the upper voices "cannot hold out in the fire" and only the tenor is "obedient until death." In M15 the word *desconfiture*, the "defeat," may have provoked the dissonant ending. And in M17 it is impossible to sing the tenor a second time precisely as long as the first; to avoid a dissonant clash one has to cheat by shortening the tenor. The concluding words of the triplum are suggestive: *Qui .ii. fois vuet avoir denree / Le marcheant conchie* ("he who wishes to have the same wares twice / fouls the merchant"). Such disharmonic endings form the point of the piece and surely were meant to stimulate the contemporary performers to think about the seeming mistake. But clashes often also occur during the piece and should usually be understood as a call to attention to a particular passage. The transgressions of notational and contrapuntal conventions suggest that the motets belong to an experimental phase in Machaut's compositional career, perhaps as part of a playful exchange of ideas with fellow-composers who were capable of appreciating such bold experiments. In performance the continual short-circuiting of ideas between text and music sets in motion a gradual process of discovery of the many facets of the subject, which often converge into a central image, capturing and summarizing it all.[74]

---

[72] Hexachords are scales of six notes, named *ut-re-mi-fa-sol-la*, with a semitone only between *mi* and *fa*, that helped the singer to find the correct intervals of a melody. A hexachord could start on C (natural), G (durum, hard, with the note b-natural as *mi*) or F (molle, soft, with the note b-flat as *fa*); changing from one hexachord to another via a pivot note was called "to mutate." See further in *New Grove* sub "Hexachord," "Solmization," and "Musica ficta." A particularly revealing example of the use of solmization terms in Machaut's poetry is found in the complaint that follows on the Explicit of the *Confort d'amy*. All of its 26 lines end on –*mi* and at its center Charles complains that his enemies have *Mon b mol de be fa be mi / Mis en b dur* ("have changed my b-molle of be fa be mi into b-durum," i.e., have changed the sweet pleasure I had into hardship).

[73] See below under Editorial Policy: Mensuration.

[74] See about the representation of the subject also Zayaruznaya, *The Monstrous New Art*, especially the Epilogue, pp. 227–34.

THE ORDER OF THE CORPUS

Order, and the ordering of his works in particular, proved a major preoccupation for Machaut throughout his career.[75] His personal intent is demonstrated by the famous heading of the index of manuscript *A*: *Vesci l'ordenance que M. de Machau vuet qu'il ait en son livre* ("See here the order as G. de Machau wishes it to be in his book"). In all the musical genres a tendency to a fixed arrangement can be seen,[76] but only in the motets was the order established from early on and remained identical in the successive manuscripts, except in the last, the posthumous and non-authorially organized *E*.

The motets were apparently considered complete at two moments: first as a series of twenty, as was probably the case in *C* (assuming that M4 indeed belonged to the finished motets at that stage),[77] and finally as a corpus of 23 works, as in the later manuscripts.[78] Assuming that Machaut intended a fixed order raises the question: according to which criteria was this conceived? Although the addition of M21-23 at the end of the corpus could suggest otherwise, the order clearly is not chronological since M18 very probably is one of the oldest works.[79] In the following examination the most important clues to Machaut's ordering of his motet-œuvre will be discussed, with the contention that it was arranged according to both thematic and structural criteria.[80] The principal division of the motet corpus is a bipartition according to language, entailing both the general subject matter and the speaking person. In the seventeen French and French-Latin motets the narrator is the lyric *I*, and they all treat subjects of courtly love. The six entirely Latin motets have various ceremonial, political, and occasional subjects and in these works the narrative voice belongs to a *We*, representing the community. The original corpus, as in *C*, contained only three Latin motets (M9, 18, and 19).

Of the seventeen amorous motets three have French texts in all the voices (M11, 16, and 20, with a French chanson tenor). Fourteen have a Latin tenor, two of which also feature a Latin motetus; the other twelve have French upper voices. Remarkably, the series M1–M17 includes one all-Latin motet (M9), while the series M18–23 has one all-French motet (M20). Possibly, this was so arranged in order to bear out that the linguistic-thematic domains are not entirely mutually exclusive.

As can be expected in an ordered corpus, the opening and closing works occupy key positions. The opening works of the two language groups both mark an initiation: in M1 the *I* (Guillaume?) is initiated in love, in M18 Bishop Guillermus is instated in his function. A common structural feature is that in both motets the stanzaic and musical forms show an exemplary correspondence found in no other work; in both, the diminished talea in the music corresponds to a reduced strophic form in the poem. Moreover, both share the same number

---

[75] The basic article on the arrangements of the various manuscripts is Earp, "Machaut's Role."

[76] See e.g., Huot, *From Song to Book*, pp. 260–72, about the rationale behind the ordering of the lays in *C*. About the order of the various genres see Earp, "Introductory Study," pp. 14–19.

[77] Earp suspects that M4 probably was accidentally left out when the manuscript was rebound. M20 was originally conceived as a closing work, as will be argued further below.

[78] The attribution of the motet *Li enseignement de Chaton / De touz les biens / Ecce tu pulchra* to Guillermus de Mascandio in MS Fribourg, Fcu 260 is generally rejected on stylistic grounds and because none of the main manuscripts contains the work. See Zwick, "Deux motets."

[79] Only one bishop with the name Guillermus (Guillaume de Trie) served in Machaut's time and he was enthroned in 1324 or 1325. Robertson argues, unconvincingly, that the motet — which is clearly addressed to a bishop Guillermus whose name is in rhyme position — could have served for several bishops' enthronements (*Machaut and Reims*, p. 55 ff.) by changing the name and could thus be of later date. Even if such reuse occurred, the motet's first addressee must still have been Guillaume de Trie, which fixes the date of composition.

[80] The order of the motets was first discussed in my article "Love's Unstable Balance, Part II," of which the main arguments were elaborated in Brown's "Another Mirror," as well as in footnotes 106–7 of Boogaart, "Encompassing" and in id., "L'accomplissement." Robertson's interpretation, in *Machaut and Reims*, as an allegorical and spiritual journey inspired by the successive stages of a pilgrim's quest in Heinrich Suso's *Horologium Sapientiae* appeared in the same year. Hers is the most generally cited explanation of the ordering and interpretation of their message, although not accepted without reservations. My critical review of Robertson's interpretation appeared in *Early Music* 2004 (Boogaart, "Review of Robertson, *Machaut and Reims*"). Since the main arguments against her interpretation are summed up in that review, they will not be repeated here; suffice it to say that the musical structures play no part in her explanation.

of breves, 144, a traditional symbolic number pointing to perfection and stability.[81] The mensuration of M1 is entirely perfect. Perhaps highlighting their special status, M1 and 18 are the only motets in the index of MS *A* to be listed by their triplum incipit and not, as are the others, by that of the motetus.

The placement of M17 and 23 as the closing works of the two language groups can probably be explained by the liturgical association of their tenors: both were taken from a Marian antiphon, and in Machaut's time, just as nowadays, these antiphons were sung after compline, at the closure of the liturgical day; the *Ave regina cœlorum* (used for the tenor of M17) during Lent, and the *Salve regina* (M23) between Trinity Sunday and Advent. It was, however, apparently not Machaut's initial idea. M20 concludes the oldest manuscript of his works, *C*. Its closing function is emphasized by the religious *Amen* in the otherwise secular texts of the upper voices. The tenor text expresses the ideal of courtly love, a lover loyally waiting for his lady's grace, and in that respect refers back to the first motet in which striving for love's perfection is a key concept. Like M1, M20 has a symbolic number for its length, in this case of 153 semibreves;[82] its mensuration is also entirely perfect. From the fact that all-perfect mensuration is thus found exclusively at the outer ends of the original corpus it can be concluded, first, that Machaut still felt a qualitative difference between perfect and imperfect mensuration and, second, that perfect mensuration was chosen with regard to the texts, since both motets highlight the theme of perfect love.[83] Thus it seems warranted to assume that at the time *C* was being copied, Machaut considered these twenty motets as a complete cycle and that only later he decided to take instead the Marian antiphons of M17 and M23 to mark the closure points of two thematic groups.

Themes

Thematically, the corpus can be subdivided into groups of three consecutive motets with related subjects, except for M16 and 17, which form a pair. To make this clear an extensive interpretation of all the motets would be necessary, for which this is not the place.[84] The thematic sequence of M1–3 should suffice as a brief example.

In the opening motet, *Quant en moy / Amour et biauté parfaite / Amara valde*, the texts evoke the initiation in love of the lyric *I* and his striving for perfection, both in the sense of fulfillment and of becoming a perfect lover. He is confronted with the essential problem of courtly love: for its fulfillment he must await his lady's *mercy*, her grace, and as a perfect lover he may not ask for it or he would impair her honor. This anxious waiting — because the beloved might also refuse him — turns Love's sweetness into bitterness. The tenor words *Amara valde*, from a responsory for matins of Holy Saturday, the day of expectation before the fulfillment of the Salvation of mankind through the Resurrection, have an apocalyptic ring, magnifying the amorous problem to a cosmic scale: the words refer to that other day of fulfillment, the Last Judgment, a day which "will be great and very bitter"; some will be rescued, others refused. At the same time, the Latin word *amara* alludes by its sound to a classical pun in trouvère-chansons, which itself is given as the conclusion of the triplum text: *amer* = *amer*, to love is bitter. In the motetus text the lover accepts, however, the unfulfilled state of his feelings by pronouncing his willingness to languish and even to die for the purity of his beloved's honor: *languir et morir*.

---

[81] The breves are perfect only in M1; M18 has imperfect breves, so there is still a hierarchic difference. For the meanings of the apocalyptic number 144 (12x12), see Meyer and Suntrup, *Lexicon der mittelalterlichen Zahlenbedeutungen*, pp. 807–8.

[82] Its symbolic meaning of completeness derives from the number of fishes in the Miraculous Draught of Fish (St. John 21:11); see Meyer and Suntrup, *Lexicon der mittelalterlichen Zahlenbedeutungen*, pp. 814–16. It is also the sum of the first seventeen integers; since there are seventeen amorous motets, this could be significant. Arguments to consider the final of the motet as a perfect longa (defining the length of 51 breves) are presented below. However, the rondeau structure of the tenor defines a length of 50 breves, so the quality of the longa, perfect or imperfect, ultimately remains undecided, perhaps in accordance with the tenor text in which uncertainty and certainty are thematized.

[83] The difference in quality between perfect and imperfect is in accordance with De Muris' statement in his early *Notitia*, Secunda pars, Capitulum II: "Quod autem in ternario quiescat omnis perfectio, patet ex multis veresimilibus coniecturis." (That all perfection rests in the ternary [number] appears from many trustworthy conjectures.)

[84] References to articles or book chapters with interpretations of individual motets are given in the commentaries to each piece.

These trials are the subject of the two following motets. Both the tenors of M2 and 3 originate from the history of the suffering Job, whose patience serves as example for the impatient lover. Languishing (*languir*) is vividly evoked in the sighs of M2, *Tous corps / De souspirant cuer / Suspiro*; in this work body and heart of a lover struggle with each other whether to transgress the norm of courtly behavior by asking openly for *mercy* or to remain silent in languishing and, as a consequence, to die. Fear of death (*morir*), but at the same time a longing to offer one's life for love, is the subject of M3, *Hé! Mors! / Fine Amour / Quare non sum mortuus*. This work has a subtle mirror-form, reflecting the contrasting aspects of dying for love. In the texts the mirror is visible in the opposition of Love and Death at the beginning and end of the motetus and triplum texts.

Similar thematic groupings in threes, though not always as explicit, or even only perceptible as a connection by a common denominator, can be argued for the following motets. In M4–6 the themes of hope and subjection take central place. In M4, *De Bon Espoir / Puis que la douce / Speravi*, the lover gradually loses all hope but professes his enduring loyalty; M5, *Aucune gent / Qui plus aimme / Fiat voluntas tua*, features the beginning of new hope by subjection to the will of the lady and of Love, and in M6, *S'il estoit nuls / S'Amour tous amans / Et gaudebit cor vestrum*, a promise of future joy is given the lover, on the condition of long suffering. Moreover, M5 and 6 contain quotations from the same chanson by the trouvère Perrin d'Angicourt. M7, 8, and 9 all have a vice or vices as their subject, although they are otherwise very different in character: the lady's punished pride and remorse are the subject of M7, *J'ai tant mon cuer / Lasse! je sui / Ego moriar pro te*; a diatribe against Fortune's treachery, symbol of love's capriciousness, is heard in M8, *Qui es promesses / Ha! Fortune / Et non est qui adjuvat*, the most popular of Machaut's motets. It is followed by another tirade, against the fallen angel Lucifer's pride and envy in M9, *Fons totius Superbie / O Livoris feritas / Fera pessima*. Thus, although it is a linguistic outsider in the French group, thematically this motet nevertheless appears to be right in place.

M10–12 concentrate on the heart and eyes: in M10, *Hareu, hareu! / Helas! ou sera pris / Obediens usque ad mortem*, the lover's burning heart fears to die; in M11, *Dame, je sui cils / Fins cuers dous / Fins cuers dous*, the lady's sweet heart forbids the lover to see her, and in M12, *Helas! Pour quoy / Corde mesto / Libera me*, the lover complains about his sad heart, first wishing never to have seen his beloved but finally accepting his fate. M13–15 treat the subject of false seeming: of the lady in M13, *Tant doucement / Eins que ma dame / Ruina*, of the lover in M14, *Maugré mon cuer / De ma dolour / Quia amore langueo*, and of Love herself in M15, *Amours qui a le pooir / Faus Samblant / Vidi Dominum*. M16 and 17, the only group of two, deal with the problems of faith when a third person is involved: in M16, *Lasse! comment / Se j'aim / Pour quoy me bat mes maris*, it is a husband, in M17, *Quant Vraie Amour / O Series / Super omnes speciosa*, a second suitor. M18–20 are laudatory motets: Bishop Guillermus is praised at his enthronement in M18, *Bone pastor Guillerme / Bone pastor / Bone pastor*; in M19, *Martyrum gemma / Diligenter / A Christo honoratus*, reverence is paid to Saint Quintinus. In M20, *Trop plus est bele / Biauté paree de valour / Je ne sui mie certeins d'avoir amie*, the lover exalts the superb qualities of his adored lady, to whom he declares his unwavering faith, although he remains uncertain of her love. As with M9, this linguistic "outsider" motet within the Latin group is thematically in place.

The closing group M21–23 consists of invocations for help in times of war and despair; all three end with an outcry for peace. An urgent appeal to Christ and the Holy Spirit is heard in M21, *Christe, qui lux / Veni Creator / Tribulatio proxima est et non est qui adjuvet*; M22, *Tu qui gregem / Plange, regni res publica / Apprehende arma et scutum et exurge*, is an exhortation to an unnamed *dux*, probably the dauphin Charles who was duke of Normandy, to act as a firm leader; finally, in M23, *Felix virgo / Inviolata genitrix / Ad te suspiramus gementes et flentes*, the Virgin Mary is desperately beseeched for divine intervention against the disasters of war.

Tenors and their Liturgical Contexts[85]

Three motets are built on a chanson melody (M11, 16, and 20), while twenty have tenor melodies chosen from liturgical chant. Except for the Marian antiphons used in M17 and 23 (as argued above), the tenors themselves and their contexts do not seem to give direct clues to an ordering principle but their pertinence will appear in the discussion of the ordering after musical criteria.

---

[85] For an extensive discussion of the sources and their liturgical context, see Clark, "Concordare cum materia"; for a possible rationale for the order of the corpus according to the tenors, see pp. 93–96.

Of these twenty tenors at least two remain unidentified (M13 and 18); for the proposed identifications of M2 and 5 considerable modifications or different versions of the source melisma have to be assumed. Two tenors stem from the Marian antiphons sung after compline (M17 and 23); one is from a Marian office, mostly associated with the Assumption of the Virgin (M14). One tenor chant belongs to the Commune for One Martyr (M22) and one (M19) to the feast of Saint Quintinus (31 October). Strikingly, eight of the remaining thirteen source chants belong to the penitential season: Lent (M9, 12, and 15) and Holy Week (M1, 5, 8, 10, and 21). Two chants belong to the weeks in September when the book of Job is read, which itself is associated with the Office of the Dead (M2 and 3). Two are from the time shortly after Pentecost (M4 and 7), and only one belongs to Advent (the hopeful tenor of M6). Significantly, not a single chant was chosen from the liturgical time of joy and fulfillment, the seven weeks between Easter and Pentecost.

The most frequent biblical figures are David (as the psalmist or as the king) in M4, 7, 8, 21, and 22, and Christ (as the apocalyptic Lord from the books of the Prophets in M1 and 6, or as the suffering Christ from the Gospels in M5 and 10). In M18 the words *Bone Pastor* (Good Shepherd) could refer to Christ as well, but the chant remains unidentified;[86] in M19 Saint Quintinus is "Honored by Christ." The other figures are Jacob in M9, 12, and 15, Job in M2 and M3, Mary as the Bride from the Song of Songs in M14, Mary as *Sapientia* (Wisdom) in M17, and the Virgin Mary in M23.

Musical Structure and Tenors

The finals of the motets give no hint of an ordering principle according to mode. The most frequent mode by far is *F*, in M1, 2, 4, 5, 8, 10, (14),[87] 15, 18, 20, 21, and 22; in M17 the melisma's original Lydian is transposed up a fifth, to *C*. The other two modes are *D*, in M3, 7, 12, 16, and 23, and *G* in M6, 9, 11, 13, 14, and 19. M3 and 12 emphasize at first *F* as the central tone but halfway through the piece the melisma moves to *D*; in M8 the reverse takes place (*D* to *F*). In all three the ever-changing Fortune plays a role, which may be relevant for the choice of these modally fluctuating melismas.

An inventory of the mensuration, construction, and length of the motets, on the other hand, does indeed betray signs of an ordering system. A connection with the thematic order can be established via the tenor figures and their liturgical provenance. This structural criterion suggests a main grouping of the original corpus into two times ten works, to which the three late motets were added. A first caveat is that sometimes matters are slightly confused because the compositional plan of a motet is disturbed in its final shape by a small deviation; thus, relationships between some motets have remained unobserved and it is probably the planned form of the works which should be taken as the norm for the ordering, not their final state in which Machaut sometimes had altered tiny details (such as the omission of a final rest). Secondly, the semibrevis, not yet the minima, is to be considered as the basic unit of equivalence and of calculation in the motets.[88]

Similarities and proportional relationships between individual motets determine the main outline of the order. M1, 5, and 10 have a very close structural kinship. All three have tenor diminution in the proportion 3:1 (to one-third, perfect modus diminishing to perfect tempus). This is, however, really the case only in M1 and, only in sheer numbers, in M10 and 5, whereas their real proportion of diminution is 2:1 (to one-half): in the tenor of M5 96 *imperfect* breves are diminished to 32 *perfect* ones (192:96 semibreves) and in M10 72 *imperfect* breves to 24 *perfect* ones (144:72 semibreves). The proportion in length between these three motets is thus 144:96:72 perfect breves or 432:288:216 semibreves; interestingly, reduced to 6:4:3 it is the harmonic proportion of the intervals octave, fifth and fourth. Of these three M1 and 10 have the strongest similarities, since the tenor structure of M10 reflects that of M1: both tenors have 2x 30 color notes divided by six *integer valor* and six diminished taleae, each containing 5 notes; upper-voice isorhythm couples every two taleae into a super-talea containing 10 notes. Both motets are built on a tenor from the *Triduum sacrum*, M1 from a responsory for matins of Holy Saturday and M10 from an antiphon for the Tenebrae. M5 and 10 have several further connections in addition to the proportional one. Their taleae share a rhythmic pattern of three perfect

---

[86] A possible source is suggested in Robertson, *Machaut and Reims*, pp. 62–63.

[87] The final note of M14 is *G* but its real central tone throughout the piece is *F*. See for the subject of mode in Machaut's motets especially Fuller, "Modal Tenors and Tonal Orientation."

[88] See Michels, *Die Musiktraktate*, p. 116 and Rastall, *The Notation*, p. 71.

longs, albeit in differing rhythmical contexts, and, as just argued, both tenors give the impression of perfect, that is, ternary, diminution. Moreover both works contain references to the same motet by Philippe de Vitry (*Douce playsence / Garison / Neuma quinti toni*) through quotations and modeling; M10 in its texts and M5 in its music.[89] Therefore, it seems at least possible and, indeed, likely that M5's tenor, which as yet is not securely identified, stems from the same liturgical context as the other two works, the *Triduum sacrum*, in this case from the responsory *In monte Oliveti* for Maundy Thursday.[90]

M11, 16, and 20 are a similarly related group of three: they are the only works with chanson tenors and with French texts in all three voices. M11 and 20 exhibit a similar kind of relationship as M1 and 10, since their proportion in length is 2:1 (102:51 breves) and both works share the structural feature of a division of the motet by three isorhythmic hocket passages.[91] The two works are complementary in the sense that M11 contains very few minimae so that only modus and tempus are relevant mensural levels, whereas M20 has just one longa, so that the modus mensuration is irrelevant. M16, however, has a quite different structure. The proportion in length of all three chanson-motets is dissimilar to that of M1-5-10, because of the deviating length of M16 (the proportion in length of the three works is 102:150:51 in breves, in semibreves 306:300:153).[92] Yet, the refrains of their chanson tenors show the same proportion in length as the tenors of the first group, 72:48:36 (=6:4:3) semibreves.

These groups frame two series of ten motets in the old corpus. Moreover, they exhibit an apparent symmetrical design since the distances between M11, 16, and 20 mirror those of M1, 5, and 10. Perhaps the maker of *A* was aware of this arrangement: on the miniature which illustrates M1 a music scroll is shown on which two words can be read, referring to text and music of a motet: *Dam(e)* and *tenor*. The only motet beginning with *Dame* is M11, and in its tenor's historiated initial F (of *Fins cuers dous*) a head may represent an old woman's face looking back or, as Domenic Leo suggests, a hunting horn player; does the face look back to M1 and is it meant to draw attention to the relationship of these two motets?[93]

The series M1–10 consists mainly of works with mensural transformations in the tenor, in most cases by diminution; the exceptions are M8 and 9. M6 has no diminution either but features instead a complex mensural re-reading of the tenor in its second section. The series M11–20 is more divergent in structure but, except for M18, none of these motets has tenor diminution. The great four-part motets 21–23 are very similar in structure; of these, M22 has no diminution section.

Within the first group of ten the relationship between M2 and 3 is clearest in their themes and in the shared tenor figure of Job. Structurally, they are characterized by experimentation in talea construction: M2 has a puzzling tenor diminution that, when properly read, turns out to be half binary and half ternary. M3 has an intriguing tenor structure with a broken-off last talea, which functions in a symmetrical form defined by the upper voices. In M6 as well the tenor structure displays an experimental construction, with a telescopic design

---

[89] Both Vitry's motet and M10 treat the theme of love's fire, and M10 clearly refers to the older work by its opening words *Hareu, hareu*. In M5 Machaut cited Vitry's talea and complicated it by adding a contratenor with the talea in retrograde. Moreover he speculated on the paradox of perfection and imperfection (the perfect longae of the tenor/contratenor are imperfect for the upper voices). See Boogaart, "Encompassing," pp. 51–72.

[90] This specific context, of the suffering Christ on Mount Olivet who trembles before his coming suffering but subjects himself to the will of his Father, fits the message of the motet like a glove; it is the biblical parallel of the lover's fear to suffer and his subsequent subjection to his lady and the god of Love. It means, however, that the melisma had to be considerably modified (like that of M2). See the commentary of this motet.

[91] Assuming that M20 has a length of 51 breves, with a perfect longa as its closing note, which is entirely defendable since the hocket sections which divide the motet recur at a period of 17 breves; and also the closing *Amen* might be a justification to consider the final as a perfect longa.

[92] Brown's suggestion that M16 might have a length of 153 breves is attractive but it would spoil the otherwise very precise proportions in this piece. It has a phrase periodicity of 15 (motetus) and 25 breves (triplum) causing a bisection in the middle of the motet; one minor deviation prevents a complete division by two at bar 75 in this piece of 150 breves, which is precisely the point of its meaning: a faithful lady's heart cannot divide itself into two. See Brown, "Another Mirror," p. 131.

[93] For an extensive interpretation of the miniature, see the commentary by Domenic Leo and myself after the Editorial Policy.

in which the beginning of the new talea is at the same time the end of the preceding one; again, it is the upper voices that invite this perception of the form. Thus, all three motets are characterized by experiments in talea-construction.

Of the remaining motets in this group, M4 and 7 clearly were conceived as a pair. This is evident from several connections, beginning with their tenor figures: David as the psalmist in M4 and David as the king in M7. Both the source chants belong to the liturgical time following Pentecost. They have a similar complex talea-color construction: in both works the talea length is a mensurally irrational number, 17 and 19 longae respectively, which makes a regular division by the mensural numbers 2 or 3 impossible. Both have two colores divided by three taleae (expressed by the formula 2C=3T), repeated in diminution. The reason why they were placed so far apart may be the following: together with M1 and 10 these two motets form a group of four equidistant works, 1-4-7-10. Both the biblical figures and the liturgical contexts of the tenor pairs are complementary: David — as the suffering psalmist and as the mourning king, Christ's prefiguration in the Old Testament — in M4 and 7, whose tenor chants belong to the time just after Pentecost; Christ — as the apocalyptical Judge and as the dying Christ, the fulfillment of David's prefiguration in the New Testament — in M1 and 10, whose chant tenors belong to Holy Week, just before Easter. Within the series of motets with diminution, M1 and 7 are both exceptional; they have completely perfect (M1) or completely imperfect mensuration (M7), whereas M4 and 10 are thematically related by the motif of the amorous fire.[94]

The thematically related M8 and 9 both feature varied color-talea proportions: the 12 taleae of M8 are combined by upper voice isorhythm to 4 super-taleae which span 3 colores (3C=4T), so that only at the end do color and talea close together. In M9 the relationship 2C=3T is repeated twice, from which three cycles result.

Within the second series of ten motets M13, 14, and 15 are obviously related, not only through their themes of false seeming but also through their construction in four lengthy taleae, in M13 and 15 dividing a single long color, and, at the other extreme, in M14 dividing six short colores (two cycles with the scheme 3C=2T). Iambic prolatio patterns, otherwise rare, appear in both M14 and 15.[95] All three works have a greater amount of isorhythm than the average of the motets. In M18 and 19 no common structural principle is apparent; their connection is only thematic, as ceremonial motets. Finally M12 and 17 are also not related through their musical construction but through the Boethian connotations of their texts.

A similar group of four equidistant works in the second series of ten to that of the first (M1-4-7-10) would be formed by M11, 14, 17, and 20. However, this relationship is rather tenuous: the only clear common element is the presence of a female figure in the tenor. In the tenors of the chanson-motets the courtly Lady (called *Fin cuer dous* in M11 and *amie* in M20) is the object of adoration, while the texts in M20 have an almost religious tone; in M14 and 17 the tenor stems from a Marian antiphon. The tenor figure in M14 is the Bride from the Song of Songs; in M17 it is Wisdom (*Sapientia*), who in the biblical context is also longed for as a bride.[96]

With the musical construction and the tenors as combined criteria, the original corpus thus appears to be governed by a mirror-symmetrical plan, through the position of M1, 5, and 10 on the one side, and of M11, 16, and 20 on the other. In between, similarities of theme and structure form subsets of works. To this main

---

[94] Moreover, the sum of the lengths of the two motet-pairs 1–10 and 4–7 is equal (that is, assuming for M7 a planned length of 171 breves, as if the isorhythmic structure were carried out completely, so not taking account of the omission of the final rest) namely 648 semibreves: 432+216 for M1 and 10, and 306+342 for M4 and 7. Admittedly, this depends on the above-mentioned assumption about the length of M7 and the semibreve as the unit of calculation.

[95] Otherwise these are only found in M20 and 22, both arguably late works.

[96] Sapientia 7:29 probably was the source for the tenor words in the antiphon: "Est enim haec *speciosior* sole, et *super omnem* stellarum dispositionem, luci conparata invenitur prior. 8:2 Hanc amavi, et exquisivi a iuventute mea, et quaesivi sponsam mihi adsumere, et amator factus sum formae illius." ("For she is more beautiful than the sun, and above all the order of the stars: being compared with the light, she is found before it. Her have I loved, and have sought her out from my youth, and have desired to take her for my spouse, and I became a lover of her beauty.") See Boogaart, "Encompassing," p. 46, notes 99–100.

corpus a set of three grand motets was added.[97] The close thematic relationship of M21-23 is answered on the structural level by their common four-voice structure, lengthy introits and imposing design.

Several authors have written about the midpoint of the corpus of motets, since the midpoint often forms an important position in medieval works.[98] Once the three late works were added — but only then — M12 became the midpoint of the complete corpus. The midpoint of M12 itself (its length is 162 breves) is marked by a brief melodic imitation between triplum and motetus, where they exchange roles: before bar 81 the triplum is generally lower than the motetus; thereafter it regains its normal higher register. No doubt this construction was inspired by the biblical context of the tenor words *Libera me*, which express Jacob's fear of Esau, his first-born twin brother whose precedence he had taken fraudulently, a deed that was afterwards justified. The signification of the register change in both texts is that the *I*, who until this midpoint complains about his miseries, in the second half learns to accept his fate, the lesson of virtually all the motets. However, since in the original corpus M12 did not have that central place it is a mystery whether this was so planned or is just a happy coincidence.

Thus, two concurring ordering principles in Machaut's series of motets can be distinguished: one thematic, the other structural. The two complement each other, while also the tenors and their contexts play a role. The question of whether Machaut devised the plan for his series of motets beforehand is difficult to answer. The order seems more an attempt at rationalization after the composition of certain groups than the result of an overall pre-compositional plan that was gradually filled in. Had there been a pre-conceived plan, one would expect greater precision and more outspoken similarities within the corpus, like those principally found in the first group of ten. Nevertheless, the existence of an organized cycle of 23 motets by a single composer from the late Middle Ages is in itself already an extraordinary fact, from a music-historical as well as from an aesthetic point of view.

❧ ❧ ❧

Guillaume de Machaut's collected motets form a unique corpus, both in quantity and in quality. No comparable ensemble from the fourteenth century, showing the same degree of thematic unity in so great a number of works, has been preserved. Their uniform sequence in the manuscripts suggests that Machaut considered the motets a finished part of his oeuvre, even at two different points in his career; the last three motets are a later addition to the original series of twenty works as it stands in the earliest complete-works manuscript *C*. As argued above, the corpus was ordered according to both thematic and musical criteria.

The majority of the motets are the fruit of Machaut's early years as a composer, at the time he was in court service; perhaps they even represent his first achievements in the field of polyphony. His explorations of the modern notational system betray astounding insight into its possibilities. In most of the works featuring subjects of courtly love he incorporated and further developed the French poetic tradition of bygone centuries, reflecting on the problems and paradoxes of that love. The motets show a remarkable combination of poetic philosophy and musical refinement. With its polytextuality, the motet formed the ideal genre to consider the various subjects from different angles in the texted voices. A smaller number of works in Latin, originally destined for various ecclesiastical or political occasions, nevertheless still fit the thematic order of the amorous motets. The three compositions added later display a much grander design that elaborates on the more subtle construction of the earlier works.

In all his motets Machaut shows himself a bold experimenter with counterpoint and large-scale rhythms. Within the fairly restrictive template of the isorhythmic motet, developed by composers before him, he

---

[97] Leech-Wilkinson has observed that M23 has similarities in text division with M10; see Leech-Wilkinson, *Compositional Techniques*, p. 132. More links between older and newer works can certainly be discovered (e.g., textual references in M23 to M9). Striking with respect to the distances between the female tenor figures in M11, 14, 17 and 20 is that with M23 the same distance is conserved.

[98] Brown sees a dead point between M10 and 11 and draws a comparison of the dead lover in M10 with the death of the first author of the Rose, Guillaume de Lorris, described in the centre of the *Roman* after which the work is said to be taken over by Jean de Meung; see "Another Mirror," p. 129. For Robertson the midpoint is M9, the nadir of her allegorical pilgrimage; *Machaut and Reims*, p. 151 (M20 plays no part in her interpretation of the order).

succeeded in surmounting its constraints and created works of an astonishing variety and fantasy that are already impressive at first hearing but reveal their subtlety further after detailed analysis and consideration. Each composition exhibits an individual character, in accordance with its subject. Poetry and music are on a par. No less than composers in later centuries Machaut devised the means to translate his poetic reflections in ingenious musical constructs and gestures of great expressiveness. Machaut's most imposing achievement is the highly inventive way in which he wove his complex literary deliberations with musical threads into harmonic webs of thought and song. It is the challenge to the performer to realize in sound the aesthetic potential of the written notes.

❧ Editorial Policy

Choice of Base Manuscript

Machaut's motets appear in all six extant complete-works manuscripts; for only a few works concordances in anthologies or fragments exist.[1] These manuscripts are, in the generally accepted chronological order and with their customary sigla:

C (Paris, Bibliothèque nationale de France [BnF], fonds français [fr.] 1586), c.1350–1356 but very possibly earlier. 19 motets (M4 and 21–23 missing), written in two columns: on the verso the triplum, continuing into the left column of the recto and followed by the tenor; on the recto right column the motetus, where necessary continuing on staves over the entire width at the bottom of the page. All initials one staff tall.

W (Aberystwyth, National Library of Wales, MS 5010 C), severely damaged but originally an early complete-works codex like *C*, has, besides other damage, lost practically all of its music and contains only a fragment of M1, from which the initial was torn off. To judge from the fragment the layout of the motets must have been similar to that of *C*.

Vg (Ferrell-Vogüé, private ownership of James E. and Elizabeth J. Ferrell). Main body c.1365–1370, with later addition of *La Prise d'Alixandre* (copied from *B*). 23 motets: no columns, staves occupy the entire width of the page; on the verso the triplum, where necessary continuing onto the recto and followed by motetus and tenor. Initials two staves tall for the triplum, one staff for motetus and tenor. Spellings are more "modern" than in *C*, *A*, and *F-G*, approaching the etymologizing spellings of the late *E* (e.g., *doulz* instead of *dous*, *resgardant* instead of *regardant*).

B (Paris, BnF, fr. 1585), paper copy of *Vg*, except for the *Prise d'Alixandre*; formerly dated c.1370–1372 but recently a later date has been proposed, c. 1388; with seven replacement folios from the early fifteenth century. Same layout and spellings as in *Vg*. Cursive script (in contrast to the *littera textualis* of the other manuscripts).

A (Paris, BnF, fr. 1584), c. 1375–1377, possibly written in Reims. 23 motets: two columns, verso left column for the triplum, continuing onto left column of recto or, if necessary, the full width of the recto page; verso right column for the motetus, continuing on recto right column; followed on recto right column by the tenor and contratenor (where present). Initials one staff tall for triplum and tenor, two staves for the motetus (in the index the motets are listed by their motetus incipit except M1 and 18). Miniature heading the triplum of M1; small face-like drollery in the capital F of the tenor of M11.

---

[1] On the affiliation and ordering of the manuscripts containing the music, see Earp, "Machaut's Role"; for a complete description and inventory of all the manuscript sources, see id., *Guillaume de Machaut*, pp. 77–128; on the different layouts and orderings in the main manuscripts, id., "Interpreting the Deluxe Manuscript" and id., "Introductory Study," pp. 29–35. For a later dating of *B*, see id., "Introductory Study," pp. 44–46.

F-G (Paris, BnF, fr. 22545–6), illuminated c.1390 but probably written still within Machaut's lifetime and possibly left unfinished at his death (certainly copied from authorially controlled materials).[2] **G** contains the musical œuvre. 23 motets, layout as in *A* but all initials one staff tall. Above the beginning of the triplum of M1 two staves are left empty; perhaps a miniature was originally intended, as in *A*, but not executed. Spellings in general similar to *C* and *A*.

E (Paris, BnF, fr. 9221), c. 1390. 22 motets (M23 missing). As in *Vg* and *B* the staves occupy the entire width of the page. Initials one staff tall, often slightly different in size. Spellings are typical for the late fourteenth and early fifteenth centuries. The order diverges from the other manuscripts and, due to the much larger page size, which for a number of works left considerable empty space, the motets are combined with rondeaus. Order of motets: M20, 1, 2, 8, 3, 4, 5, 6, 17, 16, 7, 9, 11, 10, 12, 13, 14, 15, 19, 18, 22, 21.

A few motets are also found in surviving anthologies and fragments; other codices, now lost, may have contained more works.

Trem (Trémoïlle, Paris, BnF, nouv. acq. fr. 23190), according to its preserved index, once had M8, 9, 10, 14, 15, 16, 19, 20, and possibly M23; in addition it transmitted ten of Machaut's chansons. In the surviving fragment now only the triplum and tenor of M8 and the motetus and tenor of M15 remain. **Iv** (Ivrea, Biblioteca Capitolar 115) contains M8, 15, and 19. The fragment **CaB** (Cambrai, Bibliothèque municipale B.1328) transmits the entire M8. Lastly, **St** (Stockholm, Kungliga biblioteket V.u. 22) preserves the texts only of M8.

In choosing which manuscript version to use as the best source, different considerations offer themselves. Regarding the motets, no great difficulties are encountered since the versions in the four most important manuscripts are fairly uniform; differences are usually due to scribal errors or misunderstandings, and fundamentally divergent musical readings are very rare. Most of the differences concern ficta signs, plicae, and spellings.

The oldest source, **C,** might be closest to Machaut's original conception, yet it lacks four motets. The source that often has the clearest readings, especially for the text underlay, is **Vg**. Its hastily made and less correct copy **B** and the posthumous and often faulty **E**, whose versions are for the most part based on those in **B**, can be ruled out. Although **F-G** seems to be the last codex to have been copied from authorial materials and could therefore present the latest versions, we have after much deliberation opted for the earlier **A** as the base source for the entire edition; current scholarly research posits it as the most recent and possibly the last copy that was produced during Machaut's lifetime, perhaps in Reims itself and thus close to the poet-composer's person. There are a few passages where other versions seem more correct and these have been amended accordingly, but in general **A** is a good and reliable source and has been preferred for all the volumes of our edition. It is also the earliest manuscript to contain all of Machaut's major literary works. Moreover, its index bears a rubric, unique among all the Machaut manuscripts, that reads *Vesci lordenance que G. de Machau wet quil ait en son livre* (literally "See here the order as G. de Machau wishes it to be in his book" or, in Barton Palmer's translation, "This is the arrangement that Guillaume de Machaut wishes his book to have"). Although such a prescriptive index surely does not imply that the author controlled every detail (and some deviations from its order are indeed found in *A*),[3] the rubric may be understood as testimony to the authenticity of the manuscript and thus as a witness to the author's intentions (depending, though, on what exactly Machaut understood by *ordenance*).

Layout and Barring

Since texts and musical structure are equally important, an edition of the motets should ideally present both the texts and the music in an easily readable and conveniently arranged way for performers. At the same time it must clarify the mensuration and its intricacies for the scholar and student. Reflecting the problems and

---

[2] See Earp, "Introductory Study," p. 32 and p. 35n44; also Yolanda Plumley and Uri Smilansky, "A Courtier's Quest for Cultural Capital: New Light on the Original Owner of Machaut MS *F-G*," forthcoming.

[3] See Earp, "Machaut's Role," pp. 480–88; see also Cerquiglini, "*Un engin*," pp. 15–16.

notational games of the composer may not only help analysis and interpretation but also enhance an expressive performance of the work.

The scale of reduction is the customary 1:4, which renders the musical structure in an easily comprehensible shape for a modern performer, much as the fourteenth-century performer may have experienced his notation:

Maxima	longa	brevis	semibrevis	minima

The bar numbering follows the tempus units, which are indicated with "ticks" through the upper line of the staves of triplum and motetus (except in the larger note values in the introitus of M21-23, where they would be visually distracting).

The tenor always operates on a larger mensural level than the upper voices, that is, in modus or maximodus (major modus, depending on whether or not maximae are used). Its measuring scale and barring are thus usually twice or thrice that of the upper voices, in which modus is the largest level, with tempus and prolatio as the most common mensurations. The modus bars are marked by bar lines in all the voices and are the only ones shown in the tenor staves. In the case of tenor diminution the mensural scale shifts down one level, so that then bar lines indicate tempus units (or those of modus in the tenor when in undiminished form it was maximodus) and the ticks disappear, except for a few cases in the tenor/contratenor parts where they serve to clarify the subdivision. The diminution section thus has a busier appearance, but this corresponds with its content and structure: not only does the rhythmic activity accelerate, but the problems discussed in the texts and also the contrapuntal tension in the music both acquire more urgency.

Laying out motets in modern score format presents the problem of combining widely diverging values in the different voices and, thus, of their spacing; in this respect the original manuscript layout in parts was much more economical and practical. In *A*, as in most of the manuscripts, all the motets except M23 fit onto one opening (two facing pages) whereas a layout in score format requires from three to eight pages.

It is the tenor (in four cases complemented by a contratenor) in which most of the mensural problems and notational intricacies are found. In the present edition the tenor voice has been distributed over the staves in such a way that its modus bars — and with it, the comprehensibility of its structure — are not broken at the transition from one system to the next; only in two cases (M13 and 21) did it prove unavoidable to break off an occasional bar, which is then indicated by a dashed bar line. Far more often modus bars have had to be broken off in the upper voice parts (also indicated by a dashed bar line); this occurs where their mensuration and barring differ from that of the tenor, in which cases the tenor bars have been left intact.

As many tenor bars as possible have been placed on a system while maintaining the readability of the upper-voice texts; this has resulted in a sometimes uneven division of time-units per system. Particularly in the four-part works, where the coordination of the lower voices is crucial, often the choice had to be made between a certain number of bars or twice that amount. The melodies of the triplum parts with their long texts are sometimes difficult to space in a consistent way. Especially the larger values of this voice part tend to suffer; because they carry one syllable only they are given much less space than their sounding length would justify. In this respect the transcription is actually closer to the text division and spacing of the manuscripts than to that of a typical modern score. The more compact Latin texts present fewer difficulties in this respect than the French ones.

Mensuration

In Machaut's music the mensuration must be deduced from the notes and rests, and from their combination and grouping; although mensuration signs were available at the time, they are rarely found in the Machaut manuscripts and nowhere in the motets.[4] The time signatures in the transcriptions have the sole purpose of indicating the mensuration — the way of measuring the different note shapes, of establishing their perfection

---

[4] See the relevant chapters in Apel, *The Notation* and Rastall, *The Notation*. On meter in the chansons see also Maw, "'Trespasser mesure.'"

or imperfection and how they relate to each other — and should not be regarded as modern signatures with implications for accentuation. They function as follows: single time signatures indicate tempus, the division of the brevis: 3/4 for perfect tempus, 2/4 for imperfect tempus. The larger divisions, modus and maximodus, indicating the division of longa and maxima respectively, are presented as multiplications (like 2x 3/4). The first number indicates ternary or binary division of the level indicated by the lower number of the following fraction; that lower number indicates modus by a 4, maximodus by a 2 (only in those pieces that have maximae in the tenor and contratenor).[5] The upper number indicates the perfection or imperfection of modus or tempus:

3/4 = perfect tempus

2/4 = imperfect tempus

3x 3/4 = perfect modus with perfect tempus

3x 2/4 = perfect modus with imperfect tempus

2x 3/4 = imperfect modus with perfect tempus

2x 2/4 = imperfect modus with imperfect tempus

3x 2/2 = perfect maximodus with imperfect modus

2x 3/2 = imperfect maximodus with perfect modus

2x 2/2 = imperfect maximodus with imperfect modus

(3x 3/2, perfect maximodus with perfect modus, does not occur)

The upper voices never have maximae, so for them the signatures always indicate minor modus and tempus, or tempus only. The quality of the prolatio — which in the motets consists of only a few standard patterns, mostly trochaic, rarely iambic — can be seen from the presence or absence of triplets. Ludwig's practical solution to transcribe the prolatio major by triplets has been followed here since it allows for transcribing the original values so that the larger perfect notes are simpler in appearance (with fewer dots and ties), and that subtleties as in M5, where the black longae in the tenor and contratenor are perfect with respect to each other's red longae but imperfect with respect to the upper voices, can easily be perceived. Only in the rondeau-motet M20, where modus mensuration is virtually irrelevant (except for the final longa), perfect tempus and prolatio have been transcribed in 9/8 since in this work, which features subtle syncopations on the prolatio-level, the triplet notation would have been confusing (the same holds for the chansons in the following volumes of the edition). Double-dotted notes are used to indicate that a particular brevis or longa is perfect in all its subdivisions. An entirely perfect maxima, which would be difficult to transcribe by a single sign, never occurs; in M18, the only motet where a dotted maxima, transcribed as a double whole note, appears, it is worth two perfect longae and equals three imperfect longae in the upper voices. The most common mensural combination is perfect modus, imperfect tempus, and perfect prolatio. Only two motets have perfect mensuration on all levels (M1 and 20), and only one has overall imperfect mensuration (M7).

Earlier editors took for granted that Machaut permitted himself many notational licences, such as unheralded changes of modus. Some of these assumptions were criticized in 1960 by Richard Hoppin; the original notation often precludes a transcription according to the modus which, for those editors, the music seemed to suggest (e.g., they assumed perfect modus or maximodus but overlooked, or supposed that Machaut ignored, the first rule of perfect mensuration, *similis ante similem perfecta*, "like before like is perfect"). Their method, confusing the mensural system with modern time signatures, has obscured several of Machaut's notational tricks and his play with the performer, elements that are important for the understanding of his music. The present edition strives to show the mensuration as indicated or implied by rest signs and configuration of values. Only in rare cases one must one indeed conclude that Machaut changed the modus without warning. His use of the dot of

---

[5] The perfection or imperfection of the maximodus cannot always be established with certainty, just as is often the case with the modus in the chansons.

perfection is interesting in this respect. Two examples: in the motetus of M4 a dot of perfection following a longa influences also the surrounding notes, which are to be read in perfect mensuration; the imperfect longa-rest signs of the contratenor of M21 conventionally suggest an imperfect modus, yet dots of perfection cause alterations and thus in fact realize perfect modus (see the commentaries of these motets).

A consistent modus division often entails large-scale syncopations that exceed the modus bars (and bar lines) and makes ties necessary in the upper voices, although this occurs less frequently than we might expect; especially in works in whose texts with the theme of *trespassing measure* syncopations are likely to occur and seem to serve an expressive purpose (e.g., in M2, M7, M8);[6] such syncopations should therefore be clearly visible.

For the syncopations and other mensural complications in the tenor parts a different solution has had to be found for each piece. The easiest case was M10, where beginning with an "upbeat" suffices to make the structure visible. A problematic case is M4, where a very simple rhythm in perfect maximodus is complicated by four inserted brevis rests; in our transcription this simple rhythm is shown enclosed by the supernumerary rests which are marked and isolated by ticks. Another problem occurs in those tenors whose number of maximodus measures cannot be divided by 2 or 3 (M3, M4, M7, in M17 the minor modus) and thus are not in regular perfect or imperfect mensuration; in those cases different solutions had to be devised for each piece, as explained in the commentary. The incomplete (or, in M4, the surplus) bars have not been indicated with a change of time signature since they often can be supposed to function in a long-term syncopation (see e.g., the commentary for M17). The regular exchanges of mensuration — indicated by red and black color — between tenor and contratenor in M5 and M23 have, as a reminder, been marked by time-signatures in small type above the staff (full-size time signatures within the staves would have created difficulties with the text spacing). Coloration has been indicated by the customary square brackets.

Structure

It has not always been possible to arrive at a layout with one talea per page (although this was the ideal). However, each undiminished talea begins on a new system, so that it is easy to perceive the (ir)regularities. For the diminished taleae this would sometimes have resulted in too wide a spacing of notes and text, so that the diminished taleae may also begin halfway across a system.

The colores and taleae are numbered continuously, in Arabic numerals for the colores, in Roman for the taleae; in the diminished sections the Roman numerals are repeated for the taleae but in lower case (e.g., C2, i, ii, and iii). When isorhythm in the upper voices combines several taleae into one "super"-talea (e.g., M1, M8, M10, M15) its subdivision into single taleae is indicated by the letter a or b after the talea-number, e.g., Ia, Ib etc. (in M12 super-talea and color coincide completely). A motet like M9 has three cycles, each of 2 colores divided by 3 taleae (2C=3T), with no diminution, so that an extra indication for these cycles is needed: A, B and C in bold. A comparable case is M14 with 6 colores and 4 taleae (3C=2T) in two cycles, A and B. The tenor phrases in the chanson-motets are marked by a double bar line in the staff, without numbers or letters; their structure is explained in the commentary.

Pitch Names, Musica Ficta, and Plicae

The note names used in this edition are those of the medieval diatonic scale:

Graves	Acutae	Superacutae
ΓA B C D E F G	a b♭♮ b c d e f g	aa b♭♮b♭ bb cc dd

In the domains of musica ficta and plicae the manuscripts differ most. The general policy followed is that musica ficta signs — accidentals — are treated as referring to a single note and that extensions of their effects are given as editorial additions, even where they seem obvious.[7]

---

[6] On M7 see also Maw, "Trespasser mesure," pp. 112–13.

[7] About the thorny subject of musica ficta, see the various opinions in e.g., Bent, "Musica recta and musica ficta;" ead., "The Grammar of Early Music;" ead., "The 'Harmony' of the Machaut Mass;" Harden, "Sharps, Flats and Scribes;" ead., "Musica ficta in Machaut;" Berger, "Musica ficta"; Cross, ed., *Machaut: La Messe*, pp. i–iv; Brothers, *Chromatic Beauty*; Leach, "Counterpoint and Analysis;" Bain, "Theorizing the Cadence;" ead., "Tonal Structure."

All accidentals that appear in MS *A* are given within the staff.

A sign within the staff with "(-) sigla" above the staff indicates that it is in *A* but is missing from the sources specified.

"*A only*" above the staff means of course that it is missing in all the other sources.

A sign above the staff with sigla indicates that it occurs in the sources specified but not in *A* and that it is recommended.

A sign above the staff with no sigla indicates that it is not in any source but is recommended. This is often the case in cadential situations.

A sign above the staff within round brackets suggests that the performer may consider applying it (i.e., the inflection is open to debate).

A sign above the staff between square brackets plus sigla indicates that it is found in the specified source(s) but that applying it is not recommended.

Sometimes it appears that Machaut steered his counterpoint into an impasse, by writing strictly forbidden dissonances. This may already be seen and heard in the first three motets. The problem follows from the convention that the tenor — whose melody was borrowed from sacred plainchant — is not to be altered. An accidental in the upper voices may thus cause severe dissonances (e.g., by an f♯ in an upper voice against an F in the tenor which cannot be altered); such clashes probably had an expressive function and challenged the performers to find a solution, if at all possible. Clashes of this kind and their possible solutions are discussed in the commentaries.

The same policy as for ficta signs has been followed in indicating plicae, with the caveat that its absence in MS *E* has not been marked, since that manuscript contains no plicae at all. The old *custos* sign has been given a new life and has been used for the transcription of the plica, with upward tail for an ascending plica: ⌁, downward for a descending plica: . The performance of this ornamental sign is still open to debate. It usually has been performed as an auxiliary passing note bridging intervals of (very often) a third; however, Machaut used it also for very wide intervals. Recently it has been proposed that it could be a kind of vibrato or trill.[8] On the grounds of its frequent use in certain motets (M2, 5, 17) one might conclude that it had an expressive function. Performers are thus advised to experiment with the ornamental aspect of the plica, perhaps realizing it as a discreet trill, followed by a filler note. The plica longa is usually explained as a longa with reversed stem and for that reason in the older editions was not transcribed as a plica. It is true that two manuscripts, namely *Vg* and *B*, fairly consistently draw low-positioned longae with upward tails, in order not to go through the text; but the others, *C, A,* and *G,* generally do not follow this practice and they often agree on the plica longa. The scribe of *G* in particular did not hesitate to draw the stem through the underlaid text. An ambiguity is created because very low notes may in themselves also suggest a state of depression and so, as if to enhance their expressiveness, may be reinforced by a plica. Where these three manuscripts agree on a plica longa it has been transcribed as such; doubtful cases are discussed in the commentary.

Text Underlay and Translation

The text underlay also often differs slightly from manuscript to manuscript; only in rare cases where alignment of note and syllable is unclear do hairlines connect a syllable to a note. In general *A* has been followed except in the few cases where this manuscript is plainly wrong; in doubtful cases *C, Vg,* and *G* have been consulted. In principle the metrical form of the verse has been respected; as a consequence unwritten elisions have often been applied, except where a rest would split a word for an unnaturally long time or where the manuscripts clearly set all the (metrically superfluous) syllables. Apparently some freedom existed in the hocket sections where it is not always clear on which note a syllable should be sung and where often only a few syllables must

---

[8] See Haines, "Lambertus' Epiglotus."

be divided over many notes; the Latin works in particular are rather vague in this respect.[9] Performers may try other solutions than those proposed here and judge for themselves which sounds best.

Each motet is followed by the texts and their translation. Translations are by the present editor but have been refashioned into more fluent and lively English versions by R. Barton Palmer.

Commentaries

At the end of the volume the reader will find the commentary and critical notes for each piece. It presents the concordant sources, the tenor source with its context and the structure of the texts; quotations as far as these can be identified; the tenor's mensuration and musical structure, and the mensuration of the upper voices, which sometimes differs from the tenor's; discussions of special problems; and a list of variants. An asterisk within the score refers to an emendation, which is explained in the commentary. Finally, references to the most important literature on a particular piece are given. More complete references to literature through 1995 can be found in Earp, *Guillaume de Machaut,* of which the relevant pages are given. Text variants will be given in the volumes of the present edition devoted to the lyric poetry.

NOTE FOR THE PERFORMANCE

Performers are advised to choose a tempo that allows the texts to be clearly articulated. Part of the pleasure in singing motets is the clash of different texts, which only at rare moments come together in a common verbal sound. The tenor is the foundation of the piece directing the whole movement, so the singer of this voice may experiment with timbre and volume to increase the tension. The ensemble should not (in the opinion of the present editor at least) necessarily strive for a harmonic and blended consonant sound but rather for a lively confrontation of the three or four different melodies and rhythms.

PRONUNCIATION

Although it is impossible to know precisely how Middle French was pronounced an attempt must be made.[10] It was a relatively well-notated language: specialists assume that on the whole all the letters, with a few exceptions, corresponded to a sound and were pronounced. The following minimal indications cover most cases.

Vowels and Dipthongs

In general, vowels sounded as in modern French except for the following cases:

> *e* was never completely mute (except in elision) but sounded more or less like it still does in Southern France and Italy (close to *è*). In transcription an acute accent is given where confusion between *e* and *é* could arise.
>
> Most diphthongs, although written with two letters, usually had only one sound: *ai = é, ue* and *eu = œ, oi* and *oy = wè*. Only those diphthongs that resulted from a former *l* continued to be pronounced as two sounds: *autre* (=aoutre), *biaus* (=biaous).
>
> In nasalized vowels the final *n* was pronounced, as in Southern France (*paiñ, bieñ*).

Consonants

All consonants were pronounced, with the exception of:

> *s* within a word before another consonant (*isle = ile*);
>
> *r, s,* and *t* at the end of a word following a consonant and followed by a consonant in the next word.

---

[9] See on the problem of the texting of hockets especially Zayaruznaya, "Hockets as Compositional and Scribal Practice," and Schmidt-Beste, "Singing the Hiccup."

[10] The following is based on the instructions in Hasenohr, *Introduction,* pp. 11–13 and on the still useful E. and J. Bourciez, *Phonétique française: Étude historique.*

However, where *r*, *s*, or *t* are followed by a vowel or are at a point of rest (caesura, musical rest) they were pronounced.

ch and *j* were pronounced as in modern French.

h, when aspirated in modern French (*haïr*, in general in words of Germanic origin) was probably fully pronounced, as in English *hate*.

l in words like *altre* is an alternative way of writing *u*.

ll sounded like *gl* or *ll* in in modern Italian or Spanish; *fille* (=fillye).

r was a rolling tongue-tip *r* as in modern Italian or Spanish.

x was often a way of writing *–us*, like in *Diex* (Dieus), *miex* (mieus).

In Latin texts all vowels and consonants were probably pronounced as in French; *u* sounded as *ü*, *qu* as *k*, like in que; *gn* as *ñ* (like in *agneau*).

THE MOTET MINIATURE: A COMMENTARY

BY DOMENIC LEO AND JACQUES BOOGAART

Figure 2. *A*, fol. 414v (A153). Opening miniature for the motets.
Bibliothèque nationale de France, with permission.

There were dynamic, creative forces at work in the planning and execution of *A*. One of the more prominent examples is the miniature at the opening of the motets (fig. 2[1]). It displays innovations in composition, iconography, placement, and content. Parsing the image in light of its contemporary reception reveals an internal dialogue which synthesizes the images, texts, and music found in the microcosm of this manuscript. Machaut may very well have been at the center of this activity. The artist ingeniously adapted pre-existing iconographic moduli to suit his purposes. In light of the motet beneath the image, and of this section as a whole, the image embodies the tension so integral to this genre. It is a unique creation, which betrays profound consideration and reflection on the part of the artist. Unlike a painting, this is a miniature in a manuscript that contains 155 other miniatures. It thus gives the richest enjoyment to the viewer who is most familiar with the manuscript's diverse contents as a whole.

In the motet image, a fashionably attired nobleman, with a long, forked beard, stands casually. He is leaning on a tonsured cleric with short hair (fig. 2). Of interest is the nobleman's physical rapport with the cleric: he has one arm draped over the cleric's shoulder and his hand resting on the cleric's extended forearm. It is as if they are acting in harmony — a church and court group, if you will. Their faces are placid as they watch a group of four singers. The attire of these singers, the floor-length robe and *capuchon*, marks them as clerics, and the figure at far right is tonsured. They probably represent trained clerical singers, able to cope with works as complex as motets. Each singer is differentiated in some way from the other by physiognomy, gesture, and hairstyle; this last aspect, perhaps, denotes disparities in age. At far right, one singer's mouth is open wide in an ungainly fashion. All sing from music on a scroll which extends over a barrel; on the scroll, notes and two words are visible, *dam[e]* and *tenor* (figs. 2, 5). The singer on the right, who holds it, is likely to be the leader; his gesture, holding his hand to his ear as if to control tuning, identifies him as such. This underlines the participation of the nobleman and elder cleric as *audience*, not performers.

To enhance the prestige of the nobleman, a valet stands behind him pouring wine from a ewer into a *hanap*, an elaborate medieval goblet (fig. 3). The attention to detail here is astonishing: the artist has depicted the wine being poured with bright red striations (see the cover of the volume). The pleasurable combination of wine and music is, of course, age-old, not only in coarse tavern songs, but also in an (admittedly parodic) trouvère chanson like *Chanter me fait bons vins et resjoïr* ("Good wine makes me sing and enjoy myself");[2] the wine surely was meant to add a humorous note to the scene.[3]

Figure 3. *A*, fol. 414v, detail. A valet pouring wine. Bibliothèque nationale de France, with permission.

---

[1] "A153" conforms to Lawrence Earp's system of numbering the miniatures in this manuscript. For a concordance of miniatures from all extant illuminated Machaut manuscripts, see Earp, *Guillaume de Machaut*, 1995, pp. 145–88.

[2] Raynaud-Spanke, no. 1447; edited in Jeanroy and Långfors, *Chanson satyriques et bachiques*, pp. 77–78. It is a parody of *Chanteir me fait Amors et resjoïr* (ed. ibid., pp. 86–87).

[3] The *Roman de Fauvel* ends with a drinking motet, with a refrain in all three voices: *Cis chans veult boire* ("This song wants [us] to drink").

Two early-fourteenth-century documents provide compelling evidence of the mixed groups of expert performers and learned audience. Around 1300, Johannes de Grocheio writes in his treatise, *Ars musicae*, of just such a company:

> Cantus autem iste non debet coram vulgalibus propinari. eo quod eius subtilitatem non advertunt nec in eius auditu delectantur. Sed coram litteratis et illis, qui subtilitates artium sunt quaerentes. Et solet in eorum festis decantari ad eorum decorationem, quemadmodum cantilena, quae dicitur rotundellus, in festis vulgalium laycorum.

> This *cantus* ought not to be celebrated in the presence of common people, because they do not notice its subtlety, nor are they delighted in hearing it, but in the presence of the educated and of those who are seeking out subtleties in the arts. And it is customarily sung at their feasts for their enhancement, just as the *cantilena* that is called *rotundellus* at feasts of the common laity.[4]

Jacques de Liège (Jacobus de Ispania)[5] mentions in his *Speculum musicae* (late 1320s) a society of clerics and literate laymen who constitute both the performers and the audience of motets:

> Vidi ergo, in quadam societate, in qua congregati erant, valentes cantores et laici sapientes. Fuerunt ibi cantati moteti moderni et secundum modo modernorum, et veteres aliqui. Plus satis placuerunt, etiam laicis, antiqui quam novi, et modus antiquus quam novus

> In a certain company in which some able singers and judicious laymen were assembled, and where new motets in the modern manner and some old ones were sung, I observed that even the laymen were better pleased with the ancient motets and the ancient manner than with the new.[6]

Pre-existing group-singing iconographic moduli include the ubiquitous motif of clerics singing in psalters, usually nestled into a historiated letter "C" from *Cantate* (Psalm 97: "Sing to the Lord a New Song"). The use of a scroll or *rotulus* is not exceptional. Both codices and scrolls can either be resting on lecterns or held by the singers.[7] A simultaneous representation of performers and audience is, however, unusual. The nobleman and cleric in *A* are physically enmeshed as friends, whereas one would expect to see the latter in a subservient role, presenting or offering his writing, painting, or musical composition (is this a comment on Machaut's role?). The cleric, instead, is holding a ewer (a vase-shaped pitcher). Does this mark him as a "server," or, with a *jeu de mots* on singing, as an *eschanson*, a cupbearer, rather than a "drinker"?

Known as a *tonne* or *ton[n]ele* in Middle French, could the barrel perhaps, again as a *jeu de mots*, refer to the musical *ton* ("tone," "sound of the voice")? The triplum text of M1 ends with a comparable pun, on *son*, which can mean "one's," "sound" or "song": *que de son dous face on amer* ("that you make your sweetness bitter / that you make a sweet sound/song bitter"). An intriguing further interpretation can focus on the shape of the barrel: *rond comme un tonnelet* ("round as a barrel") was a proverbial expression.[8] The barrel itself, the round hole in its center, and the circular disposition of the group around it, could refer to the circle as a symbol of perfection (the

---

[4] Johannes de Grocheio, *Ars musice*, pp 84–85. For a broad-ranging discussion of the motet in its contemporary perception, see Dillon, *The Sense of Sound*.

[5] The *Speculum* was formerly dated somewhat earlier, c. 1321–1324. Margaret Bent, in *Magister Jacobus de Ispania*, has argued that this theorist was not a Liégeois at all, but may be identified as Jacobus de Ispania, from Spanish descent, and educated and living mainly in England. Recently, however, Rob Wegman has convincingly counter-argued that Jacobus lived and worked in Liège and had nothing to do with Spain; a part of the diocese of Liège, the archdeaconate of Hesbaye, is also known in Latin as Hispania (in various spellings) and Jacobus' intimate knowledge of local chant practices points to his presence in Liège. ("Jacobus de Ispania and Liège," in *Journal of the Alamire Foundation* 8/2, 2016, 153–74). This may reset the date to the earlier assumption, but see about the date also Desmond, "New Light," p. 35.

[6] Bragard, ed., *Jacobi Leodiensis Speculum musicae*, Vol. 7, p. 95. Trans. in Strunk, *Source Readings*, Vol. 2, pp. 167–68.

[7] For an example of a scroll with an actual motet, see Page, "Around the Performance of a Thirteenth-Century Motet"; idem, "An English Motet."

[8] See Hassell, *Middle French Proverbs*, p. 238 (T58).

notational sign to indicate perfect mensuration was a circle); the barrel even has three series of hoops. The first motet, above which the miniature is placed, has entirely perfect mensuration (i.e. all mensural divisions are by three) and could almost serve as a model of motet composition; the number 3 and ternary proportions pervade the entire structure of the work.[9] If these assumptions are correct, it would strongly point to Machaut himself, lover as he was of *jeux de mots*, as the deviser of the imagery.

But what is the context? Does the motet image convey a scene from a dining hall? None of the participants are seated, and the top of a massive barrel serves as a sort of table. Is this a tavern image? Or are there no commonly known precedents? Machaut uses the word *tavern* only once, in his final poetic work, the *Prologue*. This poem appears for the first time in *A*:

> Rhetoric makes the lover
> Versify and metrify,
> …
> And it ornaments his language
> In a pleasant and wise way.
> For Good Sense is present there to rule over all
> In the bedchamber, dining hall, and tavern.
> (*Prologue*, ll. 261–62, 271–74)[10]

There is a literary topos for the tavern, but no established iconographic source.[11] Andrew Cowell writes that the literature of the tavern "represents the possibility of escape from ecclesiastical models of economic and literary exchange that insisted on equality, utility, and charity by offering a vision of exuberant excess."[12] It is tempting to see a parodic reference to the blood of Christ on an altar, although this seems highly improbable if Machaut participated in creating this image. However, such sacrilegious comedy does appear in the historiated initial "T" (for the tenor in Rondeau 10 – *Rose, lis*) in which a standing fox, mimicking a priest giving a blessing above an altar, appears to be celebrating Mass (fig. 4). Instances of the topsy-turvy world where animals perform human functions, including participation in the mass — as bishops, priests, clerics, or singers — are frequent in marginalia.[13]

Could this blurred context and iconographic polysemy in the motet image mirror the impact of the reception of the motet? Could individual threads of meaning or micro-narratives reflect or inform a medieval reception, one where the motet functions variously? One can perform, read, or listen to the individual lines of lyrics, the lyrics with the music, or the music alone. Sylvia Huot writes of this image:

---

[9] Machaut rarely used mensuration signs (see the discussion on mensuration under Editorial policy above); there are none in this motet (unless the image should serve as such). See also the commentary for this motet.

[10] "Rhetorique versefier / Fait l'amant, et metrefier / … / Et li aourne son langage / Par maniere plesant et sage. / Car Sens y est qui tout gouverne / En chambre, en sale, et en taverne." Palmer, ed. and trans., *Guillaume de Machaut: The Fountain of Love and Two Other Love Vision Poems*, pp. 16–17; the other two poems are the *Prologue* (pp. 2–19) and the *Story of the Orchard* (*Dit dou Vergier*, pp. 22–87).

[11] There are, however, at least two humorous depictions of drunkenness and revelry which include barrels. An early-thirteenth-century image depicts a cellarer, keys secured by a cord around his waist, drinking from a cup while he holds a ewer to catch the wine gushing out from a large barrel (London, British Library, MS Sloane 2435, fol. 44v). In a manuscript illustrated in 1344, there are numerous marginalia (Oxford, Bodleian Library, MS 264). In the bas-de-page on fol. 94v, apes are shown in a topsy-turvy world — mocking drunken humans — where they cavort and gambol about holding hanaps, goblets, and ewers that they are filling from a wine barrel on which one sits astride.

[12] Cowell, *At Play in the Tavern*, p. 5; also, see Cerquiglini, *"Un engin si soutil"*, pp. 130–31, for an exploration of the motif of the tavern and its negative connotations in literature.

[13] See Randall, *Images in the Margins*, p. 54, which lists various instances of apes representing bishops.

Figure 4. *A*, fol. 478r, detail. Initial "T" with a fox celebrating Mass.
Bibliothèque nationale de France, with permission.

Figure 5. *A*, fol. 414v, detail. The scroll.
Bibliothèque nationale de France, with permission.

This image of performance is appropriate to the motet. Although all of Machaut's musical pieces would of course have been performed, they can also be read as poems; still, the textual interplay of the motet in particular can be appreciated only through performance. Because of the multitude of singers, the performers are distinguished from both poet-composer and lover; we know that each of these characters cannot simultaneously be identified with the lyric 'I' and that the harmony of parts is due to the guiding, if invisible, hand of the author.[14]

An overarching theme in the image is, indeed, harmony. The words *dame* and *tenor*, pointing to the courtly and sacred domains, are united on the scroll (figs. 2, 5). The lay courtier and cleric are joined to the performers by it. The courtier rests his hand on the forearm of the cleric who, in turn, holds the top of the scroll while one of the singers holds a lower portion of it. The "listening cleric," based on *pentimenti* (visible traces of an earlier but rejected drawing), was at one point intended to hold the scroll from the top. The dark line at the immediate left of the scroll and an ambiguously shaded area above it reveal that the original sketch left room for a wider scroll with a higher top. The line in question appears to have confused the illuminator who, instead, carefully drew the vertical sections of wood on the side and top of the barrel which transect it. It is also apparent that the person who wrote on the scroll followed the bottom three lines of the hoops to create the red staves, resulting in an awkward lack of continuity for the lines of the hoops at right.[15] These "errors" say more about the artist, who was struggling to achieve linear continuity for the depiction of the barrel, than an iconographer giving poor directions. We doubt that this lack of precision would have had an impact on the interpretation by the original target viewer. Moreover, this raises the question of who wrote the musical notation and the words on the scroll.

Figure 6 (*left*). *A*, fol. 454r, detail (A154). Historiated initial "S" at the head of the ballades with lovers.
Figure 7 (*right*). *A*, fol. 367r, detail (A 152). Historiated initial "L" at the head of the lays with a courtly love scene. Bibliothèque nationale de France, with permission.

---

[14] Huot, *From Song to Book*, pp. 300–301. Justin Lavacek interprets the scene as follows: "In the illustration, the word *Dame* labels the upper voices, which carry the vernacular love poetry, while *Tenor* labels its staid foundation in chant. It is revealing to observe that not only the sound but the musical notation is directed at its audience. This depiction suggests that the great intricacies of *Ars nova* counterpoint, with its sophisticated rhythms, harmonies, and bilingual polytextuality, cannot at once be apprehended fully by the ears." Lavacek, "Contrapuntal Confrontation," pp. 7–8.

[15] The staves have four lines, as usual in Gregorian chant, and not the customary five for polyphony.

Located at the center of the miniature, the scroll holds a prominent place in the motet image (figs. 2, 5). In this manner, the miniature represents the whole section of motets in the way that some of the miniatures, which occur before it in the manuscript at the head of the long narrative poems, have an emblematic rather than engaging narrative value.[16] At the same time, the image demarcating the section of motets carefully meshes with the music and lyrics. This is emphasized if one compares the images that head the ballades and lays (figs. 6, 7). These are historiated initials with lovers acting out the subject matter of the lyrics and do not offer much latitude for subtle meaning.

As we have written, on the notated motet scroll are the words *dam[e]* and *tenor. Dame* does not appear in the motet copied directly below; the triplum of M11 is the only first line within Machaut's motets that opens with this word: *Dame, je sui cils qui vueil endurer* ("Lady, I'm the one willing to endure what you will as long as I'll prove able to last").[17] M11 is also the only motet with a historiated initial in the tenor (*Fins cuers dous*, fol. 425r). In it, a hooded man sounds a hunting horn (or could it be an old lady?) – which also serves as part of the letter "F" (fig. 8) – and he (or she) faces left — towards the preceding motets? This could draw attention to the ordering of the corpus, in which both M1 and M11 hold a special place.[18] Moreover, they are the only motets in which the lady is addressed in direct speech.

There are five illuminated manuscripts with Machaut's collected works. The earliest, *C*, usually dated 1350–56, possibly dates to the mid-1340s. The three artists in this instance emphasize composition via the use of scrolls.[19] *Vg*, which is probably close in date with *A*, has no imagery dealing with the representation or performance of music.[20] *F-G*, illuminated only c. 1390, has a space for an image at the head of the motets, which was

Figure 8. *A*, fol. 425r, detail. Historiated initial "F" with hooded man sounding a hunting horn (?). Bibliothèque nationale de France, with permission.

---

[16] See Leo, "BnF, fr. 1584: An Art Historical Overview," in *Guillaume de Machaut: The Complete Poetry and Music*, vol. 1, pp. 37–45, on pp. 39–40, for a commentary on the historiated initials at the openings of the ballades and lays, and the opening miniature of the *Alerion* (fol. 96v). These elements are discussed at length with color images on the website for *The Works of Guillaume de Machaut: Music, Image, Text in the Middle Ages* (<http://machaut.exeter.ac.uk>).

[17] Trans. Jacques Boogaart and R. Barton Palmer. *Dame*, however, appears in this position numerous times in the other musical genres, especially the virelai.

[18] See p. 20 above.

[19] See Huot, *From Song to Book*, p. 251, and Ruffo, "The Illustration of Noted Compendia," pp. 162–171.

[20] *B* (Paris, BnF, ms. fr. 1585), was copied from *Vg*; it has spaces left to indicate insertion points for miniatures; see Earp, *Guillaume de Machaut*, pp. 85–87, and id., "Introductory Study," pp. 44–46.

Figure 9. *G*, fol. 102v, detail. Blank staves at the opening of the motets.
Bibliothèque nationale de France, with permission.

never executed; instead, it was filled with two blank staves which serve no apparent function (fig. 9). Perhaps this "gap" demonstrates that there were directions for insertion points (placement) and subject matter, with or without sketches, which were mistakenly skipped in *F-G*. Was this due to poor planning of the *mise-en-page* at the outset?[21]

In a posthumous complete-works Machaut manuscript of the 1390s, *E* – which was not copied from *A* – one miniature has a strikingly similar use of a barrel with singers arranged around it performing from a scroll (fig. 10).[22] But the image has now "migrated" to sit with the unnotated rondeaux in the *Loange des dames* (fol. 16r, E6).[23] Based on the tonsures and fashion, the six singers are of mixed social status in *E*: three clerics wear *houpelands* (ankle-length robes with blousy sleeves); and the three men wearing bastard-length *houpelands* (with buttock-high hemlines), have varying headdresses. All have *poulaines* (long, pointed shoes). The tonsured figure at far left, dressed in blue, holds one end of a long scroll, and is likely to be the leader given his gesture. As in *A*, a nobleman embraces him with one arm.[24] The round form of the barrel in this image now clearly serves as a pun on the genre the image heads, that is, the rondeaux.

---

[21] The artist in *Vg* apparently had a different set of "directions" given the unique insertion points, the varying size of the miniatures, and the concentration of them in the *Loange des dames* and the *complaintes*. See Earp, *Guillaume de Machaut*, p. 185n210.

[22] Identified as the Master of the *Policraticus* of John of Salisbury (BnF, ms. fr. 24287) in Avril, "Les manuscrits enluminés," p. 128; also see Earp, *Guillaume de Machaut*, pp. 137–38, for a table of artists in *E* and bibliography.

[23] See Scheller, *Exemplum: Model-Book Drawings*, p. 289n15, fig. 165.

[24] Karl Kügle interprets the difference between the two images as a change in gravity center between the genres. According to him, the miniature in *A* shows the performance of a typical Ars Nova-motet, with French upper voices and Latin tenor, sung by clerics. From the image and its position at the head of the motets it would appear that for Machaut, and the older generation, the motet had pride of place as the leading genre of polyphonic music, whereas in the much later and posthumous *E* this privileged status of the motet had, for a younger public, shifted to the polyphonic chanson. Another difference which Kügle points out is that in the older image an elite group from the nobility and clergy is portrayed as the audience, whereas the later miniature shows three clerics and two courtiers (he mistakenly identifies a third courtier as a fool, apparently based on costume) as all actively participating in the performance; it would suggest that the originally clerical art of polyphony was now fully incorporated into courtly society. See Kügle, "Die Musik des 14. Jahrhunderts: Frankreich und sein direkter Einflußbereich," p. 361 (the images are reproduced there in the wrong order).

Figure 10. *E*, fol. 16r (E6). Opening image for the rondeaux in the *Loange*.
Bibliothèque nationale de France, with permission.

Figure 11. *E*, fol. 107r (E31). Opening image for the lays.
Bibliothèque nationale de France, with permission.

Another artist painted the image that heads the lays in *E* (fig. 11).[25] In it, five men stand grouped around a codex in a lush garden, which is bordered on three sides by a flower-laden bower (fol. 107r, E31). They wear the same combination of clothing mentioned above, and the figure at far left is likely the musical director, given his gestures. Although both miniatures in *E* have a clerical figure leading the performance, the *arrangement* of the figures in a group is the focal point, quite unlike the motet image in *A*, where it is the scroll.

The attention to detail in the motet image in *A* is bound up with a series of inscriptions in French within the miniatures (figs. 12–14).[26] The majority of these inscriptions accompany Machaut's *Voir Dit*, a pseudo-autobiographical love story where the protagonist is named Guillaume de Machaut. The first set is epistolary (figs. 12, 13).

Machaut's name appears on a missive sent to him by his beloved, *A Guillau[me]* (fig. 12), and, in turn, *a ma dame* appears on a missive he sends to her (fig. 13). In another instance, the beloved hovers over the protagonist, who composes a musical work for her inscribed *balade* (fig. 14). The artist's love for detail is nowhere more

Figure 12. *A*, fol. 221r, detail (A119). Guillaume receives a sealed letter inscribed with his name, *A Guillau[me]*, from a messenger. Bibliothèque nationale de France, with permission.

Figure 13. *A*, fol. 233r, detail (A123). The lady receives a sealed letter from Guillaume inscribed *a ma dame*. Bibliothèque nationale de France, with permission.

---

[25] Identified as a Master of a *Grandes chroniques de France* (BnF, ms. fr. 20350) in Avril, "Les manuscrits enluminés," p. 138; and Earp, *Guillaume de Machaut*, pp. 137–38 (Table of Artists in MS *E* with bibliography).

[26] See the commentary on the iconographic program in the volume with the *Voir dit*.

Figure 14. *A*, fol. 242r (A127). Guillaume composes a *balade* for his lady.
Bibliothèque nationale de France, with permission.

evident than here. He includes an inkwell and a leather, capped tube which will be used to transport the scroll. This degree of specificity in the inscriptions reveals an artist-iconographer who was thoroughly intimate with the texts, music, and images in this manuscript.

The motet miniature is clearly charged with meaning that is built on a dynamic interaction of music, text, and image. The more familiar viewers and performers are with *A* as a whole, the more they can appreciate the subtly fashioned image. In this capacity it transcends its iconographic forebear, a group of clerics singing in a *Cantate* initial. As we have suggested here, reflection on the cluster of written and visual references in the motet miniature puts into motion the optimal reception of this image on multiple levels, for there can never be one overriding, definitive meaning.

In retrospect, despite the word *dame* on the scroll, there are no images of women in this miniature. There are women, however, who could not be excluded from this image: they are invisible, intimately tied up in word and mental image. But real women undoubtedly viewed the motet miniature. This is a possible catalyst for the network of tensions, both subtle and dramatic, that pervade Machaut's motet, and, in some regards, his works as a whole. In this respect, the viewer, the patron, the artist/iconographer, and the poet all act in concert as performers and listeners. The person who devised the complex imagery of the motet miniature must have had a conception of the motet as a genre, full comprehension of the first work in Machaut's series of motets, knowledge of music and poetry, and a sense of humor: in our own view, Machaut himself best fits this description.

QUESTIONS ON THE DISSEMINATION OF THE ICONOGRAPHY FOR THE MOTET IMAGE IN *A*

Giovannino de Grassi (1350–1398), over the course of about ten years (c. 1380–c. 1390), compiled what is known today as his *Sketchbook*.[27] It comprises exquisite, meticulously rendered paintings and drawings ranging from birds to an anthropomorphic alphabet. In it, there are three images of musicians and singers. Two show women singing and playing the harp. The third (on fol. 5), is a drawing of five men, distinguished by an exceptionally high degree of finish. Three men sing while one holds a scroll and another listens. The animated gestures of the singers are difficult to interpret, but surely one of them is leading. The flowing scroll has musical notation and an inscription.

De Grassi's composition closely resembles the motet image in *A*. The figures exhibit the same sense of camaraderie and harmony, warmly embracing each other.[28] But, assuming we are witnessing direct influence here, it is difficult to determine the means of dissemination of Machaut's image. The marriage of Isabelle of France (1348–1373) to the Lord of Milan, Giangaleazzo I Visconti (1351–1402), in c. 1365, may hold an answer.[29] Isabelle, who brought a large collection of her own manuscripts to Pavia, was the youngest child of Machaut's early patroness, the princess Bonne of Luxembourg, duchess of Normandy (1315–1349), and her husband, the future king John II (Jehan le Bon; 1319, r. 1350–1364). Giangaleazzo was a bibliophile and may have met Machaut during his frequent trips to France. Moreover, it is possible that he saw the manuscripts in the royal collections of John II or his sons, King Charles V (1338, r. 1364–1380) and John, duke of Berry (1340–1416), and possibly even at Machaut's home in Reims. Visconti's "political, dynastic, and cultural relationships with the French court ... reached their zenith in 1387 when his daughter Valentina Visconti, duchess of Orléans (1371–1408) wed Louis of Orléans (1372–1407), brother of king Charles VI (1368, r. 1380–1422)."[30]

The connection between *A* and de Grassi's work cannot, of course, be securely demonstrated. The pictorial resemblance is mysterious and generates more questions than answers. There are at least two possibilities for the transmission of the image. The work of the artist who painted the two stunning *Prologue* images that head *A*, the Master of the Bible of Jean de Sy, marks the manuscript as a royal possession. In this scenario, these miniatures may have been commissioned by Charles V. But what role might the royal women have played? Did Isabelle bring a manuscript or a closely related image with her from France to Italy?[31] Her daughter, Valentina,

---

[27] Visible in normal and UV lighting at: <http://www.opificiodellepietredure.it/getImage.php?id=3265&w=800&h=600&f=0&.jpg> On the *Sketchbook* (Bergamo, Biblioteca Civica, MS D VII 14), see Gallo, *Music in the Castle*, pp. 64–67; Gallo writes "the parchment scroll contains a melody in notation typical of liturgical books, and syllables of text." On the *Visconti Hours* (Florence, Biblioteca Nazionale Centrale, MS Banco Rari 397), see Meiss and Kirsch, *The Visconti Hours*; the opening for BR 90v has a commentary (no page numbers). De Grassi also painted a miniature in the lavish *Visconti Hours*, on fol. 90v. There are nine beautifully dressed, singing men arranged in such a manner that there is an inner circle who sing directly from a scroll. The entire scene is tucked into the historiated initial C of Psalm 97.

[28] I am indebted to Louis A. Waldman for his help in identifying the social status of the singers based in part on fashion. The figures on the left are courtiers. Their very rich, elaborately decorated clothing recalls drawings by Pisanello. The man on the right wearing long robes and a laurel crown or wreath seems to be a musician/composer. He is presented in a way that matches depictions of humanists and poets, beginning with Petrarch. See, for example, the painting by Justus van Ghent (c. 1430–after 1480; fl. 1460–1480), *Portrait of Petrarch*, Urbino, Galleria nazionale delle Marche. The famous Florentine organist and composer, Francesco Landini (c. 1325–1397), also wears a laurel wreath over a hood or cap in a miniature from the early fifteenth-century Squarcialupi Codex (Florence, Biblioteca Medicea Laurenziana, Med. Pal. 87, c. 1410–1415). F. Alberto Gallo, *Music in the Castle*, p. 65, writes – I believe mistakenly – that "some of the [five singers] are in ecclesiastical dress."

[29] For a rare, albeit brief, history of Bonne of Luxembourg's upbringing and her possible reception of and taste in manuscripts, and of her daughter, Isabelle, see Joni M. Hand, *Women, Manuscripts, and Identity in Northern Europe, 1350–1550* (Burlington: Ashgate, 2013): 11–17. I thank Lawrence Earp for this reference.

[30] Gallo, *Music in the Castle*, p. 54. The Visconti interest in Machaut is reflected in their owning a copy of the *Dit dou lyon*. See Earp, *Guillaume de Machaut*, p. 109: cat. [39], "Pavia, lost Visconti manuscript of *Lyon*."

[31] Yolanda Plumley, personal communication, speculates that Isabelle de Valois may have had a complete-works Machaut manuscript made before her death in 1373.

was known to love the harp, which she herself played.[32] Did she see the heavily-illuminated *Dit de la harpe* in *A*? Finally, could de Grassi himself have seen *A*? I (DL) suspect that there was a list of directions and/or rough sketches for its iconographic program, as I have argued above. Would this have drawn on images from Machaut's own atelier in Reims? And what of the later complete-works *E*? Given the drastically different overall iconographic programs in *A* and *E*, there is little to suggest a connection. By itself, however, the rondeau image in *E* hints at a cursory knowledge of the motet image of *A*, perhaps via a sketch, and perhaps with directions, or possibly of another source manuscript now lost.

At present, these questions must remain unanswered. But the publication of Machaut's complete *oeuvre* in the current series, in print and in digital form, will itself become a potent means to disseminate Machaut's images, texts, and music.[33] This new accessibility to Machaut's output will surely attract new scholars, stimulate new approaches to this material, and provide new answers to old questions, among which the motet image should hold a significant position.

---

[32] Gallo, *Music in the Castle*, p. 56.

[33] For an expansive view on this phenomenon, see McGrady, "Machaut and His Material Legacy," pp. 361–86.

LES MOTÉS
THE MOTETS

1

C1, Ia **Amara valde**

Ib

51

triplum

Quant en moy vint premierement		When Love entered my heart
Amours, si tres doucettement		That first time, She so very sweetly
Me vost mon cuer enamourer,		Wished to make it fall in love,
Que d'un regart me fist present,		That She sent a look my way,
Et tres amoureus sentement	5	And gave me feelings of deep love,
Me donna avec Dous Penser:		With Sweet Thought:
Espoir		Hope
D'avoir		That I'd receive
Mercy sans refuser,		Mercy without being refused,
Mais onques en tout mon vivant	10	But never as long as I've lived
Hardement ne me volt donner;		Has She ever intended to embolden me;
Et si me fait en desirant		And so She makes me in my desiring
Penser si amoureusement,		Have thoughts so filled with love,
Que par force de desirer		That by the strength of desiring
Ma joie convient en tourment	15	My joy must change to torment,
Muer, se je n'ay hardement.		If I do not possess courage.
Las! et je n'en puis recouvrer,		Alas! and I cannot find any,
Qu'Amours		Because Love
Secours		Has no intention
Ne me vuet nul prester,		Of providing me with any help,
Qui en ses las si durement	20	As She keeps me so tightly in her nets
Me tient que n'en puis eschaper;		That I cannot escape them;

Ne je ne vueil, qu'en atendant		Nor do I want to, since as I await
Sa grace, je vueil humblement		Her mercy, my humble wish is
Toutes ces dolours endurer;	25	To endure all these pains;
Et s'Amours loyal le consent		And if faithful Love consents
Que ma douce dame au corps gent		That my sweet lady with her noble appearance
Me vueille son ami clamer,		Might wish to call me her friend,
Je sai		I know
De vray	30	Truly
Que arai, sans finer,		That I shall, without end, possess
Joie qu'Amours a fin amant		The joy that Love owes a perfect lover
Doit pour ses maus guerredonner;		As a reward for his ills;
Mais elle atent trop longuement,		But she waits too long,
Et j'aimme si folettement	35	And I love so foolishly
Que je n'ose mercy rouver,		That I do not dare beg for mercy,
Car j'aim miex vivre en esperant		For I prefer living in the hope
D'avoir mercy prochainnement,		Of soon receiving mercy,
Que Refus me veingne tuer,		Rather than Refusal coming to finish me off,
Et pour ce di en soupirant:	40	And so I say with a sigh:
Grant folie est de tant amer		It's great folly to love so much
Que de son dous face on amer.		That you make your sweetness bitter //
		That you make a sweet sound/song bitter.

motetus

Amour et biauté parfaite		Love and perfect beauty
Doubter,		Make me doubt
Celer		And dissemble
Me font parfaitement,		Perfectly,
Et vrais Desirs, qui m'afaite	5	As does true Desire, who inspires me
De vous,		To love you,
Cuers dous,		Sweetheart,
Amer sans finement;		With endless love;
Et quant j'aim si finement,		And since I love so purely
Merci	10	I beg mercy
Vous pri,		From you,
Car elle me soit faite		If only it might be granted me
Sans vostre honnour amenrir,		Without diminishing your honor,
Car j'aim miex einsi languir		For I'd prefer this kind of languishing
Et morir, s'il vous agree,	15	And dying as well, should it please you,
Que par moy fust empiree		To harming in any way
Vostre honnour, que tant desir,		Your honor, which I so highly esteem,
Ne de fait ne de pensee.		Either by deed or thought.

tenor

Amara valde

Very bitter

2

MS *A* fols 415v-16r

C1, I **Suspiro**

morsure De ses griés maus sans meffait Et sans mespresu-

mours m'estuet re-

C2, i

re, Ne lairay ja que secours Ne quiere de

traire: Ou merci

ii

mes dolours A madame pure, Car bien

prochei ne ment De

puis avoir mercy Selonc ce que j'ay servi; A ce m'asseu-

madame de bon-

iii

57

re, Et en ce qu'on dit, pour voir: Miex vient en joi-e ma-noir Par

nai - re, Ou mo -

iv

proi - er qu'a-dés lan-guir Par trop tai - re et puis mo - rir.

rir en lan - - guis - sant.

triplum

Tous corps qui de bien amer	Everyone who would attend
Vuet avoir la cure	To loving well
Doit par raison encliner,	Must follow reason and
Et c'est sa droiture,	Be inclined, for that's proper,
La ou son cuer esmouvoir 5	Toward what his heart
Se vuet, quant a bien avoir;	Feels, if he is to have what's good;
Pour ce li miens cure,	Such is the case with my own heart,
Qui de Nature est formez,	Formed by Nature,
Et oubeissance assés	And quite willing therefore
Vuet faire a Nature, 10	To pay obeisance to Nature,
Et a celle qui m'a point	As well as to the one who stung me
De male pointure,	With a malicious sting,
Puis que n'a de pité point	In that she takes no pity at all
Dou mal que j'endure,	On the pain I endure,
Qui me fait en desirant 15	Which makes me languish
Languir, quant vois remirant	With desire, whenever I gaze
La douce faiture	Upon the sweet shape
De son tres gracieus vis,	Of her so gracious face,
Par qui mes cuers est ravis	Which stole my heart
Et mis en ardure; 20	And set it to burning;

Et comment qu'Amours m'ait fait	And even though Love has made me
Souffrir la morsure	Suffer the bite
De ses griés maus sans meffait	Of Her grievous pains, despite my having
Et sans mespresure,	Not failed or gone wrong at all,
Ne lairay ja que secours 25	I shall never cease from seeking help
Ne quiere de mes dolours	For my pains
A ma dame pure,	From my lady pure,
Car bien puis avoir mercy	For I should certainly receive mercy
Selonc ce que j'ay servi;	In proportion to how I've served her;
A ce m'asseüre, 30	On that I rely,
Et en ce qu'on dit, pour voir:	And on the truth of what's said about such things:
Miex vient en joie manoir	Better it is through pleading to remain in joy
Par proier qu'adés languir	Than to languish unceasingly
Par trop taire et puis morir.	By keeping too long silent and then to die.

motetus

De souspirant cuer dolent	From my sighing, suffering heart
Me pleing, et bien le doy faire,	I complain, and so should I do,
Car, quant j'ay pris hardement	For, just when I found the courage
De ma grant doleur retraire,	To speak of my great pain,
Lors m'estuet il tout coy taire. 5	I must hold my peace about it.
Si sui pris en regardant;	Thus I am caught in gazing upon her;
Et pour ce que je doubt tant	And because I am so fearful of
Refus, qui ne me doit plaire,	Refusal, who does not intend to please me,
Et Dangier, mon adversaire,	And of Resistance, my adversary,
Qui me livre estour si grant 10	Who attacks me with such fierceness
Que d'amours m'estuet retraire:	That I must beat a retreat from love:
Ou merci procheinnement	Either I'll have mercy coming soon
De ma dame debonnaire,	From my lady nobly born,
Ou morir en languissant.	Or, languishing, I will expire.

tenor

Suspiro   **I sigh**

3

C1, I Quare non sum mortuus

Hé! Mors! com tu es ha - i - e De moy, quant tu as ra-

Fine A - mour, qui me vint na-

vi - e Ma joi-e, ma dru-e-ri-e, Mon so - las, Par qui je sui ein - si

vrer Au cuer, m'a fait grant des -

mas Et mis de si haut si bas, Et ne

- rai - son

me po-vi - és pas As - sail - lir? Las! miex a - mas-se mo-

Quant el - - - - le

III

triplum

Hé! Mors! com tu es haïe	You there, Death! how I hate you
De moy, quant tu as ravie	For robbing me
Ma joie, ma druerie,	Of my joy, my affection,
Mon solas,	My comfort,
Par qui je sui einsi mas 5	And this is why I feel so destroyed,
Et mis de si haut si bas,	Thrown down so low from on so high,
Et ne me poviés pas	And yet you could not manage
Assaillir?	Turning on me?
Las! miex amasse morir	Alas! I'd prefer dying
Qu'avoir si grief souvenir 10	To entertaining such painful imagination
Qui moult souvent resjoïr	Which often used
Me soloit,	To give me joy,
M'amour en pensant doubloit,	Which doubled the love I felt,
Mon desir croistre faisoit,	Made my desire increase,
Et toudis amenuisoit 15	And day after day decreased
Mes dolours;	My pains;
Mais c'est dou tout a rebours,	But now it's just the opposite,
Car croistre les fait tous jours	For now it makes them always increase,
En grans soupirs et en plours,	With heavy sighs and weeping,
Pour m'amour 20	Because of my love
Que scens par avoir valour,	Which I feel possesses such virtue,
Scens, courtoisie et honnour;	Good sense, courtliness and honor;
Or sçai bien que sans retour	Now I know well I've lost it
Perdu l'ay,	Beyond recovery,
Et que la mort en aray 25	And that it shall be my death
Quant Amours delaisseray	When I shall quit Love
Ne remirer ne porray	And can no longer gaze upon
Son acueil,	Her fair welcome,
Qui met en moy si grant dueil	And this plunges me into such great misery
Que riens ne desir ne vueil 30	That I want or desire nothing
Fors la mort. S'aray mon vueil	But death. If my wish
Acompli,	Will be granted,
Et se il en estoit en my	And if it were up to me
De ma mort ou de merci,	About my dying or mercy
Dou tout metroie en oubli 35	I would completely forget about
Ma vie,	My life,
Car en moy joie n'est mie;	For there is no trace of joy in me;
Et on dit, je n'en doubt mie:	And as they say, which I doubt not at all:
Qui bien aimme a tart oublie;	Whoever loves well forgets slowly;
Bien l'ottroy, 40	I very much agree,

Et pour ce qu'il ha l'ottroy
D'amours, soit sages de soy
Et si serve en bonne foy,
  Sans folie,

Car il n'est, pour voir l'affie,   45
Nulle si grief departie
Com c'est d'amy et d'amie.

And as for him to whom love
Has been granted, let him be wise
And serve in good faith,
  Without folly,

For there is, I confirm the truth of it,
No leave-taking so miserable
As that of a lover from his beloved.

motetus

Fine Amour, qui me vint navrer
Au cuer, m'a fait grant desraison
Quant elle ne voloit saner
Mon mal en temps et en saison;
Mais tant me fait en sa prison   5
Les tres griés peinnes endurer,
Car des or mais reconforter
Ne me puet, fors que nuire non,
Car Fortune ma garison
M'a tollu pour moy plus grever.   10
Helas! or me puis dementer,
Plourer et pleindre a grant foison,
En attendant, pour bien amer,
La mort en lieu de guerredon.

Pure Love, who came to pierce
My heart, did me a great injustice
In not wishing to cure my pains
At the proper time and season;
Instead in Her dungeon She forces me
To suffer its terribly grievous pains,
For from this point on She can offer
Me no comfort, only do me harm,
Since Fortune has snatched away
My cure, to grieve me still more deeply.
Alas! now I can go mad with grief,
Abandon myself to weeping and complaint,
As I expect, in return for loving well,
Death by way of reward.

tenor

Quare non sum mortuus

Why did I not die?

4

8 C1, I **Speravi**

De Bon Es - poir, de tres Dous Sou - ve - nir Et de tres

Puis que la dou -

Dous Pen - ser con - tre De - sir M'a Bon - ne A - mour main - tes fois se - cou - ru,

ce rou - se - e D'Um - bles - se

Quant il m'a plus ai - gre - ment sus cou - ru;

ne vuet flo - - - rir

Car quant De - sirs plus fort me des - train - gnoit, Moult dou - ce - ment Es - poirs m'as - se - u - roit, Et

Pi - tez, tant que me - u - re - e

70

triplum

De Bon Espoir, de tres Dous Souvenir		With Good Hope, with so Sweet Imagination
Et de tres Dous Penser contre Desir		And with very Sweet Thought, Good Love many times
M'a Bonne Amour maintes fois secouru,		Has supported me against Desire
Quant il m'a plus aigrement sus couru;		When he quite fiercely attacked me;
Car quant Desirs plus fort me destraingnoit,	5	For, whenever Desire pressed me the hardest,
Moult doucement Espoirs m'asseüroit,		Hope reassured me very sweetly,
Et Souvenirs me moustroit la biauté,		While Imagination showed me the beauty,
Le scens, l'onneur, le pris et la bonté		The good sense, honor, worth and goodness
De celle dont li amoureus penser		Of her, the source of the loving thoughts
Mon dolent cuer venoient conforter.	10	That arose to console my sorrowful heart.
Las! or m'assaut Desirs plus qu'il ne suet,		Alas! Desire now assails me more than is his custom
Mais durement endurer le m'estuet,		Yet I must endure this resolutely,
Car je sui pres de perdre le confort		For I am close to losing the comfort
De Bon Espoir, dont je me desconfort,		Of Good Hope, which discourages me,
Et Souvenirs me fait toudis penser	15	And Imagination always leads me
Pour mon las cuer faire desesperer,		To think what makes my weary heart despair,
Car Grace, Amour, Franchise, Loyauté,		For Grace, Love, Generosity, Loyalty,
Pité, Doctrine et Debonnaireté		Pity, Good Manners, and Nobility
Sont pour moy seul si forment endormi,		Have fallen fast asleep for me alone,
Car Dangiers est souvereins de Merci	20	Since Resistance is now lord over Mercy
Et que ma dame, a qui je sui rendus,		And my lady, to whom I am pledged,
Croit a Durté et orguilleus Refus,		Trusts to Severity and proud Refusal,

Pour ce, sanz plus, que m'amour ne mon cuer
Ne vueil ne puis departir a nul fuer;
Mais puis qu'estre ne puet ore autrement,   25
Face de moy tout son commandement,
Car maugré li l'ameray loyaument.

Only because I will not, cannot
In any way deny her my love and my heart;
Yet since it cannot now be otherwise,
Let her do with me whatever she wishes,
For despite her I will faithfully love her.

motetus

Puis que la douce rousee
D'Umblesse ne vuet florir
Pitez, tant que meüree
Soit Mercy que tant desir,
Je ne puis avoir duree,   5
Car en moy s'est engendree,
Par un amoureus desir,
Une ardeur desmesuree
Qu'Amours, par son dous plaisir,
Et ma dame desiree,   10
Par sa biauté coulouree,
De grace y ont fait venir;
Mais puis qu'einsi leur agree,
Je vueil humblement souffrir
Leur voloir, jusqu'au morir.   15

Since the sweet dew of Humility
Will not make Pity blossom,
So that Mercy might ripen,
As I fervently desire,
I can endure no longer,
For in me has been engendered,
Through an amorous desire,
A burning beyond any measure
That Love, through Her sweet caprice,
And my desired lady,
Through her rosy beauty,
By their grace have made appear there;
Yet since this is their pleasure,
I intend to suffer humbly
What they wish, until I die.

tenor

Speravi

I have trusted
I hoped

5

74

Aucune gent M'ont demandé que j'ai
Que je ne chant Et que je n'ai cuer gay,
Si com je sueil Chanter de lié corage;
Et je leur di, Certes, que je ne say,
Mais j'ai menti, Car dedens le cuer ai   5
Un trop grief dueil Qui onques n'assouage;

Car sans sejour Ay mise ma pensee
A Bonne Amour Faire ce qui agree,
Ne a nul fuer N'i pensasse folage;
Et je sai bien Que ma dame honnouree,   10
Que je tant crien, Si m'a ma mort juree
Par crueus cuer Et par simple visage;

Car quant je voy Son gracieus viaire,
D'un dous ottroy Me moustre .i. exemplaire,
Et si me vuet Tenir en son hommage,   15
Ce m'est avis; Mais aus dolours retraire
J'ay .c. tans pis Qu'on ne me porroit faire,
Car nuls ne puet Penser si grief damage

Com le refus Que ses durs cuers m'envoie;
Et si l'aim plus, Se Diex m'en envoit joie,   20
Que riens qui soit; Dont n'est ce droite rage?
Certes, oïl! Mais pour riens que je voie
De ce peril Issir je ne voudroie,
Car tous siens suy, Sans changement de gage,

Quant esperer Me fait ma garison;   25
Et c'est tout cler Que monsigneur Yvon
Par bien servir, Non pas par vasselage,
Conquist l'amour Dou grant lion sauvage.

Some people have asked me what's wrong
Because, no joy in my heart, I sing no more
As I used to sing with cheerful heart;
And I tell them that, for sure, I do not know,
But that's a lie, for in my heart resides a pain
Too hard to bear that never softens;

For I have fixed my thoughts unflinchingly
On doing what pleases Good Love,
And I would never contemplate any foolishness;
And now I know well that my honored lady,
Whom I respect so much, has sworn my death,
With cruel heart and affable expression;

For whenever I gaze upon her gracious face,
It's an image of sweet consent she shows me,
And so she wishes to retain me as her man,
Or so I think; but as for assuaging my pains,
I'm a 100 times worse off than anyone else could manage
For no one can imagine a misery as painful

As the refusal her hard heart sends my way;
And yet I love her more - may God send me joy -
Than anything else; so is that not perfect madness?
Surely, yes! But for nothing apparent to my eyes
Would I wish to escape from such peril,
For I am all hers, my pledge unchanged,

Because she makes me hope for my recovery;
And it's clear as crystal that sir Yvain
Through proper service, not knightly prowess,
Won the love of the grand and savage lion.

Qui plus aimme plus endure
Et plus meinne dure vie,
Qu'Amours, qui est sans mesure,
Assés plus le contralie,
Que li mauvais qui n'a cure   5
De li, einsois met sa cure
En mal et en villonnie.
Hé, Diex! que n'ont signourie
Les dames de leur droiture,
Que ceuls qui ont la pointure   10
D'Amours au cuer atachie
Choisissent sans mespresure;
S'einsi fust, je m'asseüre:
Tels est amez qui ne le seroit mie,
Et tels haïs qui tost aroit amie.   15

Whoever loves more, endures more,
And the harder is the life he leads,
Since Love, who lacks measure,
Opposes him much more than She does
The false one who heeds Her not,
But devotes himself
To wickedness and villainy.
Oh God! would that the ladies were entitled
By their rights to make
That those [lovers] who have planted
In their hearts Love's sting
Choose without going wrong;
Were it thus, I'm sure that
He who is now loved, would not then be,
While the one now hated, would soon have a sweetheart.

Fiat voluntas tua

Thy will be done

6

8 C1, I Et gaudebit cor vestrum

S'il es-toit nuls qui plein-dre se de-hust Pour nul mes - chief que d'A-mour re - ce-ust, Je me de-vroi-e bien plein-dre *(sans retraire;)* sans re-trai-re; Car quant pre - miers me vint en-a-mou-rer, On-ques en moy har-de-ment de-mou-rer Ne volt lais-sier de ma do- *(-lour retraire;)*

S'A - mours tous a - mans jo - ir Au com--man - ce-ment fai - soit, Son pris fe - roit a-men - rir, Car nuls a-mans ne sa - roit Les grans

81

triplum

S'il estoit nuls qui pleindre se dehust	If anyone had the right to complain
Pour nul meschief que d'Amour receüst,	About any mistreatment he has received from Love,
Je me devroie bien pleindre sans retraire;	I should certainly be the one to complain, and freely;
Car quant premiers me vint enamourer,	For, from the moment She first came to make me fall
Onques en moy hardemens demourer 5	She never intended allowing me to stay [in love,
Ne volt laissier de ma dolour retraire;	Bold enough to rehearse the pains I felt;
Mais ce qui plus me faisoit resjoïr	But what made me rejoice the most
Et qui espoir me donnoit de joïr	And gave me the hope to reach joy
En regardant, sans plus dire ne faire,	- By gazing, saying or doing nothing more -
Fist departir de moy; puis en prison 10	This She made depart from me; then in prison
Elle me mist, ou j'eus ma livrison	She put me, where I received my share
De Ardans Desirs qui si m'estient contraire	Of Burning Desire, which so opposes me
Que, se un tout seul plus que droit en eüsse,	That, had I just a little more of it than my fair ration,
Je say de voir que vivre ne peüsse	I know truly I could live no longer
Sans le secours ma dame debonnaire, 15	Without the help of my noble lady,
Qui m'a de ci, sans morir, respité;	Who has, not letting me die, saved me from this place;
Et c'est bien drois, car douçour en pité	And that is quite proper, for sweetness in pity
Et courtoisie ont en li leur repaire.	As well as courtliness find in her their dwelling.

motetus

S'Amours tous amans joïr	If Love transported all lovers
Au commancement faisoit,	At the outset to the point of joy,
Son pris feroit amenrir,	She would diminish her own value,
Car nuls amans ne saroit	For no lover would come to know
Les grans deduis qu'on reçoit 5	The great delights one receives
En dame d'onnour servir;	Through serving a lady of honor;
Mais cils qui vit en desir,	But he who lives in desire,
Et Bonne Amour l'aperçoit,	And Good Love notices it,
En a plus qu'il ne voudroit,	Receives more of it [i.e. desire] than he might wish,
Quant joie li vuet merir; 10	When She wants to reward him with joy;
Et pour ce nuls repentir	And so no one who loves properly
De bien amer ne se doit,	Should repent of doing so,
S'Amours le fait trop languir.	If Love makes him languish too much.

tenor

Et gaudebit cor vestrum   **And your heart will rejoice**

7

MS *A* fols 420v-21r

C1, I Ego moriar pro te

85

153

Et dou - di - re ne me doit nuls bla - mer Qu'a-mours, be-soins et de-sirs d'a-che -

et il me het, ay - my!

iii

163

ver Font tres-pas - ser me-su - re et scens ou - trer.

Te - le est des fem - mes la na - tu - re.

triplum

J'ai tant mon cuer et mon orgueil creü,		I have trusted so much to my heart and my pride,
Et tenu chier ce qui m'a deceü		Cherishing the one who deceived me
Et en vilté ce qui m'amoit heü,		And reviling the one who loved me,
Que j'ai failli		That I have missed out
Aus tres dous biens dont Amours pourveü	5	On the very sweet gifts Love has provided
Ha par pitié maint cuer despourveü,		Many a deprived heart out of Her pity,
Et de la tres grant joie repeü		Nourishing it with the very great joy
Dont je languy.		For which I languish.
Lasse! einsi m'a mes felons cuers trahi,		Alas! thus has my cruel heart betrayed me,
Car onques jour vers mon loial amy,	10	For never towards my lover, who served
Qui me servoit et amoit plus que li,		And loved me more than himself,
N'os cuer meü,		Have I let my heart be touched,
Que de m'amour li feïsse l'ottri.		So that I granted him my love.
Or say je bien qu'il aimme autre que my,		Now I am certain he loves another than me,
Qui liement en ottriant merci,	15	Who, cheerfully promising him her mercy,
L'a receü.		Has accepted him.
Si le m'estuet chierement comparer,		So I have to pay dearly for this,
Car je l'aim tant qu'on ne puet plus amer.		Loving him so much no one could do more.
Mais c'est trop tart: je ne puis recouvrer		But it's too late: I cannot win back
La soie amour;	20	His love;

89

Et s'ai paour, se je li vueil rouver,	And thus I fear that, should I implore him,
Qu'il ne me deingne oïr ne escouter	He would not deign to hear or listen to me,
Pour mon orgueil, qui trop m'a fait fier	All because of my pride, which made me trust
En ma folour;	Too much to my foolishness;

Et se je li vueil celer ma dolour,	25	And if I wish to hide my pain from him,
Desirs, espris d'amoureuse chalour,		Desire, set aflame by the heat of love,
Destraint mon corps et mon cuer en errour		Tortures my body and puts my heart
Met de finer.		On a path toward death.

S'aim miex que je li die ma langour,		So I prefer telling him that I languish,
Qu'einsi morir, sans avoir la savour	30	To dying in this way, without savoring
De la joie qu'est parfaite douçour		The joy whose taste is perfect
A savourer;		Sweetness;

Et dou dire ne me doit nuls blamer		And let nobody blame me for saying it [openly],
Qu'amours, besoins et desirs d'achever		For love, need, and desire for fulfilment
Font trespasser mesure et scens outrer.	35	Make one trespass moderation and go beyond good
		[sense.

motetus

Lasse! je sui en aventure		Alas! I run the risk
De morir de mort einsi dure		Of dying from a death as harsh
Com li biaus Narcisus mori,		As that from which fair Narcissus died,
Qui son cuer tant enorguilly		Who filled his heart with so much pride

Pour ce qu'il avoit biauté pure	5	- Because he possessed a pure beauty
Seur toute humeinne creature,		Surpassing that of all human creatures -
Qu'onques entendre le depri		That he never deigned to listen to the prayer
Ne deingna de Echo, qui pour li		Of Echo, who for him

Reçut mort amere et obscure;		Suffered a bitter and gloomy death;
Mais Bonne Amour d'amour seüre	10	But Good Love with a well-aimed [arrow of] love
Fist qu'il ama et encheri		Made him love and cherish
Son ombre et li pria merci		His own reflection, which he pleaded with

Tant qu'en priant mori d'ardure.		So much that he died from his passionate beseeching.
Lasse! et je criem morir einsi,		Alas! and I fear I'll die the same death,

Car onques de mon dous amy,	15	For never, when my sweet friend
Quant il m'amoit de cuer, n'os cure;		Loved me dearly, did I care for him;

Or l'aim et il me het, aymy!	Now I love him and he hates me, woe is me!
Tele est des femmes la nature.	Such is women's nature.

tenor

Ego moriar pro te	**Might I die for thee**
	I shall die for thee

8

MS *A* fols 421v-22r

Qui es pro-mes-ses De For-tu-ne se fi - e Et es ri-ches-ses De ses dons s'as-se-

Ha! For - tu - ne,

(-) *E Iv*

C1, Ia Et non est qui adjuvat

u - re, Ou cils qui croit Qu'el-le soit tant s'a - mi - e Que pour li soit En riens fer-

C G Vg? B?

trop sui mis loing de port, Quant en la mer m'as mis sans

Ib

(-) *Trem*

-me ou se - u - re, Il est trop fols, car el - le est non se - u - re, Sans

a - vi - ron En un ba-tel pe - tit, plat et sans bort,

Ic

(-) *Iv Trem*

foy, sans loy, sans droit et sans me - su - re, C'est fiens cou-vers de ri-che cou-ver - tu - re,

*

Foi - ble, pour - ri, sans voi-le et

IIa

91

Qui es promesses De Fortune se fie	Whoever trusts to Fortune's promises,
Et es richesses De ses dons s'asseüre,	And counts on the richness of her gifts,
Ou cils qui croit Qu'elle soit tant s'amie	Or who believes she is so much his friend
Que pour li soit En riens ferme ou seüre,	As to be steadfast or reliable for him in the least,
Il est trop fols, car elle est non seüre, 5	He is too much the fool, for she is unreliable,
Sans foy, sans loy, sans droit et sans mesure,	Without faith, without law, without justice and without
C'est fiens couvers de riche couverture,	She's dung wrapped in rich cloth, [measure,
Qui dehors luist et dedens est ordure,	A shining façade on rottenness within,
Une ydole est de fausse pourtraiture,	An idol of false portraiture is she,
Ou nuls ne doit croire ne mettre cure; 10	Whom no one should believe or trust;
Sa convenance en vertu pas ne dure,	Her propriety in virtue does not last,
Car c'est tous vens, ne riens qu'elle figure	For it's all wind, nor can anything she portrays
Ne puet estre fors de fausse figure;	Be more than a false image;
Et li siens sont toudis en aventure	And her followers always run the risk
De trebuchier; car, par droite nature, 15	Of stumbling; for, by her true nature,
La desloyal, renoÿe, parjure,	This woman disloyal, unfaithful, perjuring
Fausse, traitre, perverse et mere sure	False, treacherous, perverse, this sour-milk mother,
Oint et puis point de si mortel pointure,	First anoints, then pierces with so mortal a sting,
Que ceaus qui sont fait de sa norriture	That she leads those she has nourished
En traïson met a desconfiture. 20	Treacherously to destruction.

Ha! Fortune, trop sui mis loing de port,	Ah, Fortune, too far am I driven from port
Quant en la mer m'as mis sans aviron	Since you put me out to sea with no oar
En .i. batel petit, plat et sans bort,	In a little boat, flat and with no board,
Foible, pourri, sans voile, et environ	Flimsy, rotted through, lacking a sail, and around
Sont tuit li vent contraire pour ma mort, 5	All the winds are contrary, so as to kill me,
Si qu'il n'i a confort ne garison,	So that there is no comfort or rescue of any kind,
Merci n'espoir ne d'eschaper ressort,	No mercy or hope, no way to escape,
Ne riens de bien pour moy, car sans raison	Nor anything good for me, for I see
Je voy venir la mort amere, a tort,	A bitter death ahead, unmerited
Preste de moy mettre a destruction; 10	And unjust, ready to destroy me;
Mais celle mort reçoy je par ton sort,	But this death is dealt me through your evil spell,
Fausse Fortune, et par ta traïson.	False Fortune, and through your treachery.

Et non est qui adjuvat	**And there is no one who helps**

9

Fons to - ti - us Su - per - bi - e, Lu - ci - fer,

et ne - qui - ti - e, Qui, mi - ra - bi - li spe - ci - e De - co - ra -

tus, E - ras in sum - mis lo - ca - tus, Su - per thro - nos su - bli - ma - tus; Dra - cho fe -

O

Fera pessima   A: C1, I

rus an - ti - qua - tus, Qui di - ce - re   Au - sus es se -

Li - vo - ris   fe - ri - tas,

II

triplum

Fons totius Superbie,	Fount of all Pride,
Lucifer, et nequitie,	Lucifer, and of all baseness,
Qui, mirabili specie	You, with wondrous beauty
Decoratus,	Adorned,
Eras in summis locatus, 5	Were placed most high,
Super thronos sublimatus;	Raised above the Thrones;
Dracho ferus antiquatus,	You, of old a fierce serpent,
Qui dicere	Who dared proclaim
Ausus es sedem ponere	That you'd establish your seat
Aquilone et gerere 10	In the North and hold sway
Te similem in opere	In your works like
Altissimo;	The Most High;
Tuo sed est in proximo	Yet it was not long
Fastui ferocissimo	Before your arrogance so fierce
A judice justissimo 15	Was halted
Obviatum;	By the Judge Most Just;
Tuum nam auffert primatum;	For He bears away your pride of place;
Ad abyssos cito stratum	You saw yourself, for your sin,
Te vidisti per peccatum	Quickly thrown down into the abyss
De supernis. 20	From the greatest heights.
Ymis nunc regnas infernis;	Now you reign in deepest hell;
In speluncis et cavernis	In caverns and pits
Penis jaces et eternis	You lie, in pain and everlasting
Agonibus;	Agonies;
Dolus et fraus in actibus 25	Deceit and fraud are in your deeds,
Tuis et bonis omnibus	And all good things
Obviare missilibus	You seek to obstruct
Tu niteris;	With your shafts;
Auges que nephas sceleris	You make increase the terrible crime
Adam penis in asperis 30	That kept Adam in the harsh punishments
Tenuit Stigos carceris;	Of the dungeons of Styx;
Sed Maria	But to Mary,
Virgo, que plena gratia,	The Virgin, full of grace,
Sua per puerperia	Who through Her childbearing
Illum ab hac miseria 35	Set him free
Liberavit,	From this misery,
Precor et anguis tedia	I pray that She increase
Augeat et supplicia,	The miseries and torment of that serpent,
Et nos ducat ad gaudia	And lead us to joy,
Quos creavit. 40	Us, whom She created.

O Livoris feritas,		Oh, fierceness of Envy,
Que superna rogitas		You who strive for the heights
Et jaces inferius,		And lie in the depths,
Cur inter nos habitas?		Why do you dwell among us?
Tua cum garrulitas	5	While the torrent of your words
Nos affatur dulcius,		Sweetly flatters us,
Retro pungit sevius,		It stings all the fiercer from behind,
Ut veneno scorpius;		As does the scorpion with his venom;
Scariotis falsitas		Iscariot's falseness
Latitat interius.	10	Stays hidden within.
Det mercedes Filius		May the Son of God
Dei tibi debitas!		Give you the reward you deserve!

tenor

Fera pessima   **A most evil beast**

101

10

C1, Ia **Obediens usque ad mortem**

Ib

triplum

Hareu, hareu! le feu, le feu, le feu		Help, help! The fire, the fire, the fire
D'Ardant Desir, qu'ainc si ardant ne fu,		Of Burning Desire, never before so burning,
Qu'en mon cuer ha espris et soustenu		Which Love in my heart has set ablaze
Amours, et s'a la joie retenu		And stoked; and so She has held back the joy
D'Espoir qui doit attemprer celle ardure.	5	Of Hope, who should damp down this burning.
Las! se le feu qui ensement l'art dure,		Alas! should the fire last that burns it this way,
Mes cuers sera tous bruis et estains,		My heart will be all burnt to ashes,
Qui de ce feu est ja nercis et tains,		Blackened and stained as it is already by this fire,
Pour ce qu'il est fins, loiaus et certains,		Just because it is pure, loyal, and trustworthy,
Si que j'espoir que deviez yert, ains	10	And so I expect it will perish before
Que Bonne Amour de merci l'asseüre		Good Love assures it of mercy
Par la vertu d'Esperance seüre;		Through the virtue of certain Hope;
Car pour li seul, qui endure mal maint,		Since for my heart alone, enduring many trials,
Pitié deffaut ou toute biauté maint;		Pity lacks where perfect beauty dwells;
Durtés y regne et Dangiers y remaint,	15	There Harshness reigns and Resistance resides,
Desdains y vit et Loyautés s'i faint		Disdain lives in that place, and Loyalty grows weak,
Et Amours n'a de li ni de moy cure,		And Love cares not for it or me.
Joie le het, ma dame li est dure,		Joy hates it, my lady is harsh to it,

106

Et, pour croistre mes dolereus meschiés,   And, to increase my painful suffering,
Met dedens moy Amours, qui est mes chiés, 20   Love, my master, plants within me
Un desespoir qui si mal entechiés   A despair so diseased
Est que tous biens ha de moy esrachiés,   That it has bereft me of all good,
Et en tous cas mon corps si desnature,   And anyway so alienates my body from its nature,
Qu'il me convient morir malgré Nature.   That I must die in spite of Nature.

motetus

Helas! ou sera pris confors   Alas! where shall comfort be seized
Pour moy qui ne vail nes que mors,   For me, fit for nothing but death,
Quant riens garentir ne me puet   Since nothing can protect me
Fors ma dame chiere, qui vuet   Except my dear lady, who wishes
Qu'en desespoir muire, sans plus,   5   Me to die in despair, and that's all,
Pour ce que je l'aim plus que nuls;   Because I love her more than anyone else;
Et Souvenir, pour enasprir   And Imagination, to make more deadly
L'ardeur de mon triste desir,   The burning of my sad desire,
Me moustre adés sa grant bonté   Constantly shows me her great goodness
Et sa fine vraie biauté,   10   And her perfect true beauty,
Qui doublement me fait ardoir.   Which doubles my burning.
Einsi, sans cuer et sans espoir,   And so, lacking heart and hope
Ne puis pas vivre longuement,   I cannot live long,
N'en feu cuers humeins nullement   Nor can a human heart in any way
Ne puet longue duree avoir.   15   Survive for very long in fire.

tenor

Obediens usque ad mortem   **Obedient unto death**

11

Fins cuers dous

Dame, je sui cils qui vueil endurer	Lady, I'm the one willing to endure
Vostre voloir, tant com porray durer,	What you will, as long as I'll prove able to last,
Mais ne cuit pas que longuement l'endure	But I don't think I can endure it for long
Sans mort avoir, quant vous m'estes si dure	Without dying, with you being so hard on me
Que vous volés qu'en sus de vous me traie, 5	In that you wish me to depart from you,
Sans plus veoir la tres grant biauté vraie	And thus gaze no more on the very great beauty
De vo gent corps qui tant a de valour	Of your noble person, which is so worthy
Que vous estes des bonnes la millour.	That you are the best among the good.
Las! einsi ay de ma mort exemplaire.	Alas! thus I prefigure my death.
Mais la doleur qu'il me convenra traire 10	But the grief I shall be forced to bear
Douce seroit, se un tel espoir avoie	Would be sweet, if I entertained such a hope
Qu'avec ma mort par vo gré vous revoie;	That, in death, you'd favor me with another glimpse;
Dame, et se ja mes cuers riens entreprent	Lady, and if my heart ever attempts something
Dont mes corps ait honneur n'avancement,	To advance or honor my person,
De vous venra, com lonteins que vous soie, 15	It will come from you, no matter how far away you are,
Car ja sans vous, que j'aim tres loiaument,	For without either you, whom I love so faithfully,
Ne sans Amours emprendre nel saroie.	Or Love, I'd not be able to make the attempt.

Fins cuers dous, on me deffent	Heart sweet and perfect, I've been forbidden
De par vous que plus ne voie	On your behalf to ever look again
Vostre dous viaire gent	Upon your sweet noble face,
Qui d'amer m'a mis en voie;	Which has set me on the path of love;
Mais vraiement, je ne say 5	But truly, I cannot imagine
Comment je m'en atenray	How not to expect from this
Que briefment morir ne doie,	A death I must soon suffer,
Et si m'en faut abstenir	And yet I must abstain from seeing you,
Pour faire vostre plaisir,	For such is your pleasure;
Ou envers vous faus seroie. 10	Otherwise I'd play you false.
S'aim trop miex ma loyauté	So I much prefer remaining loyal,
Garder, et par vostre gré	And, by your leave,
Morir, se vos cuers l'ottroie,	Dying, if your heart so determines,
Qu'encontre vostre voloir,	To receiving, against your will,
Par vostre biauté veoir, 15	The complete joy
Receüsse toute joie.	Of gazing on your beauty.

Fins cuers dous   **Heart sweet and perfect**

12

He-las! pour quoy vi-rent on-ques mi oueil   Ma chie-re da-me_au

Cor-de me - sto Can - tan-do

C1, Ia Libera me

tres plai-sant a-cueil, Pour qui je vif en tel mar-ty-re Que je ne con-gnois joi-e de i-

con - que-ror, Sem - per pre - sto Ser-vi-ens ma-ce-

re? N'on-ques A - mour ne me volt en-ri-chir Tant que j'e-us-

ror, Sub ho - ne - sto Ge - stu to -

Ib

se_un es-poir de jo-ir, Ne je ne puis en-cor rien es-pe-rer Que tout ne

tus te - ror, Et

112

triplum

Helas! pour quoy virent onques mi oueil	Alas! why did my eyes ever come to gaze upon
Ma chiere dame au tres plaisant acueil,	My dear lady with her very pleasant welcome,
Pour qui je vif en tel martyre	For whom my life is such torment
Que je ne congnois joie de ire?	That I cannot tell joy from misery?
N'onques Amour ne me volt enrichir 5	Love never intended to grace me
Tant que j'eüsse un espoir de joïr,	With some hope of joy I might possess,
Ne je ne puis encor rien esperer	Nor can I still hope for anything
Que tout ne soit pour moy desesperer,	That would not sink me into complete despair,
Dont vraiement plus chier heüsse,	And so I would in truth prefer,
Quant ma dame vi, que je fusse 10	Catching sight of my lady, that I lacked
Sans yex, ou que mes corps tel cuer heüst	Eyes or that the heart within my body
Que ja mais jour dame amer ne peüst,	Was such as could never love a lady,
Qu'en li veoir je conquis mort crueuse,	For looking upon her won me a cruel death,
Et mon vivant vie avoir dolereuse,	And a sorrowful life as long as I live,
Puisqu'einsi est que pité ne merci 15	Since the situation is that her cruel heart
Ses crueus cuers ne vuet avoir de my.	Intends to show me neither pity nor mercy.
Las! Elle het mon preu et ma santé	Alas! she hates my worthiness and well-being,
Pour ce que j'aim s'onneur et sa biauté.	Precisely because I love her honor and beauty.
Et si la serf de cuer en tel cremour	And so I serve her with such respect in my heart
Que nulle riens ne li pri, eins l'aour; 20	That I ask her for nothing, but simply adore her;
Et c'est raisons, qu'on quiert souvent	And that's correct, since one often seeks out
Ce qu'on n'a de l'avoir talent.	The very thing one doesn't wish to have.

S'aim miex einsi ma dolour endurer
Qu'elle me fust plus dure par rouver;
Car s'el savoit que s'amour souhaidier   25
Heüsse osé, ja mais ne m'aroit chier.
Et si l'aim tant que s'en ce monde avoie
.I. seul souhait, einsi souhaideroie
Que s'amour fust envers tres tous d'un fuer
Fors vers celui qui l'aimme de mon cuer.   30
Par tel raison suis povres assasez,
Quant je plus vueil ce dont sui plus grevez:
Dont ne doit nuls pleindre ce que j'endure
Quant j'aim seur tout ce qui n'a de moy cure.

Thus I prefer enduring this kind of pain
To the grimmer face she'd show suppliant me,
For if she knew I was daring enough
To hope for her love, she'd never hold me dear.
And yet I love her so much that if in this world
I had but one wish, I would wish
Her love were available equally for all
Save for the one who loves her with my heart.
By such logic, I am both deprived and satisfied,
Since I desire most what grieves me the worst:
So no one should be upset about what I endure
In that I love above all the one who cares nothing
                                 [for me.

motetus

Corde mesto
Cantando conqueror,
  Semper presto
Serviens maceror,
  Sub honesto   5
Gestu totus teror,
  Et infesto
Casu remuneror.

With sad heart
Singing I complain,
  A servant always ready,
I weaken,
  By honest deeds
I waste away to nothing,
  And a hostile fate
Is my reward.

  In derisum,
Fortuna, te ponis;   10
  Das arrisum
Expars rationis
   Et obrisum
Malis; sed a bonis
  Tollis risum   15
Et abis cum donis.

  Into a laughing stock,
Fortune, you make yourself;
  You giggle,
Devoid of reason,
  And you smile
At the wicked; but the virtuous
  You deny your laugh,
Stealing away with your gifts.

  Spernens cece
Fortune tedia
  Utor prece
Cum penitencia,
  Culpe fece   20
Ut lauto venia,
  Michi nece
Promatur gloria.

  Spurning the irksomeness
Of blind Fortune,
  I take to prayer
With penitence,
  So that, scrubbed clean
Of guilt's filth by forgiveness,
  In death
Glory will be mine.

tenor

Libera me

Free me

13

I **Ruina**

Tant doucement m'ont attrait		So sweetly have attracted me
Bel Acueil et Dous Attrait,		Fair Welcome and Sweet Attraction,
Nés de Dous Viaire,		Finding their origin in Sweet Countenance,
Et Samblans d'Amour, qui, trait		And Appearance of Love - who, shot by
D'un regart riant, attrait	5	A laughing look, attracted
M'a par son plaisant attrait,		Me by her pleasant attraction -
Que clamour fait faire		That they have caused me to complain
A ma dame debonnaire		To my gentle lady
M'ont dou mal qui est en my.		About the ills inside me.
Helas! si m'ont fait einsi	10	Alas! in this way they have
Pour ma mort attraire,		Made me bring death upon myself,
Com cils qui son anemy		Like the man who leads his enemy off
Meinne noier comme amy,		To drown him, arms around his neck,
Les bras au col; et traÿ		As if he were his friend; and they have
M'ont par tel affaire;	15	Betrayed me by doing so;
Car Regars, pour moy detraire,		For Look, to mislead me,
En riant m'asseüroit		Laughingly reassured me
Et merci me prometoit;		And promised me mercy;
Et Samblans d'attraire		And too, Appearance of Attraction
Ma grant paour estraingnoit	20	Restrained my great fear
Et hardement me donnoit;		And gave me courage;
A Bel Acueil m'apelloit		She summoned me to Fair Welcome
Pour mes maus retraire,		In order to rehearse my troubles,
Mais pour moy faire mort traire:		But it was to make me draw toward my own death:
Quant ad ce m'eurent mené,	25	After leading me to this point,
Com faus traïtour prouvé		Like a traitor proven false,
Furent mi contraire,		They turned against me,
Et d'un refus sans pité,		And with a pitiless refusal,
Dur et plein de cruauté,	30	Unfeeling and full of cruelty,
D'orguilleus cuer engendré,		Brought to life by an arrogant heart,
Me firent deffaire,		They made me suffer defeat,
Pour ce que j'aim sans retraire.		Because I love without reservations.

Eins que ma dame d'onnour,		Before my honorable lady,
Que je serf et pris,		Whom I serve and value,
Sceüst la dure dolour		Learned of the unremitting pain
Dont je sui espris,		By which I was gripped,
Souvent estoie enrichis,	5	I was often enriched,
Sans avoir s'amour,		- Without having her love -
De son regart qui conquis		By her look, which has conquered me
M'a par sa vigour,		With its strength,
Et de la fine douçour		And by the refined sweetness
De son plaisant ris.	10	Of her pleasant laugh.
Or me tolt ses biens gentils		Now she takes from me her noble gifts,
Et me tient en plour,		Keeping me in tears,
Quant elle scet que j'aour		Since she knows how I worship
Son gracieus vis		Her gracious visage
Et que je l'aim sans faus tour.	15	And how I love her without any deceptive tricks.

Ruina   **Ruin**

14

MS *A* fols 427v-28r

A: C1, I **Quia amore langueo**

Maugré mon cuer, contre mon sentement Dire me font que j'ay aligement De Bonne Amour, Ceaus qui dient que j'ay fait faintement Mes chans qui sont fait dolereusement, Et que des biens amoureus ay souvent La grant douçour.

De ma dolour

Confortez doucement, De mon labour Me ris tres hautement, De grant tristour En toute joie mis, De

C2

123

He - las! do-lens, et je n'os on-ques jour, Puis que pre - miers

grief lan - gour Es - cha -

vi ma da-me d'on-nour, Que j'aim en foy, Qui ne fu nez et fe - nis

pés et ga - ris; De Bon E - ur, de Gra - ce,

en do - lour, Con - ti - nu-ez en tris - tes-se et en plour, Pleins

de Pi - tié Et de For - tu - ne a -

de re - fus pour croi - stre mon la - bour Et con - tre moy;

mis; et a mon gré Con

triplum

Maugré mon cuer, contre mon sentement	Despite my heart, against my feelings
Dire me font que j'ay aligement	They make me say that I am comforted
De Bonne Amour,	By Good Love,
Ceaus qui dient que j'ay fait faintement	Those claiming that I have feigned
Mes chans qui sont fait dolereusement, 5	In my songs which were composed in sadness,
Et que des biens amoureus ay souvent	And that I often receive the great sweetness
La grant douçour.	Of Love's goods.
Helas! dolens, et je n'os onques jour,	Alas! poor me, and I have spent not one day,
Puis que premiers vi ma dame d'onnour,	Since I first laid eyes upon my honorable lady,
Que j'aim en foy, 10	Whom I love faithfully,
Qui ne fu nez et fenis en dolour,	That did not begin and end in suffering,
Continuez en tristesse et en plour,	That did not drag on with sadness and weeping,
Pleins de refus pour croistre mon labour	Filled with refusal so as to increase my hardship,
Et contre moy;	And not to my advantage;
N'onques ma dame au riche maintieng coy 15	And never did my lady with her rich and demure
Mon dolent cuer, qui ne se part de soy,	Bring joy to my sorrowing heart, [bearing,
Ne resjoï,	Which never leaves her side,
Ne n'ot pitié dou mal que je reçoy;	Nor did she take pity on the ills I receive;
Et si scet bien qu'en li mon temps employ,	And yet she knows that I live my life for her,
Et que je l'aim, criem, serf, desir et croy 20	And that I love, fear, serve, desire and trust her
De cuer d'amy;	With a true lover's heart;
Et quant il n'est garison ne merci	And since there is no remedy or mercy
Qui me vausist, se ne venoit de li	That would help me, if not coming from her
A qui m'ottry,	To whom I have given myself,
Et son franc cuer truis si dur anemi 25	And since in her generous heart I find an enemy so
Qu'il se delite es maus dont je langui,	As to delight in the ills that make me languish, [fierce
Chascuns puet bien savoir que j'ay menti.	Everyone can easily know that I have lied.

motetus

De ma dolour Confortez doucement,	For my grief sweetly comforted,
De mon labour Meris tres hautement,	For my endeavor highly rewarded,
De grant tristour En toute joie mis,	From great sadness lifted up to perfect joy,
De grief langour Eschapés et garis;	Escaped from terrible languishing, and healed;
De Bon Eür, de Grace, de Pitié 5	By Good Luck, by Grace, by Pity
Et de Fortune amis; et a mon gré	And by Fortune befriended; also, as I'd wish,
Con diseteus Richement secourus,	Richly supported in my deprivation,
Et familleus Largement repeüs	And as a starving man generously regaled
De tous les biens que dame et Bonne Amour	With all the gifts a lady and Good Love
Puent donner a amant par honnour 10	Can in honor bestow on a lover,
Suis! et Amours m'est en tous cas aidans.	All this am I! And Love is my help in everything.
Mais, par m'ame, je mens parmi mes dens!	But, upon my soul, I am lying through my teeth!

tenor

Quia amore langueo	**For I languish with love**

15

Ia **Vidi Dominum**

130

corps d'um - bles - se pa - ré, Cuers qui est pleins de dur - té Et de cou-ver-

N'en riens n'a re - con - gne - u

IIb

tu - re; Re - fus, qui d'es-poir os - té M'a la nor - ri -

Ma do - lour ne ma gre - van -

tu - re, Et Dan - giers, qui des - pi - té M'a sans cau-se et si gre - vé Qu'il m'a

ce; Eins m'a mis

par des - daing me - né A des - con - fi - tu - re.

en non - cha - - - - - loir.

131

Amours, qui a le pooir	Love, who has the power to bring it about
De moy faire recevoir	That my lot is either joy
Joie ou mort obscure,	Or a gloomy death,
Ne fait par sa grace avoir	Does not with Her grace foster
A ma dame tel voloir 5	Any willingness in my lady
Qu'elle m'ait en cure.	To care for me.
Durer ne puis longuement,	I cannot long endure
Car pour amer loyaument	Because for neither loving faithfully
Ne pour servir liement	Nor joyfully serving
Sans penser laidure, 10	With no improper thoughts,
Ne pour celer sagement	Nor for wisely remaining discreet,
N'ay confort n'aligement	Do I receive any comfort or relief
De ma dolour dure;	For my harsh pain;
Einsois com plus humblement	Rather, the more humbly
La sueffre et endure, 15	I suffer and endure it,
De tant est plus durement	The more harshly treated
Traitiés mes cuers, que briefment	Is my heart, so that soon
Morray dolereusement	I shall die a painful death
De dueil et d'ardure,	From this misery and burning,
Et tant sui plus eslongiez 20	And the more I am made distant
De merci et estraingiés	From mercy and estranged
De ma dame pure;	From my lady pure;
Mais avec tous ces meschiés	But with all these misfortunes,
Sueffre Amours, qui est mes chiés,	Love, who is my master,
Que Raison, Droiture, 25	Does permit that Reason, Justice,
Douçour, Debonnaireté,	Sweetness, Nobleness
Franchise, Grace et Pité	Generosity, Grace, and Pity
N'ont pooir a Cruauté;	Have no power over Cruelty;
Einsois regne et dure	Instead, what holds sway and endures
En corps d'umblesse paré, 30	In a body graced with humility,
Cuers qui est pleins de durté	Is a heart full of harshness
Et de couverture;	And dissimulation;
Refus, qui d'espoir osté	Also Refusal, who has stolen from me
M'a la norriture,	The nourishment of hope,
Et Dangiers, qui despité 35	And Resistance, who has spurned me
M'a sans cause et si grevé	For no reason and so wounded me
Qu'il m'a par desdaing mené	That he has through disdain
A desconfiture.	Brought on my defeat.

Faus Samblant m'a deceü		False Seeming has deceived me
Et tenu en esperence		And given me hope
De joie mercy avoir;		Of receiving the grant of joy;
Et je l'ay com fols creü		And like a fool I have believed him,
Et mis toute ma fiance	5	Placing in him all my expectation
En li d'amoureus voloir.		Of amorous desire.
Las! or m'a descongneü,		Alas! now he has ignored me,
Quant de moy faire aligence		When he had the time to bring
Ha heü temps et pooir;		Me relief, and had the power as well,
N'en riens n'a recongneü	10	Nor has he in any way acknowledged
Ma dolour ne ma grevance;		The pain or the misery I feel;
Eins m'a mis en nonchaloir.		What he has shown me instead is indifference.

Vidi Dominum   **I have seen the Lord**

16

MS *A* fols 429v-30r

134

triplum

Lasse! comment oublieray	Alas! how shall I forget
Le bel, le bon, le dous, le gay	The fair, the good, the sweet and cheerful one
A qui entierement donnay	To whom I granted unreservedly
Le cuer de my	This heart of mine
Pour le sien que j'ay sans demi? 5	In exchange for his, which I possess, and not by half?
Et le retins pour mon amy,	And I accepted him as my lover
Einsois qu'eüsse mon mari,	Before I had my husband,
Qui me deffent	Who forbids me
Et me gaite mult durement	- Guarding me very closely -
Que ne voie son corps le gent, 10	From looking on his gentle person,
Dont li cuers en .ij. pars me fent;	And so my heart breaks in two;
Car il m'estuet	For I must
Mal gré mien faire ce qu'il vuet,	Do as he wishes in spite of myself,
Dont durement li cuers me duet;	And so my heart is in dire distress;
Mais pour ce drois ne se remuet 15	But on this account justice does not change
Ne bonne foy;	Nor does good faith;
Car puis que certeinnement voy	For since I see with certainty
Qu'il vuet et quiert l'onneur de moy	That he wishes what does me honor, and seeks it,
Et qu'il m'aimme assez plus que soy,	Loving me more than himself,
Et se le truis 20	And if I find him
Si bon qu'il prent tous ses deduis	So good that all the pleasure he takes
En moy servir, je ne le puis	Is serving me, I cannot
Laissier, se mauvaise ne suis;	Abandon him, if I am not to be wicked;
Eins le puis bien	Instead I can
Amer par honneur et par bien, 25	Love him honorably and to the good,
Quant j'ay son cuer et il le mien,	Since I have his heart and he mine,
Sans ce que je mesprengne en rien,	Without doing wrong in the least,
Ce m'est avis;	Such is my view;
Mais j'eüsse trop fort mespris,	But I would have committed a terrible wrong,
Se j'eüsse l'amer empris 30	Had I undertaken to love
De puis que j'eus a mari pris,	After taking for a husband,
Lasse! celui	Alas! the one
Qui tant me fait peinne et anui	Who causes me so much grief and pain
Qu'en tous cas toute joie fui,	That I flee at every turn from joy,
N'en ce monde n'a moy n'autrui 35	And no one in this world can comfort me,
Qui me confort,	Neither I nor anyone else,
Car mi gieu, mi ris, mi deport,	For my sport, my laughter, my pleasure,
Mi chant, mi revel, mi confort,	My songs, my delight, my comfort,
Mi bien et mi bon jour sont mort,	My well-being, and my happy days have died,
Et nuit et jour 40	And night and day

Acroist li ruissiaus de mon plour		The stream of my tears increases
Quant le plus bel et le millour		Since I do not gaze upon the fairest and best
De tous ne voy: c'est ma dolour;		Of all: this is what pains me;
Mais soit certeins		But let him be assured

Que, comment que mes corps lonteins	45	That, however far off my body,
Li soit, mes cuers li est procheins,		My heart is close to him,
D'amour et de loiauté pleins.		Full of love and loyalty.

motetus

Se j'aim mon loial amy		If I love my faithful lover,
Et il my		And he does me
Si loiaument		So faithfully

Qu'il est tous miens sans nul si		That he is all mine, and no buts,
Et je aussi,	5	And I, just the same,
Entierement,		Completely,

Sans nul villein pensement,		With no base thought,
Bonnement		Willingly
A li m'ottri,		Grant myself to him,

Pour ce qu'il m'a longuement,	10	Because he has for a long time
Liement,		Gladly,
De cuer servi,		Served me with all his heart,

Ay je pour ce desservi,		Have I therefore deserved,
Lasse! Aymi!		- Alas! poor me! -
Que tellement	15	That in such a fashion

M'en demeinne mon mari		My husband should so abuse me
Que de li		That all I get from him
N'ay fors tourment?		Is torment ?

Nennil! car certeinnement		Certainly not! For surely,
Mortelment	20	He commits
Peche celi		A mortal sin,

Qui pour bien faire mal rent.		Whoever returns evil for good.
Or m'aprent		Now he teaches me
A faire einsi,		To do just that,

Qu'il vuet que mette en oubli	25	Because he wants me to forget
Celui qui		The one who
M'a humblement		Has humbly

Doubté, celé, obey		Respected, dissembled for, obeyed,
Et servi		And served me
A mon talent.	30	As much as I could wish.

141

Pour quoy me bat mes maris?
  Lassette!
  Aymi, Diex!
Pour quoy me bat mes maris?
  Lassette!   5

Je ne li ay riens meffait,
Je ne li ay riens meffait,
Fors qu'a mon amy parlay,
  Seulette,
  Aymi, Diex!   10
Fors qu'a mon ami parlay,
  Seulette.

Pour quoy me bat mes maris?
  Lassette!
  Aymi, Diex!   15
Pour quoy me bat mes maris?
  Lassette!

Why does my husband beat me?
  Alas!
  Poor me, oh God!
Why does my husband beat me?
  Alas!

I have done him nothing wrong,
I have done him nothing wrong,
Except that I talked to my friend,
  Alone.
  Poor me, oh God!
Except that I talked to my friend,
  Alone.

Why does my husband beat me?
  Alas!
  Poor me, oh God!
Why does my husband beat me?
  Alas!

17

C1, I **Super omnes speciosa**

II

143

144

C2, IV

145

Quant Vraie Amour enflamee,	When True Love set ablaze,
D'Ardant Desir engendree,	Engendered by Burning Desire,
Pucelete mestrie	Comes to master some maiden,
Ou temps que doit estre amee,	Just when it's the right time she be loved,
Se vrais amans l'en prie 5	If then a true lover begs her favor,
Par foy de fait esprouvee,	Pledging his troth, as his actions prove,
Tant que loiautez juree	With the result that his sworn loyalty
Fait qu'elle a li s'ottrie	Makes her give herself to him
Par si parfaite assamblee	In such a perfect act of union
Qu'en dui n'ont c'une vie, 10	That the two of them share but one life,
C'un cuer ne c'une pensee,	One heart, one thought,
C'est qu'en deduit ait duree	Then this happens to make pleasure endure
Leur amour commencie.	Once their loving commences.
Se puis vient autres qui bee	If another man then turns up, eager
Qu'il en fera s'amie, 15	To make her his beloved,
Et celle dou tout li vee,	And she utterly refuses him,
Pour ce qu'avant s'est donnee,	Because she has given herself already,
S'il par sa druerie	And if he in his lovesickness
Maintient qu'Amours soit faussee,	Maintains that Love has played him false,
Quant il n'i trueve mie 20	Because he finds in her nothing
Merci d'amant desiree,	Of the lover's reward he desires,
Combien qu'il l'ait comparee	Though he has dearly paid for it
Par moult dure hachie,	With misery quite hard to bear,
N'en doit estre Amour blasmee,	Then Love should not be blamed for all this,
Mais de tant plus prisie 25	But all the more esteemed
Qu'elle ensieut, comme ordenee,	For following, as was ordained,
Nature, qui l'a formee	Nature, who formed Her
Sans estre en riens brisie;	Without showing any break;
Car qui .ij. fois vuet denree,	For he who wants to have the same goods a second
Le marcheant conchie. 30	Fouls the merchant. [time,

O Series summe rata,	O, Order perfectly proportioned,
Regendo naturam,	Who by governing Nature
Uniformam per causata	Maintains a uniform bond
Tenens ligaturam,	Through all that is generated,
Argumentis demonstrata 5	Demonstrated by proofs
Non pati fracturam,	Not to suffer breakage;
Cum sit Amor tui nata	Since Love is Thy daughter,
Spernatque mensuram,	And [yet] scorns measure,
Melle parens irrorata,	Appearing [at first] sprinkled with honey,
Post agens usturam, 10	[But] afterward scorching,
Dans quibus non est optata	Giving to those who do not desire it
Mitem creaturam,	A gentle creature
Que sola sit michi grata	Who, alone, should be pleasing to me
Michique tam duram,	And [yet] is so hard on me,
Mirans queror mente strata 15	I complain, my mind confused,
Talem genituram.	Wondering at such a begetting.

Super omnes speciosa	**Fair above all**

18

C1, I **Bone pastor**

II

Plu-ri-mi mor-den-tur. Mi - tra que ca-put cin-git Bi-no cor-nu de-pin-git Du - o te -

te - nus. O Guil-ler - me, te de-cen - ter Or - na -

C2, III

sta-men - ta, Que mi-tri-fer ha-be-re De-bet tam-quam cin-ce - re

- tum: Rex qui po - ten - ter Cun - cta

Men-tis or-na-men-ta. Et quo-ni-am im-bu-tus Et to-tus in-vo-lu-tus Es im-pre -

re - git, Su - e do - mus ad de - co - rem

IV

li-ba - tis, Fer-re mi-tram est di-gna Tu - a cer-vix, ut si-gna Sint e-qua si-gna-tis.

Re-men-si - um in pa - sto - rem Pre - e - le-git.

Cu-ram ge-rens po-pu-li, Vis ut que-ant sin-gu-li Va-gos pro-

E - le - git te, vas ho - ne - stum,

C3, i

fi - ce - re. Pri-ma par - te ba-cu-li At - tra - he - re;

Vas in - - si - - gne, De

Par - te qui-dem a-li-a Que est in-ter-me-di-a, Mor-bi - dos

quo ni - chil sit e-ge - stum

ii

re - ge - re; Len-tos par-te ter-ci-a Scis pun - ge - re.

Ni - si di - - gne; De -

150

O - ves pre - di - ca - mi - ne Et cum con - ver - sa - mi - ne Pa - scis lau -

- dit te, vas spe - ci - a - le,

C4, iii

da - bi - li, De - mum e - ro - ga - mi - ne Sen - si - bi - li.

Si - bi Re - gi; De -

Det post hoc ex - i - li - um Huic Rex a - ctor om - ni - um, Qui par - cit

- dit te, vas ge - ne - ra - le,

iv

hu - mi - li, Sta - bi - le do - mi - ni - um Pro la - bi - li.

Su - o gre - gi.

151

triplum

Bone pastor Guillerme,		Good shepherd Guillermus,
Pectus quidem inerme		Surely what was bestowed on you
Non est tibi datum,		Was no breast unprotected,
Favente sed Minerva		But one strongly armoured
Virtutum est caterva	5	By a host of virtues
Fortiter armatum.		Through Minerva's favour.
Portas urbis et postes		You guard the gates and doorposts
Tue munis, ne hostes		Of your city, so these enemies
Urbem populentur:		Might not take up residence in the city:
Mundus, demon et caro,	10	The world, the devil, and the flesh,
Morsu quorum amaro		By whose bitter bite
Plurimi mordentur.		Many are stricken.
Mitra que caput cingit		The mitre that encircles your head
Bino cornu depingit		Signifies with its double horns
Duo testamenta,	15	The two testaments,
Que mitrifer habere		Which he who bears the mitre
Debet tamquam cincere		Must possess as ornaments
Mentis ornamenta.		Of a pure mind.
Et quoniam imbutus		And since you are imbued with
Et totus involutus	20	And totally enveloped
Es inprelibatis,		By purity,
Ferre mittram est digna		Your head is worthy to bear
Tua cervix, ut signa		The mitre, so that the signs
Sint equa signatis.		Equal what is signified.
Curam gerens populi,	25	In bearing the burden of the people's care,
Vis ut queant singuli		You express the wish that individuals strive
Vagos proficere.		To help those who have gone astray.
Prima parte baculi		With the first part of your staff
Attrahere;		You know how to attract;
Parte quidem alia	30	With that other part
Que est intermedia,		Which is in the middle, you know
Morbidos regere;		How to guide those ravaged by sickness;
Lentos parte tercia		And with the third part
Scis pungere.		How to spur on the slothful.
Oves predicamine	35	You feed your sheep with sermons
Et cum conversamine		And with discourse
Pascis laudabili,		That is praiseworthy,
Demum erogamine		And in the end
Sensibili.		With sensible gifts.
Det post hoc exilium	40	After this exile here
Huic Rex actor omnium,		May the King, who brings about all things,
Qui parcit humili,		And who spares the humble,
Stabile dominium		Give him a stable dominion
Pro labili.		In place of this unsteady one.

Bone pastor, qui pastores		Good shepherd, you who surpass
Ceteros vincis per mores		The other shepherds by your morals
Et per genus,		And by your descent,
Et per fructum studiorum,		And by the fruit of your studies,
Tollentem mentes ymorum	5	Lifting the minds of those laid low
Celo tenus.		Up to heaven,
O Guillerme, te decenter		Oh you, Guillermus, so fittingly adorned:
Ornatum: Rex qui potenter		The King who powerfully
Cuncta regit,		Ordains all things
Sue domus ad decorem	10	Has, especially, chosen you
Remensium in pastorem		To grace His house as shepherd
Preelegit.		Of the people of Reims.
Elegit te, vas honestum,		He chose you, as an honorable vessel,
Vas insigne,		As a pre-eminent vessel,
De quo nichil sit egestum	15	From which nothing should be poured
Nisi digne;		If it be not worthy;
Dedit te, vas speciale,		He gave you, as a special vessel,
Sibi Regi;		To Himself, the King;
Dedit te, vas generale,		He gave you, as a general vessel,
Suo gregi.	20	To his flock.

tenor

Bone pastor   **Good shepherd**

19

Mar-ty-rum gem-ma la-tri-a, Ty-ran-ni tru-cis im-pi - a, Quin-ti-ne, sa-pi-en-ti - a, Ver-ba sper-nens ma-vor-ti-a,

Ju - ben - tis ter - ri - bi - li - a Ma - chi - na - ri sup-pli - ti - a; Ro-ma -

Di - li - gen - ter in - qui - ra - mus

C1, I A Christo honoratus

no-rum pro-sa-pi - a Ce - na - to - rum ce - le-sti - a, Ric-ti - o - va - ri so-li-

Quin - ti - ni pre-co - ni - a;

a Af - fe - ctans et Pi - ta - ni - a Ad - mo-vens su-per-ci-li-a,

Con - gau-den - ter im - pen - da - mus Nu -

154

155

triplum

Martyrum gemma latria,		Gem of martyrs in veneration,
Tyranni trucis impia,		Quintinus; you who through wisdom spurned
Quintine, sapientia,		The impieties of the harsh tyrant,
Verba spernens mavortia,		As well as the warlike words
Jubentis terribilia	5	Of him who ordered to devise
Machinari supplitia;		Those terrible tortures;
Romanorum prosapia		Coming from a most eminent house
Cenatorum celestia,		Of Roman senators,
Rictiovari solia		Seeking the dwelling of Rictiovarus
Affectans et Pitania	10	And countering
Admovens supercilia,		The Poitevin pride
Ambianensis propria		With the cheerfulness
Gentis alacrimonia,		Native to the folk of Amiens,
Humilitate socia,		With humility as its companion;
Victis volens martyria	15	Wishing to suffer tortures for the ones defeated,
Oleique ledentia		And the pains from the [boiling] oil,
Martirii redolentia:		And the fragrance of martyrdom:
Quibus fit appoplecia,		To the apoplectics
Prece cujus anadia		By your [his] entreaty medicine is given,
Datur cecis et gracia;	20	As well as assuagement to the blind;
Cunctorum purgans vicia		You [He] purge[s] all the sick
Infirmorum pernicia,		Of their pernicious defects,
Sospitati vestigia		Enabling cripples to walk;
Claudorum filocalia		Through your [his] love of beauty
Prebentur morbis gravia;	25	Powerful medicines are provided for deadly diseases.
Cujus fulget provincia		The province of Vermandois is set aglow
Virmandorum presentia,		By the presence of this [saint],
Quo livor, advaricia		Through whom envy, greed,
Cadunt, gula, luxuria,		Gluttony, lust,
Ira, fastus, accidia	30	Anger, pride and sloth are brought low,
Malaque cuncta noxia;		As well as all poisonous evils;
Quo viget pacientia,		Through whom patience reigns,
Fides, spes et prudencia,		As well as faith, hope, and wisdom,
Quo simus ad palatia		And through whom we may be counted present
Celorum refulgentia,	35	In the resplendent palaces of heaven,
Ubi pax est et gloria.		Where peace is, and glory too.

motetus

Diligenter inquiramus		Let us diligently set about
Quintini preconia;		Praising Quintinus;
Congaudenter impendamus		Let us joyfully dedicate
Numini suffragia. .		Signs of affection to his sanctity.
Fuit vite mirabilis,	5	In life, he was to be marvelled at,
Despuit obnoxia;		Shunning disgusting sins;
Fuit Deo laudabilis,		God found him worthy of praise,
Meruit suppedia.		And he merited His rich gifts.
Illimis bacca fons erat,		His mouth was a clear spring,
Bargueries nobilis.	10	His rhetoric[?] noble.
Animis Deo venerat		In his mind had come to God
Mollicies fragilis.		The frailty of his flesh.
Colentes hunc karissime		Those who revere him with great love,
Exultabunt suaviter;		Their rejoicing will be sweet;
Canentes nobilissime	15	Their singing will be sublime,
Dabunt laudes dulciter.		Harmoniously will they render him praise.

tenor

A Christo honoratus　　　　　　　　**Honored by Christ**

159

20

Trop plus est bele que Biauté		Far lovelier than Beauty,
Et millour que ne soit Bonté,		And better than Goodness itself,
Pleinne de tout ce, a dire voir,		Graced with - and it's truth I speak - everything
Que bonne et bele doit avoir,		A good and beautiful lady must possess,
Ce m'est vis, celle que desir	5	All this, it seems to me, is the one whom I desire
Et aim sans nul villain desir;		And love without any base desire;
Dont se je l'aim, et je, qu'en puis,		So, if I love her - and could I do otherwise,
Quant en sa fine biauté truis		Since in her perfect beauty I find
De tous mes maus la garison,		The cure for all my ills,
Leesse, confort, guerredon	10	Joy, comfort, reward
Et secours de tous les meschiés		For all the misery
Dont par Desir sui entechiés,		Desire afflicts me with,
Comment qu'elle n'en sache rien;		Although she is unaware of it;
Car toute la joie et le bien		For all the joy and the good
Que j'ay, de sa grace me vient	15	I receive, is brought me
Sans plus, quant de li me souvient,		By her favor alone when I think of her,
N'autre bonté de li n'en port;		No other benefit do I take from her -
Si pri Amours qu'en tel acort		So I pray Love to consent,
Soit, pour ce que miex l'aim que my,		Since I love her more than myself,
Qu'elle me teingne pour amy.	20	That she accept me as her lover.
Amen		Amen

Biauté paree de valour,		Beauty adorned with excellence,
Desirs qui onques n'a sejour		Desire that never rests
D'acroistre, eins croist de jour en jour		From increasing, but grows, day in day out,
En plaisance et en douce ardour;		In pleasure and sweet passion;
Dous Regars, pris par grant savour,	5	Sweet Look, received with great delight,
Tous pleins de promesse d'amour,		Overflowing with love's promises,
D'espoir de joie, de tenrour		With hope for joy, with tenderness,
Et de pointure de douçour,		And with the sting of sweetness,
Font que j'aim des dames la flour.		These make me love the very flower of ladies.
Or me doint Diex grace et vigour	10	God give me now both grace and power,
Que au gré d'Amours et a s'onnour		So that, as Love wishes and to her honor
La puisse servir sans folour.		I may serve her beyond any folly.
Amen		Amen

Je ne sui mie certeins d'avoir amie,	**I am not certain I have a sweetheart,**
Mais je suis loiaus amis.	**But a loyal lover is what I am.**

21

C1, I **Tribulatio proxima est et non est qui adjuvet**

165

166

triplum

Christe, qui lux es et dies,		Christ, You who are light and day,
Fideliumque requies,		As well as the repose of the faithful,
Nos visita;		Come among us;
Tu furoris temperies,		You who assuage anger,
Tu dulcoris planities,	5	You who moderate sweetness,
Nunc excita		Summon up now
Posse tuum, precipita		Your power, cast down
Depredentes qui nos ita		The rapacious, who so badly
Vituperant.		Rail against us.
Sicut per te fuit vita	10	Just as through You life
Patribus nostris reddita,		Was given back to our fathers,
Qui tunc erant		Who lived in days gone by

Nec tueri se poterant,		And could not effect their own salvation,
Sed ad te reclamaverant,		But called upon You,
Deus fortis,	15	Mighty God,
Sic cave, ne nos atterant		So prevent from destroying us
Qui nos in guerris laxerant		Those who are cutting us to shreds
Nunc subortis,		In the wars that have now sprung up,

Et adire nexu mortis,		And from enduring the embrace of death,
Cuius sumus jam in portis,	20	In whose portals we are already standing,
Nos protegas;		Protect us;
Gentem serves tue sortis,		Safeguard the people You have chosen
Tui fratris ac consortis		And take charge of the cause
Causam regas;		Of your brother and consort;

Qui malos a te segregas	25	You who separate the evil ones from You,
Nec justis opem denegas,		And do not refuse aid to the just,
Legis lator;		You, maker of laws;
Proditores nunc detegas		Make now the traitors known
Horumque visum contegas,		And cloud their sight,
Consolator;	30	O Consoler;

Danielis visitator		You who visited Daniel
Puerorumque salvator		And saved the three boys
In fornace,		In the furnace,
Per Abacuc confortator:		You, comforter through Habakkuk:
Sis pro nobis preliator	35	Be the one who battles for us,
Et dimittas nos in pace.		And send us on our way in peace.

motetus

Veni, Creator Spiritus,		Come, Creator Spirit,
Flentium audi gemitus,		Listen to the groans of those who weep,
Quos nequiter gens misera		Whom a wretched people wickedly
Destruit; veni, propera!		Is destroying; come, make haste!
Jam nostra virtus deficit	5	Already our strength is failing
Nec os humanum sufficit		And no human mouth suffices
Ad narrandum obprobria		To tell of the disgrace
Que nobis dant vecordia,		That is brought to us by madness,
Divisio, cupiditas		By strife, by greed,
Fideliumque raritas,	10	And by the paucity of the faithful,
Unde flentes ignoramus		So that we, weeping, do not know
Quid agere debeamus;		What we should do;
Circumdant nos inimici,		Enemies surround us,
Sed et nostri domestici		But even our compatriots
Conversi sunt in predones:	15	Have turned into beasts of prey:
Leopardi et leones,		Leopards and lions,
Lupi, milvi et aquile		Wolves, vultures, and eagles
Rapiunt omne reptile;		Snatch away every creeping creature;
Consumunt nos carbunculi.		Boils consume us.
Ad te nostri sunt oculi:	20	To You our eyes are turned:
Perde gentem hanc rapacem,		Destroy this rapacious tribe,
Jhesu, redemptor seculi,		Jesus, Redeemer of the world,
Et da nobis tuam pacem.		And give us Your peace.

tenor

Tribulatio proxima est
et non est qui adjuvet

Trouble is near
and there is no one to help

22

MS *A* **fols 435v-36r**

C3, IV **Apprehende arma**

Tu qui gregem tuum ducis,		You who lead your flock,
Opera fac veri ducis,		Do the work of a true leader,
Nam ducere et non duci,		For to lead and not to be led,
Hoc competit vero duci;		Is what befits a true leader;
Dux prudentium consilio,	5	Following the counsel of the wise,
Ducat nec sit in octio		Let the leader lead and not be idle,
Debetque dux anteire,		And the leader must go in front,
Ductus autem obedire;		While the one led must obey;
Sed si ductor nescit iter,		But if the leader does not know the way,
Ambo pereunt leviter,	10	They will both readily perish,
Nam ambulat absque luce		For whoever is led by a blind leader
Qui ducitur ceco duce,		Walks outside the light,
Sed qui habet verum ducem		But whoever has a true leader
Omni hora habet lucem,		Has light at every hour,
Et ille bene ducitur	15	And that man is well led
Qui a nullo seducitur;		Who is misled by no one;
Unde qui ducum ductor es:		And so you, who are the leader of leaders:
Contere nunc seductores,		Destroy now the misleaders,
Et taliter nos deducas,		And lead us in such a way,
Ut ad pacem nos perducas.	20	That you lead us to peace.

Plange, regni res publica!		Weep, commonweal of the realm!
Tua gens ut scismatica		Your people, as schismatics,
Desolatur;		Are damned;
Nam pars eius est iniqua		For part of them is iniquitous
Et altera sophistica	5	And the other reputed
Reputatur.		To offer false arguments.
De te modo non curatur,		No one is taking care of you,
Inimicis locus datur		To your enemies a free hand is given
Fraudulenter;		Through trickery;
Tui status deturpatur,	10	Your standing is denigrated,
Sua virtus augmentatur		Their strength now openly
Nunc patenter.		Increased.
Te rexerunt imprudenter,		They have ruled you imprudently,
Licet forte innocenter,		Albeit perhaps in innocence,
Tui cari;	15	Those who are dear to you;
Sed amodo congaudenter		But from now on they will make
Te facient et potenter,		It happen, gladly and forcefully,
Deo dante, dominari.		God willing, that you have the upper hand.

Apprehende arma et scutum	**Take hold of arms and shield,**
et exurge	**and rise up**
Apprehende arma	**Take hold of arms**

23

triplum

Felix virgo, mater Christi,		Blessed Virgin, mother of Christ,
Que gaudium mundo tristi		Who has brought joy to the sad world
Ortu tui contulisti,		By Your childbearing,
Dulcissima;		Lady most sweet;
Sic hereses peremisti,	5	You destroyed the heresies then,
Dum angelo credidisti		Trusting to the angel
Filiumque genuisti,		And giving birth to Your Son,
Castissima.		Lady most chaste.
Roga natum, piissima,		Implore Your Son, Lady most pious,
Ut pellat mala plurima,	10	To drive off evils in their many kinds,
Tormentaque gravissima,		And the most terrible torments
Que patimur;		That we endure;
Nam a gente ditissima,		For by a people of great wealth,
Lux lucis splendidissima,		Light of lights most brilliant,
De sublimi ad infima	15	Are we dragged from supreme heights
Deducimur;		Into abysmal depths;
Cunctis bonis exuimur,		We are bereft of all good,
Ab impiis persequimur,		And are persecuted by the impious,
Per quos jugo* subicimur		Through whom we are subjected
Servitutis,	20	To the yoke of slavery,
Nam sicut ceci gradimur		For like the blind we walk
Nec directorem sequimur,		And are following no guide,
Sed a viis retrahimur		But are drawn away from the paths
Nobis tutis.		That are safe for us.
Gratie fons et virtutis,	25	Fount of grace and virtue,
Sola nostre spes salutis:		Only hope of our salvation:
Miserere destitutis		Have mercy on those deprived
Auxilio,		Of help,
Ut a culpis absolutis		So that, forgiven for our sins,
Et ad rectum iter ductis,	30	And led to the right path,
Inimicisque destructis		After the destruction of our enemies
Pax sit nobis cum gaudio.		Peace may come to us with joy.

Inviolata genitrix,		Inviolate childbearer,
Superbie grata victrix,		Gracious conqueress of pride,
Expers paris,		Eminent among Your peers,
Celestis aule janitrix,		Door-keeper of the celestial palace,
Miserorum exauditrix,	5	You who listen to the miserable,
Stella maris,		Star of the sea,
Que ut mater consolaris		You who provide a mother's consolation,
Et pro lapsis deprecaris		And humbly intercede for
Humiliter,		The fallen,
Gracie fons singularis,	10	Singular fount of grace,
Que angelis dominaris:		You who rule over the angels:
Celeriter		Hasten
Para nobis tutum iter		To make our journey safe
Juvaque nos viriliter;		And stand firm in helping us;
Nam perimus,	15	For we perish
Invadimur hostiliter;		While the enemy invades;
Sed tuimur debiliter,		Yet we defend ourselves only weakly,
Neque scimus		And we know not
Quo tendere nos possimus		To whom we might appeal,
Nec per quem salvi erimus	20	Or who will save us
Nisi per te.		If not You.
Eya, ergo poscimus		Well then, therefore we call upon You
Ut sub alis tuis simus:		To take us under Your wings:
Et versus nos te converte!		And turn Yourself towards us!

Ad te suspiramus gementes
  et flentes etc.

To You we sigh, lamenting
  and weeping etc.

CRITICAL COMMENTARY

M1 *Quant en moy vint premierement / Amour et biauté parfaite / Amara valde*

Musical concordances

C fols 206v-207r *G* fols102v-103r *Vg* fols 260v-261r *B* fols 258v-259r
E fols 131v-132v *W* fol. 74v (fragment of the triplum)

Tenor source

Repetenda of the responsory *Plange quasi virgo* for matins of Holy Saturday (Sabbato sancto, ad Mat. in I. Nocturno, Resp. iii; *CAO* IV:7387). Text (a compilation of Joel 1:8, Jeremiah 6:26, Jeremiah 25:34 and Zephaniah 1:14):

Plange quasi virgo, plebs mea.	Lament like a virgin, my people.
Ululate, pastores, in cinere et cilicio;	Howl, shepherds, in ashes and sackcloth;
quia veniet dies Domini	for the day of the Lord is near, which shall be
magna et *amara valde*.	great and very bitter.
V. Ululate, pastores, et clamate;	*V.* Howl, shepherds, and cry out;
aspergite vos cinere. [- Quia. *R.* Plange.]	sprinkle yourselves with ashes.

Quotation

The triplum text ends with a time-honored *rime équivoque* in trouvère poetry: *amer=amer* ("to love=bitter"). Motets often conclude with a proverb or quotation from an older poem, functioning as an *auctoritas* to confirm the truth of the text, and usually introduced by an *On dit* ("it is said") or a comparable expression. As an exception, the poet himself poses as the *auctoritas* in this first motet: *Et pour ce di* ("and therefore I say"), quoting this *rime équivoque* but extending it to a triple wordplay by the sound of the surrounding words: *que de son dous face on amer. Son* can mean: "his" ("one's"), "sound" or "song"; *face on* can also be heard as *façon*. The word *Amer* in the sense of "bitter" refers back to the tenor word *Amara*. Another *rime équivoque* is found in the motetus text, in the word *finement* (meaning both "perfectly, purely" and "ending"). Thus, equivocality is a characteristic quality of this motet.

Text structure

Triplum	a8 a8 b8 a8 a8 b8 c2 c2 b8 a8 b8	a: -ment; b: -er; c: -oir; d: -ours; e: -ai
	a8 a8 b8 a8 a8 b8 d2 d2 b8 a8 b8	
	a8 a8 b8 a8 a8 b8 e2 e2 b8 a8 b8	
	a8 a8 b8	
	a8 a8 b8	
	a8 b8 b8	

Motetus	a7' b2 b2 c6	a: -aite; b: -er; c: -ement; d: -ous; e: -i; f: -ir: g: -ee
	a7' d2 d2 c6	
	c7 e2 e2 a6'	
	f7 f7	
	g7' g7'	
	f7 g7'	

Tenor structure

Two colores of 30 notes, each divided by six taleae. The second color and its taleae are diminished to one-third. The identical rhythmic patterns in the upper voices combine every two taleae into one super-talea. The undiminished talea measures 18 perfect breves, diminished to 6 perfect breves, doubled by the isorhythmic patterns of the upper voices to super-taleae of 36 and 12 breves respectively. Color 1 measures 108 breves, color 2 36 breves. Length of the motet: 144 perfect breves.

Mensuration

Perfect modus, diminished to perfect tempus for the tenor; for the upper voices perfect modus, perfect tempus and major prolatio. In this all-perfect "model"-motet, in which the number 3 and its multiplications are heavily emphasized, the mensural levels clearly characterize the voices: modus in the tenor, modus and tempus in the motetus (six minimae forming the exception) and modus, tempus and prolatio in the triplum. Dots of division, to make the perfections clear, are not consistently used. The motetus has six textless ternariae (ligatures) in syncopated position marked by dots of division; they form the connection between the taleae. Such textless passages occur otherwise only in the motetus of M12.

Variants and errors not marked in the score

Bar	Voice	MS	
1	Tr	*Vg B*	left-tailed brevis.
1	Mo	*E*	the first note is a brevis, not a longa.
9	Tr	*Vg*	the differently shaped mi-sign at staff-beginning seems to be by another hand than the mi-sign before it (in b. 8); a later addition?
12	Tr	*A*	since the mi-sign is placed at staff-beginning it may possibly apply only to f in b. 5, similar to the other MSS.
13	Mo	*Vg B*	left-tailed brevis.
16-18	T	*B E*	imperfect longa rest (in *B* the hairline is a little longer, but *E* interpreted it as imperfect and repeated the mistake in the next talea, bb. 34-36).
22-30	Mo	*B E*	the text underlay of the hockets is misplaced (*doubter* is under the preceding textless ternaria), probably due to the copying of the slightly misplaced text in *Vg*.
26	Tr	*W*	left-tailed brevis.
34-6	T	*E*	imperfect longa rest.
37	Mo	*Vg B E*	the dot is wrongly placed before the rest instead of after it.
*37-42	T	*A*	emendation: the two notes are written a third too high.
42	Tr	*G*	the fourth and sixth note are semibreves, not minimae.
44	Tr	*B, E*	the brevis c♯ is missing.
44	T	*A C*	fa-sign at staff-beginning which can only – but wrongly – apply to b in b. 62.
45	Tr	*C W*	the third semibrevis (c) is d.
46	Tr	*G*	the fourth and sixth note are semibreves, not minimae.
52	Tr	*Vg B E*	the mi-sign is written before and on the line of g; it should apply to f in b. 53.
55	Tr	*E*	the brevis rest is missing.
58	Mo	*A*	the text is slightly misplaced, under the preceding ternaria.
61	T	*A C*	no mi-sign for b as in the other MSS; see b. 44.
62	Tr	*E*	the f♯ is a brevis instead of a semibrevis.
65	Tr	*Vg*	the mi-sign seems written by another hand (cf. b. 9, the same hand).
*72	Mo	*A Vg?*	the d seems an error caused by the difficulty of drawing the ligature properly; in *Vg* it is not entirely clear.
73-76	T	*Vg G B E*	binaria; in *B* and *E* this wrongly became a binaria longa-brevis; the right tail is missing.
75	Mo	*A*	the text is slightly misplaced, under the preceding ternaria.
76	Tr	*B E*	the last note is a minima instead of a semibrevis.
79	Mo	*A*	the mi-sign unusually is notated before the clef; a later addition or an afterthought?
85	Tr	*Vg B*	up-stemmed longa.
94	Mo	*A*	the text is slightly misplaced, under the preceding ternaria.
96	Tr	*B E*	*B* has a dot after the minima c; the last note (semibrevis) is a minima in *E*.
98	Tr	*E*	the second note of the ligature is e (instead of d).
111	Mo	*A*	the text is slightly misplaced, under the preceding ternaria.
113	Tr	*E*	the second note of the ligature (beginning in b. 112) is an a (instead of g).
116	Tr	*G*	the fifth note (a) is a semibrevis, not a minima.

116	Mo	*E*	the last note (c) is a minima, not a semibrevis.
117	Tr	*E*	the first minima is an a (instead of g).
119	Tr, T	all	the clash between T and Tr seems intentional, expressing a contrapuntal tension between finals F and G which continues until the end; M2 contains more examples of such clashes.
123	Tr	*B E*	erroneously first a minima (on *j'aim*) and then the two minima rests.
125-26	Tr	*E*	no ligature.
129	T	all	no MS gives the mi-sign; however, since the second color should be identical with the first it is supplied here.
135	Mo	all	different from the setting in b. 112, all the MSS split the word *vostre* in hocket.
136	Mo	*A*	the semibrevis rest is missing.
139	Mo	*E*	erroneous minima rest after the d.
143	Mo	*A*	up-stemmed longa; was a sound effect intended, comparable to the plica? A downward tail would not have interfered with the text.
144	T	*A*	a superfluous perfect longa rest follows the last ligature. The scribe may have been wondering why this motet, mensurally perfect on all levels, would end with an imperfect longa and have added the rest sign. His awareness of the work's emphasis on perfection may also be seen from the three decorative *fines punctorum* (double strokes through the whole staff) following this longa rest.

Literature

Editions of text: Chichmaref, *Poésies lyriques*, pp. 483-84; Wilson, *Music of the Middle Ages*, pp. 311-12 (trans. in id., *Anthology*, pp. 210-11); Robertson, *Machaut and Reims*, pp. 294-96.

Editions of music: Wolf, *Geschichte* 2, pp. 16-18 (diplomatic transcription); id., *Geschichte* 3, pp. 28-32; Ludwig, *Werke* III, pp. 2-5; Schrade, *Works*, pp. 1-4; Wilson, *Music of the Middle Ages*, *Anthology*, pp. 206-9; Clark, "The Motets Read and Heard," pp. 200-8.

Tenor sources: Clark, "Concordare cum materia," p. 186 and pp. 236-37.

Discussion/interpretation (texts only): Robertson, *Machaut and Reims*, pp. 110-13; Leech, *Machaut, Secretary*, p. 288n86.

Analytical studies (text- and text/musical structure): Machabey, *Guillaume de Machault* 2, pp. 63-68; Reichert, "Das Verhältnis," pp. 203, 205-6, 209; Clarkson, "On the Nature," pp. 212, 263, 267, 271, 292-93; Newes, "Imitation in the Ars nova," pp. 47-48; ead., "Relationship of Text," pp. 84-85; Mulder, *Guillaume de Machaut*, pp. 88-90; Wilson, *Music of the Middle Ages*, pp. 296-306; Zayaruznaya, "Hockets as Compositional and Scribal Practice," pp. 494-95.

Analytical studies (musical structure, counterpoint): Gombosi, "Machaut's *Messe*," p. 220; Pelinski, "Zusammenklang und Aufbau," p. 70; Clark, "Concordare cum materia," pp. 54-56; Hartt, "Tonal and Structural Implications," pp. 64-66.

Analysis and interpretation of text/music relationship: Boogaart, "O series," pp. 211-39; id., "L'accomplissement," pp. 47-54; Clark, "The Motets Read and Heard," pp. 195-208.

See also Earp, *Guillaume de Machaut*, pp. 360-61.

M2 *Tous corps qui de bien amer / De souspirant cuer dolent / Suspiro*

Musical concordances

C fols 207v-208r *G* fols 103v-104r *Vg* fols 261v-262r *B* fols 259v-260r
E fols 132v-133r

Tenor source

Not identified with certainty but possibly the repetenda of the responsory *Antequam comedam suspiro* from the *Historia de Job*, read during the first half of September (Kalendae Septembris-medio Septembris; *CAO*

IV:6106); identification suggested by Huot ("Patience in Adversity") and Clark ("Concordare cum materia"). Text (a compilation of Job 3: 24-26 and 23: 6-7):

Antequam comedam *suspiro*,	Before I eat I sigh,
et tamquam inundantes aquae sic rugitus meus,	and as overflowing waters, so is my roaring,
quia timor quem timebam evenit mihi,	for the fear which I feared hath come upon me,
et quod verebar accidit.	and that which I was afraid of, hath befallen me.
Nonne dissimulavi, nonne silui?	Have I not dissembled? have I not kept silence?
Et iam quievi,	And I have been quiet,
et venit super me indignatio tua, Domine.	and your indignation is come upon me, Lord.
V. Nolo multa fortitudine contendat mecum,	*V.* I would not that he should contend me with much [strength,
nec magnitudinis suae mole me premat,	nor overwhelm me with the weight of his greatness;
aequitatem proponat contra me.	let him propose equity against me.

Only the first seven notes of the tenor correspond to the melody of the responsory; Machaut may have known another source or have manipulated the melody very strongly.

Quotations

The last three lines of the triplum are a quotation from the jeu-parti *Je vous pri, Dame Maroie*, between two women-trouvères, Dame Margot and Dame Maroie (edited in Långfors, *Recueil général*, pp. 171-74, and more recently in Doss-Quinby, *Songs of the Women Trouvères*, pp. 74-78). The expression in the last line of the motetus, *morir en languissant*, probably is a quotation from a *chanson de geste*, the *Chanson d'Aubery le Bourgoin* (ed. Tobler, p. 184, line 19).[1]

Text structure

Triplum	a7 b5' a7 b5' c7 c7 b5' d7 d7 b5'	a: -er; b:-ure; c: -oir; d: -ez (és); e: -oint;
	e7 b5' e7 b5' f7 f7 b5' g7 g7 b5'	f: -ant; g: -is; h: -ait; i: -ours; j: -i; k: -ir
	h7 b5' h7 b5' i7 i7 b5' j7 j7 b5'	
	c7 c7 k7 k7	
Motetus	a7 b7' a7 b7' b7' a7 a7 b7' b7' a7 b7' a7 b7' a7	a: -ent; b: -aire

Tenor structure

Two colores of 28 notes, each divided by four taleae of 24 imperfect breves; the second color is diminished partly to one-half, partly to one-third (from 24 imperfect breves to 10 imperfect breves), due to the intricacies of the notational system: in diminution the signs combine in a different way from the integer valor section (see below). The alteration of the brevis before the maxima in the integer valor section must be a notational licence, in order to complete the perfection. Length of the motet: 136 imperfect breves.

Mensuration

Imperfect maximodus, perfect modus for the tenor; for the upper voices imperfect modus (as indicated by the notation of the rests in the triplum), imperfect tempus, major prolatio; diminution to imperfect modus, imperfect tempus in the tenor. The present edition differs in this respect from the older editions which assumed perfect modus also for the upper voices and perfect tempus for the tenor in diminution. Since the contrast in modus between upper voices and tenor is more important to show here than the maximodus, the barring is according to modus; in imperfect maximodus the only maxima is also in syncopated position. The resulting syncopations and the many rests in the motetus are an illustration of Machaut's vision of the ideal sighing lover who must "interrupt and syncopate his words by deep sighs, making him mute and

---

[1] <http://www.archive.org/stream/ausderchansondeg00tobl#page/n5/mode/2up>. The *Chanson d'Aubery* was still copied and read in the fourteenth century; see Weill, "Les « merveilles » de la cour de Flandre," pp. 37-47.

silent" (*Remede de Fortune* ll. 1761-64: "...Et qu'il lui couvient recoper / Ses paroles et sincoper / Par souspirs puisiez en parfont / Qui mut et taisant le parfont"). The notation of the tenor suggests that the perfect modus diminishes to perfect tempus, but after four "perfections" the last brevis and longa of the talea appear to be imperfect for which no warning is given by coloration; the only correct solution is to read the entire diminution section of the tenor in imperfect tempus with syncopations, in accordance with the upper voices (of which the notation of the rests in the motetus, in turn, wrongly suggests that it is to be read in perfect tempus). The scribe of *A* perhaps thought that the perfect longa should be diminished to a perfect brevis and put a dot of perfection after the fourth brevis, in order to make the rhythm equal to that of the undiminished talea. It is not repeated in the following taleae and no other manuscript has it. The triplum text at this point (bb. 100-104) contains even a warning ("sans meffait et sans mespresure"; in *C* with the eloquent mistake "sans mesure").

Variants and errors not marked in the score

General remark: MSS *A*, *C* and *G* differ from the group *Vg*, *B* and *E* by having many more plicae and fewer ficta-indications. The motet contains many dissonant moments, which serve for text expression.

Bar	Voice	MS	
9	Tr	*E*	the brevis rest is missing.
16	Mo	*A C G*	*A* has a left- and up-tailed brevis probably meant as a plica, *C* and *G* have a clear plica brevis.
20-21	Tr	*E*	brevis instead of longa.
23	Mo	*B E*	brevis instead of longa.
29	Tr	*E*	the last minima is d instead of c.
34	Mo	*E*	brevis instead of longa.
37	Tr	*E*	white spot following the g; perhaps an erasure?
42-43	Tr	*A*	brevis rest instead of longa rest.
43-44	Mo	*B*	the longa rest is missing.
61	Mo	*C*	longa instead of brevis.
66-67	Tr	*A*	brevis rest instead of longa rest.
68-69	Mo	*A*	brevis rest instead of longa rest.
78	Tr	*C*	the first minima is an e.
83	Tr	*B E*	mi-sign instead of fa-sign.
92	Tr	*Vg B*	up-stemmed longa.
97	Tr	*B E*	the first minima looks like a corrected e in *B* and <u>is</u> an e in *E*.
101-02	T	*A*	the brevis is incorrectly followed by a dot of perfection; see above.
116	Mo	*A*	the brevis e is missing.
120	Mo	*C*	the first minima looks like d which was corrected to e.
129	Tr	*E*	the second note is a semibrevis, not a minima.
126	Mo	*Vg B*	left- and down-tailed brevis.

Literature

Editions of text: Chichmaref, *Poésies lyriques*, pp. 485-86; Robertson, *Machaut and Reims*, pp. 296-97.

Editions of music: Wolf, *Sing- und Spielmusik*, pp. 9-13; Ludwig, *Werke* III, pp. 6-8; Schrade, *Works*, pp. 5-7.

Tenor sources: Huot, "Patience in Adversity;" Clark, "Concordare cum materia," pp. 56-57, 187, 237; ead., "New Tenor Sources," p. 120.

Discussions/interpretations (texts only): Poirion, *Le poète*, p. 508; Huot, "Patience in Adversity;" Robertson, *Machaut and Reims*, pp. 113-15.

Analytical studies (text- and text/musical structure, counterpoint): Machabey, *Guillaume de Machault* 2, pp. 68-71; Reichert, "Das Verhältnis," pp. 200-1, 209; Günther, "The 14th-Century Motet," p. 32; Clarkson, "On the Nature," pp. 268, 271; Dobrzańska, "Rola tenoru," pp. 56-59; Koehler, *Pythagoreisch-platonische*

Proportionen 1, p. 106; Leech-Wilkinson, "Related Motets," pp. 13, 16; Earp, "Declamatory Dissonance," p. 114, ex. 9.10; Zayaruznaya, "Hockets as Compositional and Scribal Practice," pp. 494-95..

Analysis and interpretation of text/music relationship: Boogaart, "O series," pp. 319-39; id., "*Folie couvient avoir*," pp. 23-31; id., "L'amant confus;" Lavacek, "Contrapuntal Confrontation," pp. 42-56.

See also Earp, *Guillaume de Machaut*, p. 381.

M3   *Hé! Mors! com tu es haïe / Fine Amour, qui me vint navrer / Quare non sum mortuus*

Musical concordances

C fols 208v-209r	Vg fols 262v-263r	B fols 260v-261r	G fols 104v-105r
E fols 133v-134r			

Tenor source

Repetenda of the responsory *Inclinans faciem* from the *Historia de Job* (Kalendae Septembris-medio Septembris (*CAO* IV:6947). Text (adapted from Job 3:11, 6:11 and 9:28-29):

Inclinans faciem meam ingemisco,	Bowing down my face I groan;
commovebor omnibus membris meis;	I shall tremble in all my limbs.
scio enim, Domine, quia impunitum me non dimittis;	For I know, Lord, that thou wilt not let me go [unpunished;
et si sum impius, *quare non sum mortuus* sed laboro?	and if I be wicked, why then did I not die but [do I labour?
V. Quae est enim fortitudo mea ut sustineam,	*V.* For what is my strength that I can hold out?
aut quis finis meus ut patienter agam?	Or what is my end that I should keep [patience?

The tenor words have a double meaning, relevant for the interpretation of the motet: in the responsory they express despair and incomprehension, whereas in their biblical context they betray a longing for death in order to find peace.

Quotations

Triplum line 39, *Qui bien aimme a tart oublie*, is a well-known refrain (Van den Boogaard, no. 1585, Hassell, no. A63) which Machaut used at least five times; the *Lay de plour* even opens with it, and both in the *Remede de Fortune* and *Le livre dou Voir Dit* it is cited, in the latter even three times. The ending of the triplum probably paraphrases a poem by Thibaut de Champagne (with doubtful attribution; ed. Wallensköld, *Les chansons*, Appendix, Chanson VII). Although the last line of the motetus is a very common expression in trouvère poetry, it may well stem from Perrin d'Angicourt's *Biau m'est du tens de gaïn qui verdoie* of which the last line of the first stanza reads "Et si m'ocit en lieu de guerredon" (ed. Steffens, *Die Lieder*, no. 23); Machaut quoted more extensively from this chanson in M5 and 6.

The opening lines of the triplum were paraphrased by Chaucer in his *Book of the Duchess*, ll. 481-86.

Text structure

Triplum	a7'a7'a7'b3	b7b7b7c3	a:-ie; b:-as; c:-ir; d:-oit; e:-ours; f: -our;
	d7d7d7e3	e7e7e7f3	g: -ay; h: -ueil; i: -i; j: -oy
	g7g7g7h3	h7h7h7i3	
	i7i7i7a3'	a7'a7'a7'j3	
	j7j7j7a3'	a7'a7'a7'	

Motetus	8 ababbaa bbaabab	a: -er; b: -on
	(mirrored rhyme scheme with exchange of rhyme sound)	

Tenor structure

Two colores of 25 notes, each divided by three taleae of 7 notes plus a shortened talea of 4 notes; the second color is diminished to one-half. Length of the talea: 11 imperfect longae, diminished to 11 breves; the shortened talea measures 6 longae and is diminished to 4 breves by the omission of the final rest. Length of the motet: 115 imperfect breves. When the conspicuous simultaneous rests of the upper voices (bb. 17, 39 and 61) are taken as a sign of demarcation a symmetrical form can be observed in the undiminished part, with the proportions of 17-22-22-17 breves, a form which corresponds with the curve of the melody and with the double meaning of the text.

Mensuration

Probably perfect maximodus, imperfect modus for the tenor, although it is difficult to define the quality of the maximodus since the talea contains 11 longae, not divisible by 2 or 3; assuming perfect maximodus results in three perfections plus one imperfect measure; diminution to perfect modus, imperfect tempus. In the upper voices imperfect modus, imperfect tempus, major prolatio; in the undiminished part the motetus contains in each talea one perfect longa by way of exception, indicated by a dot of perfection.

Variants and errors not marked in the score

Bar	Voice	MS	
1	T		*A* has a fa-sign only once at the beginning, *C* has it on all of its three staves, *G* once at the beginning and then, too late, after b. 91 and after b. 95; *Vg* and *B* at the beginning of both their two staves and *E* on its only staff.
1-6	T	*G Vg*	the first three notes are written as a ternaria ligature in *G*; in *Vg* the three longae are written very close to each other.
5	Tr	*A*	the mi-sign is repeated on the next staff.
9	Tr	*E*	a minima for the first d, but corrected by a stroke through the stem.
12	Tr	*E*	the second note (minima) is f.
12-15	Mo	*C Vg B E*	after the c.o.p.-ligature (a binaria with upward stem, worth two semibreves) *C* has a longa without dot of perfection; *Vg* and *B* first have a longa without, then a longa with dot, followed by a brevis; *E* has two longae without dot followed by a brevis (a longa with dot, followed by two breves, as in *A* and *G*, would have been correct).
24	Mo	*Vg B*	the mi-sign is repeated on the new staff.
27-30	T	*G*	binaria in *G*.
30-31	Tr	*E*	the last two notes of b. 30 are an a and b; in b. 31 the brevis is an a.
30	Mo	*E*	longa instead of brevis.
31	Tr	*E*	a instead of c.
34	Tr	*A*	the second semibrevis is a minima.
42	Tr, Mo	all	this long-held dissonance is in all the MSS; if unacceptable one could perhaps sing c in Mo or f in Tr.
44	Tr	*C*	the last minima is f.
45-48	T	*G Vg*	binaria in *G*, ternaria (or almost) in *Vg*.
52	Mo	*A*	the strange dot after the brevis is probably just an ink-blot.
56	Tr	*B E*	a superfluous brevis rest after the c.
58	Tr	*G*	the last note (e) is a semibrevis.
59	Tr	*E*	the first note is d.
59	Mo	*A*	left-tailed brevis, probably meant as a plica.
60	Mo	*A*	the brevis has a small upward left-tail; it might have been a plica of which the tail was incompletely erased.
63-64	Mo	*Vg B E*	a longa instead of the two breves of the other MSS.
67-70	T	*G Vg B*	binaria.
71	Mo	all	up-stemmed longa except *E*. Since especially *G* but also *A* and *C* often

transmit a longa in low position with downward stem and since this g♯ is a very sensitive note it can be assumed that indeed a plica longa was meant. *E* has an a instead of g♯.

74	Mo	*B*	the first note is a brevis.
81	Mo	*G*	the semibrevis rest is missing.
84	Mo	*E*	the rhythm is ◆◆♪♪
86	T	*G*	the fa-sign seems to be missing but it is notated after the next ligature (b. 91) and on the following staff.
90	Tr	*G*	the mi-sign for f is on the g-line.
91	T	*G*	fa-sign written after g; it should have been before b in b. 86.
96	Tr	*A*	the first two notes are e and d only in *A*, all the other MSS have c b.
*110	Tr	*A C G*	emendation: all three MSS have the rhythm ◆ ♪♪♪; although possible, it seems, considering the declamation, that the version of the other three MSS (◆♪ ◆♪) is better. *Vg* may originally have had this same rhythm since it looks as if the stem of the second minima was erased to change it into a semibrevis.
*111	Mo	*A*	d e c d, while all the other MSS have c d b c; although it is possible, the transition to the next bar (resulting in d / d) would be strange; hence the emendation, making the passage conform to the majority of the sources.
*112	Mo	*A*	the brevis d is missing.
115	T	*A*	in comparison to the other MSS, *A* has an additional imperfect longa rest, probably a mistake, due to an expected exact repeat in diminution of the integer valor section which ended on a maxima rest.

Literature

Editions of text: Chichmaref, *Poésies lyriques*, pp. 487-88; Robertson, *Machaut and Reims*, pp. 297-99.

Editions of music: Wolf, *Geschichte* 2, pp. 19-21 (diplomatic transcription); id., *Geschichte* 3, pp. 33-36; Ludwig, *Werke* III, pp. 9-12; Schrade, *Works*, pp. 8-11.

Tenor sources: Anderson, "Responsory chants," pp. 122, 126; Clark, "Concordare cum materia," pp. 188, 239.

Discussions/interpretations (texts only): Poirion, *Le poète*, p. 551n22; Wimsatt, *Chaucer and His French Contemporaries*, pp. 129-30; Huot, "Patience in Adversity"; Robertson, *Machaut and Reims*, pp. 116-18.

Analytical studies (text- and text/musical structure): Machabey, *Guillaume de Machault* 2, pp. 71-73; Reichert, "Das Verhältnis," pp. 200-1, 209; Clarkson, "On the Nature," pp. 244-45, 264; Ziino, "Isoritmia musicale," p. 443n11; Koehler, *Pythagoreisch-platonische Proportionen* 1, pp.106-7; Zayaruznaya, "Hockets as Compositional and Scribal Practice," pp. 494-95.

Analytical studies (musical structure, counterpoint): Fuller, "Tendencies and Resolutions," pp. 232-34; Clark, "Concordare cum materia," p. 57; ead., "Observations;" Brown, "*Flos / Celsa* and Machaut's Motets;" Hartt, "Tonal and Structural Implications," pp. 70-84.

Analysis and interpretation of text/music relationship: Boogaart, "O series," pp. 341-61; id., "Speculum mortis;" Lavacek, "Contrapuntal Confrontation," pp. 71-74.

See also Earp, *Guillaume de Machaut*, pp. 324-25.

M4　*De Bon Espoir, de tres Dous Souvenir / Puis que la douce rousee / Speravi*

Musical concordances

Vg fols 263v-264r　　　*B* fols 261v-262r　　　*G* fols105v-106r　　　*E* fols 134v-135r
The work was probably inadvertently left off in *C*; see Earp, "Scribal Practice," pp. 140-42.

Tenor source

Introit of the Mass for the first Sunday after Pentecost. Text (from Ps. 12:6 and 1):

Domine, in tua misericordia *speravi*:	Lord, I have trusted in Thy mercy.	
exultavit cor meum in salutari tuo:	My heart shall rejoice in Thy salvation:	
cantabo Domino, qui bona tribuit mihi.	I will sing to the Lord, who giveth me good things.	
Ps. Usquequo, Domine, oblivisceris me in finem?	*Ps.* How long, O Lord, wilt Thou forget me unto the [end?	
Usquequo avertis faciem tuam a me?	How long dost Thou turn away Thy face from me?	

The word *speravi* is generally considered to be a perfectum durativum (as translated above) but isolated from its proper context it could also mean "I hoped (but do no longer)." The ambiguity is relevant for the interpretation of the upper-voice texts.

Text structure

Triplum

10 aa bb cc dd ee ff gg ee dd hh ii jj kkk		a: -ir; b: -ouru; c: -oit; d: -té; e: -er; f: -uet; g: -ort; h: -i; i: -us; j: -uer; k: -ent

Motetus	a7'b7a7'b7a7' a7b7a7'b7a7' a7'b7a7'b7b7	a: -ee; b: -ir

Tenor structure

Four colores of 18 notes; two colores taken together are divided by three taleae (2C=3T), the third and fourth color are diminished to one-half. The undiminished talea measures 17 imperfect longae, diminished 17 imperfect breves. Color 1 measures 52 imperfect breves, color 2 50, color 3 26, and color 4 25 breves. Length of the motet: 153 imperfect breves.

The upper voices arrive at the final note earlier than the tenor; since this seems a case of text expression (*jusqu'au morir*, *malgré li l'ameray loyaument*), found in comparable ways in three other motets (M10, M15, M17), the performers may choose whether they wish to end together on a consonance by lengthening the penultima of the upper voices, or leave the ending as notated. The final rest in the tenor is in all the sources but should be ignored.

Mensuration

Perfect maximodus, imperfect modus for the tenor (but see below), diminished to perfect modus, imperfect tempus; imperfect modus, imperfect tempus, major prolatio for the upper voices. Mensurally this motet has the most "advanced" notation of all the French-language motets, with *imperfectio a parte remota* in the upper voices, unsignalled temporary changes to perfect modus in the motetus, caused by a dot of perfection after the longa in bb. 19-21, which forces alteration of the surrounding breves (bb. 16-24, 50-58 and 84-92, hence the different barring at these places) and a complex syncopation in the tenor. The tenor talea of 17 longae cannot possibly be divided regularly in any of the two maximodi (the older editions assumed several changes of modus minor and major). The tenor actually has a very simple ternary rhythm in perfect maximodus, which is, however, complicated by the insertion of four brevis rests, in bb. 19, 23, 27 and 34 (and the corresponding bars in the following taleae). Although the bars in which they occur thus exceed the regular mensuration this is more likely to be understood as a long-term syncopation; the rests are an "extraneous" complication, extending the tenor bars to four units but without really changing the ternary mensuration (for this reason no change of mensuration has been indicated; the interpolated rests are isolated by ticks on the staff). An interesting detail is that in *G* the maximae originally were longae and only later were turned into maximae, as the difference in ink color shows.

Variants and errors not marked in the score

General remark: in *G* most maximae apparently initially looked too much like longae and were made clearer by enlarging the body; the color difference is clearly visible.

Bar	Voice	MS	
1	Mo	*Vg B*	left-tailed brevis.
3	Mo	*E*	brevis.

7-8	Tr	*E*	the last note of b. 7 and the first of b. 8 have reversed values (♦♪ instead of ♪♦).
9	Tr	*A*	a semibrevis was erased and the brevis added.
15	Tr	*A*	four extra notes are interpolated after this bar: a f a g, with the rhythm ♦♦♦♪; an unclear oblique stroke indicates that something should be omitted but it remains doubtful precisely what the scribe intended.
20-22	T	*E*	no ligature.
27	Tr	*G Vg*	the last minima is b.
28	Tr	*G*	the third note (a) is b only in this MS; one may try which sounds better.
28-33	T	*G*	no ligature.
35	Tr	*A*	the brevis seems to be a plica, although its right tail is rather short.
35-40	T	*G Vg B E*	no ligature.
37	Mo	*Vg B*	up-stemmed longa.
40	Tr	*B*	the last note is a minima.
41-44	T	*G Vg B E*	no ligature.
46	Tr	*B*	the last note is a minima.
47-52	T	*G Vg B E*	no ligature.
48	Mo	*E*	the whole rhythm of this bar is replaced by a single brevis g.
49	Mo	*A G*	dot of division after the ligature.
51	Mo	*E*	erroneous mi-sign.
55	Mo	*A*	superfluous brevis rest after the dotted longa.
56	Mo	*A G*	no sign in *A*, mi-sign in *G*.
62-67	T	*G Vg B E*	no ligature; in *G* the maxima is almost indistinguishable from a longa.
63	Tr	*E*	the second note is g.
64	Mo	*B*	the last note is a semibrevis, not a minima.
69	Tr	*B*	dot after the rest.
69-74	T	*G Vg B E*	no ligature.
77	Mo	*Vg*	dot of division after the minima.
78	Mo	*E*	the last minima (d) is missing.
81-86	T	*G*	no ligature.
87-88	Tr	*B E*	these bars are missing.
87-89	Mo	*A G B E*	*A* and *E* have an undotted brevis f♯ instead of a longa; *G* and *B* have a longa but without dot. Only *Vg* has the correct version (dotted longa).
94	T	*Vg B E*	the first note of the binaria has two tails in *Vg* (it should have had none; it now looks like a plica); *B* at first took this over but later "corrected" it (to a binaria worth ⎰⎱) by an (incomplete) erasure of the left tail; *E* took it over.
98	Tr	*E*	the last note is cc.
104 ff.	Mo	*B*	a third too high (the scribe forgot a clef change at the fa-sign); from here until b. 120 it is a mess in *B* anyway (see further remarks below).
106	Mo	*A*	brevis with short downward tail; perhaps a plica was meant.
109	Mo	*B E*	dot after the minima.
110	Tr	*A*	a superfluous semibrevis f was crossed out.
114	Mo	*B E*	the first note initially was a minima in *B*, the stem was crossed out in an unclear way; *E* still saw a minima in it and took that over.
114-18	Mo	*B E*	from the first semibrevis in b. 114 until the second half of b. 118 this entire passage is missing.
118	Mo	*B E*	the last two notes are a semibrevis g and a minima a in *B*, followed by a brevis f in b. 119 due to the erroneous clef, and a superfluous brevis rest; *E* has the correct pitches e f d (but copied the superfluous rest).
123	Tr	*G*	the second note is a semibrevis.
130	Mo	*Vg B E*	imperfect semibrevis a is followed by a minima g instead of a perfect

197

137-39	T	*G Vg B*	semibrevis a; this reading was adopted in previous editions. the first note is unligated.
146	Tr	*Vg*	curious clef change for just four notes (from C^1 to C^2); then, in b. 148,
146-48 ff.	Tr	*Vg B E*	again a clef change occurs in *Vg*, now a small G-clef; *B* overlooked or misunderstood this second clef and thus, from b. 148 until the end, copied the notes a third too low. *E* followed *B* in its pitches; moreover already in b. 146 *E* has a (wrong) note g for the first minima, probably because in *B* the a is written so low as to be very similar to g.
150	T	*A E*	wrong ligature: obliqua with left-tail (meaning ▪▪ instead of ▜▪); in *E* erased but still vaguely visible.
151	Tr	*B E*	erroneous semibrevis rest between the two semibreves; in *B* this may be a small ink-blot but *E* took it to be a rest.

Literature

Editions of text: Chichmaref, *Poésies lyriques*, pp. 489-90; Robertson, *Machaut and Reims*, pp. 299-301.

Editions of music: Wolf, *Geschichte* 2, pp. 21-23 (diplomatic transcription); ib. 3, pp. 36-41; Ludwig, *Werke* III, pp. 13-17; Schrade, *Works*, pp. 12-15; Harman, *Mediaeval and Renaissance Music*, pp. 132-37; Burkhart, *Anthology*, pp. 12-17; Wilson, *Music of the Middle Ages*, *Anthology*, pp. 212-16.

Tenor sources: Clark, "Concordare cum materia," pp. 189, 239-40.

Discussions/interpretations (texts only): Poirion, *Le poète*, p. 536; Sonnemann, "Die Ditdichtung," p. 63; Brownlee, "Textual Polyphony;" id., "Polyphonie et intertextualité;" Robertson, *Machaut and Reims*, pp. 118-20.

Analytical studies (text- and text/musical structure): Machabey, *Guillaume de Machault* 2, pp. 73-75; Reichert, "Das Verhältnis," pp. 201 and n2, ex. 2, 212; Reaney, *Guillaume de Machaut*, pp. 50-51; Clarkson, "On the Nature," p. 262; Ziino, "Isoritmia musicale," pp. 444n13, 448-49; Earp, "Declamatory Dissonance," pp. 116-17, ex. 9.14; Zayaruznaya, "Hockets as Compositional and Scribal Practice," pp. 494-95.

Analytical studies (musical structure, counterpoint): Gombosi, "Machaut *Messe*," p. 221; Günther, "The 14th-Century Motet," pp. 31-32, 34n7; Hoppin, "Notational Licences," p. 26; Pelinski, "Zusammenhang und Aufbau," pp.70-71; Dobrzańska, "Rola tenoru," p. 64; Wilson, *Music of the Middle Ages*, pp. 316-17; Fuller, "Tendencies and Resolutions," pp. 234-41; Clark, "Concordare cum materia," p. 57-58; Hartt, "Rehearing Machaut's Motets," pp. 216-25.

Analysis and interpretation of text/music relationship: Fast, "God, Desire;" Boogaart, "O series," pp. 391-419; id., "Encompassing," pp. 19-23, 34-35; Lavacek, "Contrapuntal Confrontation," pp. 76-80, 86-99.

See also Earp, *Guillaume de Machaut*, p. 308.

M5　*Aucune gent m'ont demandé / Qui plus aimme plus endure / Fiat voluntas tua / Contratenor*

Musical concordances

C fols 209v-210r	*Vg* fols 264v-265r	*B* fols 262v-263r	*G* fols106v-107r
E fols 135v-136r			

Tenor source

Not identified with certainty. Leech-Wilkinson ("Related Motets") proposed that it is a conflation of a version of the *Pater noster* chant with borrowings from the *Neuma quinti toni* melisma as used by Philippe de Vitry in his motet *Douce playsence / Garison / Neuma*. Since the *Pater noster* is liturgically most unspecific, it seems possible that the source instead is part of the repetenda of the Maundy Thursday responsory *In monte oliveti* (*Coena Domini*; *CAO* IV:6916); this context corresponds far better with the message of the upper voice texts. Musically, however, one has to suppose extensive manipulation and/or conflation with Vitry's tenor.[2] Text of the responsory (adapted from Matth. 26: 39-42):

In monte Oliveti oravit ad Patrem:	On mount Olivet he prayed to his Father:
Pater, si fieri potest, transeat a me calix iste;	My Father, if it be possible, let this chalice pass from me;
spiritus quidem promptus est,	the spirit indeed is willing,
caro autem infirma. *Fiat voluntas tua*.	but the flesh is weak. Thy will be done.
V. Verumtamen non sicut ego volo,	Nevertheless, not as I will,
sed sicut tu vis.	but as Thou wilt.
(Fiat. Spiritus quidem. Pater.)	

Quotations

This motet is particularly rich in quotations and paraphrases, sometimes with reversed signification. In the triplum ll. 1-5 are quotations or paraphrases from the chanson *Poinne d'amors et li maus que j'en tray* by Thibaut de Champagne (ed. Wallensköld, *Les chansons*, Appendice, Chanson 1, stanzas i, v); ll. 11-12, 15, 21, and 24 are quotations from Perrin d'Angicourt's chanson *Il ne me chaut d'esté ne de rousee* (ed. Steffens, *Die Lieder*, Chanson 1, stanzas ii-v), and ll. 26-28 from the same poet's *Biau m'est du tens de gaïn qui verdoie* (ed. Steffens, *Die Lieder*, Chanson 23, stanza v). The beginning of the motetus is a quotation from Thibaut de Champagne's *Qui plus aime plus endure* (ed. Wallensköld, *Les chansons*, Chanson 35, stanza i) and the closing lines (ll. 8-15) paraphrase or quote Robert de Castel's *Pour çou se j'aim et je ne suis amés* (ed. Melander, "Les poésies," Chanson 4, stanza iv). A musical borrowing is the talea rhythm (see below).

Text structure

Triplum (with continuous internal rhyme until the last strophe, decasyllables divided into 4+6)

a10 a10 b10' a10 a10 b10' c10'c10'b10' c10'c10'b10' d10'd10'b10' d10'd10'b10' e10'e10'b10' e10'e10'b10' f10 f10 b10'b10'	a: ai; b: -age; c: ee; d: -aire; e: -oie; f: -on

Motetus	a7'b7' a7'b7'a7'a7'b7' b7'a7'a7'b7'b7'a7' a7'b10'b10'	a: -ure; b: -ie

Tenor and contratenor structure

Two colores of 28 notes, each divided by four taleae, the second diminished to one-half. The undiminished talea measures 24 imperfect breves, diminished to 8 perfect or 12 imperfect breves respectively. Color 1 measures 96 imperfect = 64 perfect breves, color 2 32 perfect = 48 imperfect breves. Length of the motet: 96 perfect = 144 imperfect breves. The bar numbering is according to the perfect breves in triplum and motetus. The talea rhythm was borrowed from Philippe de Vitry's motet *Douce playsence / Garison / Neuma quinti toni* (*The Works of Philippe de Vitry*, ed. Schrade, p. 16-19). Machaut made it more complex by adding a contratenor with the same talea rhythm but in retrograde. The rhythmic structure of tenor and contratenor perhaps was inspired by the Ivrea motet *In virtute / Decens carmen / Clamor meus / Contratenor*, ascribed to Vitry (Leech-Wilkinson, "Related Motets,", pp. 5-8).

---

[2] Another proposal, in Maury, "A Courtly Lover," that it could be the responsory *Domine adhuc* for the feast of St Martin, supposes even more melodic manipulation; in Boogaart, "O series," p. 277, this possibility was already considered but rejected. Moreover, Machaut seems to have had no particular reverence for this saint, or at least is it not perceptible in his works, where St Martin is never mentioned, in contrast to other saints (such as St Rémi or St Nicaise).

Mensuration

Perfect modus alternating with imperfect modus for the tenor and contratenor exchanging roles each half-talea but both with imperfect tempus (in contrast to Vitry's tenor which has perfect tempus); diminished to alternating perfect and imperfect tempus; for the upper voices imperfect modus, perfect tempus, major prolatio. The notation is deceptive: in the integer valor section the brevis rest sign is a perfect brevis for the upper voices, but imperfect for the lower voices (note that the difference cannot be seen). The notation of the rest strokes in the triplum (an imperfect longa rest followed by a brevis rest) indicates imperfect modus for the upper voices. Tenor and contratenor are written in black and red, indicating perfect versus imperfect modus but their brevis is imperfect in the integer valor section; hence the different transcription of the brevis rests in upper and lower voices.

Dots of division are not consistently given in any MS. Places where all or most of the MSS have a dot are: in the triplum after bb. 6 (not in *A*), 22, 26, 29, 32 (not in *A*), 34 (not in *A*), 38, 47 (not in *A* or *G*), 55, 61 (not in *A*), 62 (not in *A*); in the motetus after bb. 25, 33 (not in *A*), 46 (not in *A*), 54, 67, 83 (not in *A*), 91. Those in *B* are sometimes so thick as to look like semibrevis rests and were sometimes copied as such in *E* (see remarks below).

Variants and errors not marked in the score

In general: the motet contains unusual contrapuntal conflicts, possibly caused by calculation errors (as supposed by Leech-Wilkinson). A few suggestions for emendation marked by an * are given in the score but performers should feel free to choose other solutions or to sing the piece as transmitted.

A fa-sign in the tenor is notated in *A* only at the beginning of the second staff, so that in the diminution section it is missing; in *C* it is at the beginning of the first and third staves, in *G*, *Vg*, *B*, and *E* correctly at the beginning of all the staves. In the contratenor *A* has it at the beginning of the first staff only, so that in the diminution section it is missing; *C* and *G* have it correctly at the beginning of the first and third staves, *Vg*, *B* and *E* only before the affected note in diminution (b. 83), but not in b. 37. It seems best to sing b♭ consistently in both the tenor and contratenor. In *E* all the rests in the contratenor, except the first pair of imperfect rests, have the wrong color (black instead of red or vice versa).

Bar	Voice	MS	
7	Mo	*C*	the semibrevis e is missing.
3-32	Ct	*E*	the first 14 notes are notated a third too high (wrong clef?).
*9	T	*C Vg B E*	b♭ instead of a; at the corresponding place in the second color (b. 69) all the MSS have a. Since b♭ contrapuntally works better this might be an option at both places.
16-19	Mo	*A*	in comparison with the other sources the whole passage is notated a third too low; although this is possible, it would end on b against the b♭ of the tenor, hence the emendation.
17-18	Ct	*A*	the red longa rests are missing.
25-26	T	*G Vg B E*	binaria.
26	Tr	*G*	the last note is a semibrevis.
*27	Mo	all	the dissonant c is in all the MSS: Ludwig suggested an emendation to d, but the a proposed here could also be a plausible emendation.
27-29	T	*G Vg B E*	binaria.
27-29	Ct	*G E*	no ligature.
29	Tr	*B E*	the division dot in *B* after the b is drawn as a semibrevis rest stroke and was copied as such in *E*.
30	Mo	*E*	no mi-sign.
33-34	Ct	*A*	the red longa rests are missing.
35-36	Mo	*Vg B*	left-tailed breves.
35-37	T	*G*	binaria.
41-42	T	*G Vg B E*	no ligature. *B*, which used no red color and drew the imperfect values as hollow notes, has the remark *rouge clef* in both T and Ct parts.

*43	Mo	all	the d which is in all the MSS seems wrong but it is difficult to find a non-dissonant solution; f might be the most acceptable emendation.
43	T	*Vg B*	*Vg* has an enigmatic mi-sign for the longa b; *B* did not know what to make of it and gave the longa b an extra tail to the left (turning it into a plica brevis).
49-51	T	*G*	binaria.
50	Tr	*B E*	*B* seems to have a semibrevis and a rest after the brevis but it may also be a too thickly written rest; *E* copied it as a semibrevis followed by a semibrevis rest.
51-53	Ct	*C G Vg B E*	binaria.
53	Tr	*Vg B E*	the fourth note is a semibrevis in *Vg*, *B*, *E*; the sixth note is a semibrevis in *B* and *E*.
54	Mo	*E*	superfluous semibrevis rest after the semibrevis d, caused by a misreading of the thick dot in *B*.
55	Mo	*C G Vg B E*	all have the rhythm ♦♩ ♦ for the first three notes; *A*'s version seems preferable. Moreover *B* and *E* have a superfluous semibrevis rest preceding these notes.
58	Mo	*C*	the third note (minima e) is f (or a negligently written e).
57-58	T	*G Vg B E*	binaria.
59-61	Ct	*C*	no ligature.
61	Tr	*E*	e instead of f.
62	T	*G*	longa rest and brevis rest instead of two longa rests.
65	Ct	*C*	the longa rest is missing.
65-66	Tr	*A*	the passage is a third too low in *A* (wrong clef?); from the last note in b. 66 onward the pitches are correct.
67	Mo	*E*	superfluous semibrevis rest after the e (same cause as in b. 54).
68	Tr	*E*	the second note is f.
*69	T	all	see remark at b. 9; emendation to b♭ might be preferred although no MS supports it here.
72	Tr	*C*	the last note is a semibrevis, not minima.
74	Tr	*C*	the third note (minima g) is missing.
75-77	Ct	*C*	two binariae.
76	Tr	*C*	the last note is a semibrevis, not minima.
76	Tr	*B E*	different version: after two superfluous minima rests the rhythm is ♦ ♦♩ ♦♩ ♦♩, with pitches d dc de de.
79	Tr	*A C*	only *A* has this version which nevertheless seems preferable; the other MSS have b a b c b a. In *C* the second note (minima) is a semibrevis.
80-81	T	*A*	a perfect longa rest instead of an imperfect one.
81-82	Ct	*A*	the red longa rest is missing.
82-84	Ct	*B E*	in *B* the remark *rouge clef*; two ligatures in *E*.
88	Tr	*C*	the last note is a semibrevis, not a minima.
91	Tr	*G Vg B E*	the last minima is d, not e.
91	Mo	*E*	superfluous semibrevis rest after the b (same cause as in bar 54).
93	Tr	all exc. *G*	the first note is a brevis in *Vg*, *B*, *E* and the following minima is missing; this minima (f) is also missing in *C* (the first note is, then, a perfect semibrevis); the fourth note (minima g) is a semibrevis in *A*.
*95-96	T	all	singers may ignore the rests and hold the last note on.
96	Ct	all	all the MSS have a superfluous imperfect longa rest after the final note.

Literature

Editions of text: Chichmaref, *Poésies lyriques*, pp. 491-92; Robertson, *Machaut and Reims*, pp. 301-2.
Editions of music: Ludwig, *Werke*, pp. 18-23; Schrade, *Works*, pp. 16-19; Leech-Wilkinson, *Compositional Techniques* II, pp. 64-66.
Tenor sources: see above.
Discussions/interpretations (texts only): Poirion, *Le poète*, pp. 198n 21, 611; Cerquiglini, "Un engin si soutil," p. 6n3; Huot, "Patience in Adversity," p. 223; Robertson, *Machaut and Reims*, pp. 120-23.
Analytical studies (text- and text/musical structure): Machabey, *Guillaume de Machault* 2, pp. 75-77; Reichert, "Das Verhältnis," pp. 198-99, 201; Reaney, *Guillaume de Machaut*, pp. 56-57; Clarkson, "On the Nature," pp. 262-63; Lühmann, "Versdeklamation," pp. 444-45, 451; Ziino, "Isoritmia musicale," pp.440n6, 444-45, 451; Leech-Wilkinson, *Compositional Techniques* I, pp. 96-98, 102-3; Zayaruznaya, "Hockets as Compositional and Scribal Practice," pp. 494-95.
Analytical studies (musical structure, counterpoint): Gombosi, "Machaut *Messe*," p. 223; Günther, "The 14th-Century Motet," p. 34; Apfel, *Beiträge* 1, pp. 40-41; Hoppin, *Medieval* Music, pp. 413-14; Reaney, *Guillaume de Machaut*, pp. 56-57; Leech-Wilkinson, *Compositional Techniques* I, pp. 88-104. 131-34; Newes, "Writing, Reading," p. 226; Koehler, *Pythagoreisch-platonische Proportionen* 1, pp. 102-4; Maury, "A Courtly Lover."
Analysis and interpretation of text/music relationship: Boogaart, "O series," pp. 265-303; id. "Encompassing," pp. 56-86; Lavacek, "Contrapuntal Confrontation," pp. 145-52.
See also Earp, *Guillaume de Machaut*, pp. 293-94.

M6   *S'il estoit nuls qui pleindre se dehust / S'Amours tous amans joïr / Et gaudebit cor vestrum*

Musical concordances

C fols 210v-211r	*Vg* fols 265v-266r	*B* fols 263v-264r	*G* fols107v-108r
E fol. 136v			

Tenor source

Repetenda of the responsory *Sicut mater* for the second Sunday of Advent (*CAO* IV:7660). Text (adapted from Isaiah 66:13-14):

Sicut mater consolatur filios suos,	As a mother caresseth her sons,
ita consolabor vos, dicit Dominus;	so will I comfort you, saith the Lord;
et de Jerusalem, civitate quam elegi,	and from Jerusalem, the city which I have chosen,
veniet vobis auxilium;	help will come to you;
et videbitis, *et gaudebit cor vestrum*.	and you shall see, and your heart shall rejoice.

Quotations

In the triplum ll. 11-14 are a paraphrase of a few lines from the same chanson by Perrin d'Angicourt as quoted in M5, *Biau m'est du tens* (ed. Steffens, *Die Lieder*, Chanson 23, stanza iii, ll. 4-6).

Text structure

Triplum	a10a10b10' c10c10b10' d10d10b10' e10e10b10' f10f10b10' g10g10b10'	a: -eüst; b: -aire; c: -ourer; d: -oïr; e: -ison; f: -eüsse; g: -pité
Motetus	7 a b a b b a a b b a a b a	a: -ir; b: -oit

Tenor structure

Two colores of 29 notes, each divided by three taleae containing 7 notes each, after which the remainder of 2 notes is set in a seemingly new talea-beginning. Only one color is notated, with a repeat sign; no diminution. Taleae I and II in both colores measure 15 imperfect breves, talea III, with the addition of the seemingly new beginning, measures 18 breves in color 1, 21 breves in color 2. The reason behind this structure is the following: in a telescopic process every first three breves of talea II and III serve at the same time as the last three of the preceding talea; the complete taleae thus would actually have a length of 18 breves (see the example below). The triplum text, whose stanzas 1 and 4 define this length, alludes to the process by the repeated rhyme sound *traire* ('to draw, to stretch'; see the example below), but stanzas 2, 3, and 5 span only 15 breves. I have tried to render the idea in the transcription by leaving blank the last part of the system but completing the triplum text belonging to the illusory talea-ending. However, in reality the triplum stanza begins, from talea II onward, on the fourth brevis of the tenor talea; at the beginning of the second color this process starts afresh. Since the very last triplum stanza still would count only 15 breves, Machaut has, by his subtle construction, added an extra longa that compensates for the feeling of incompleteness and gives it the length of the expected 18 breves; although the second color thus becomes three breves longer than the first, it would seem that equal proportions are restored. This is in accordance with the message of the motet where the conclusions of the texts allude playfully to this paradox: *trop* ("too much") in the motetus is set against *paire* ("equal") in the triplum.

Color 1 measures 48 breves, color 2 51 breves. Length of the motet: 99 imperfect breves.

Mensuration

Perfect modus for the tenor; perfect modus, imperfect tempus, major prolatio for the upper voices. Although the many imperfect longa rests would seem to indicate imperfect modus for the tenor within which no alteration would take place, the upper voices make clear that alteration is needed to arrive at the correct length. Machaut used an interesting procedure: the color ends on a rest which in reality functions as the beginning of the taleae of the second color. Through this addition the following values combine in a new way, so that the second color and taleae are rhythmically entirely different and are three breves longer than the first. Only *Vg* notates a dot of division after the first note of each quinaria; this is correct for the first color but wrong for the second. The values combine as follows into perfections (and require a free interpretation of the rules of alteration):

Color 1: 3x (B Ba / L-rest B / L B / B B B / B L-rest) / B Ba
Color 2: 3x (L-rest B / B L-rest / B L / B B B / B Ba) / L-rest B / B L-rest (see below for the transcription).

Figure 15. *A*, fol. 420r, detail. The tenor of M6.
Bibliothèque nationale de France, with permission.

203

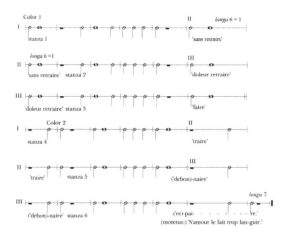

M6: Correspondence of taleae and triplum stanzas

Variants and errors not marked in the score

Bar	Voice	MS	
6	Tr	A	fa-sign instead of mi-sign.
10	T	E	the note b is missing (quaternaria instead of quinaria).
11	Tr	G	dot after the brevis.
15	Tr	E	the last note (minima) is aa, not bb.
17-20	Tr	G	the whole passage is a third too low.
35	Tr	C	the second semibrevis is bb, not aa.
*38	Tr	A	emendation; compared with the other MSS all four notes are a third too high; although this would be possible, leaps of a seventh are rare in Machaut's triplum parts.
40	Mo	G E	the mi-sign is notated a tone too high.
54-61	Mo	B E	the whole passage is a third too low.
60	Tr	all	the syllables *De ar(dans)* cause an excess in the meter; *De* could easily be elided but clearly isn't (cf. especially *G* where the words are on different pages; perhaps it is an expression of the "a little more than is proper," mentioned in the next line, where the letter –e in *Se un*, although written out in full, yet is elided.
69	Tr	Vg	only this MS has a (unnecessary) dot of division after the two semibreves.
92	Mo	Vg B	dot after the brevis rest.
94	Mo	C	the first note is a semibrevis, not brevis.

Literature

Editions of text: Chichmaref, *Poésies lyriques*, pp. 493-94; Robertson, *Machaut and Reims*, pp. 302-4.

Editions of music: Ludwig, *Werke*, pp. 24-26; Davison/Apel, *Historical Anthology*, pp. 46-48n44; Schrade, *Works*, pp. 20-22; Hamburg, *Musikgeschichte in Beispielen*, pp. 17-19 no. 22.

Tenor sources: Anderson, "Responsory chants," pp. 122, 126; Clark, "Concordare cum materia," pp. 190, 240-41.

Discussions/interpretations (texts only): Poirion, *Le poète*, pp. 198n21, 611; Robertson, *Machaut and Reims*, pp. 123-25.

Analytical studies (text- and text/musical structure): Besseler, "Studien zur Musik II," p. 224; Machabey, *Guillaume de Machault* 2, pp. 77-79; Reichert, "Das Verhältnis," p. 208, ex. 10; Wernli, "La percettibilità," pp. 16-19; Ziino, "Isoritmia musicale," pp. 443, 444-45, 451; Clarkson, "On the Nature," p. 264; Clark, "Concordare cum materia," p. 83; Zayaruznaya, "Hockets as Compositional and Scribal Practice," pp. 494-95.

Analytical studies (musical structure, counterpoint): Gombosi, "Machaut *Messe*," pp. 220-21; Günther, "The 14th-Century Motet," p. 30n16; Apel, "Remarks," pp. 141, 143; Powell, "Fibonacci and the Gold Mean," pp. 242-52; Clark, "Concordare cum materia," p. 59; Zayaruznaya, "Form and Idea," pp. 152-65.

Analysis and interpretation of text/music relationship: Boogaart, "Love's Unstable Balance," pp. 3-23; id.,"O series," pp. 305-18; id., "Encompassing," pp. 23-26; Lavacek, "Contrapuntal Confrontation," pp. 81-83.

See also Earp, *Guillaume de Machaut*, pp. 371.

M7   *J'ai tant mon cuer et mon orgueil creü / Lasse! Je sui en aventure / Ego moriar pro te*

Musical concordances
C fols 211v-212r	Vg fols 266v-267r	B fols 264v-265r	G fols 108v-109r
E fols 138r-139v			

Tenor source
The antiphon *Rex autem David*, from the *Historia de libris regum*, read during the weeks after Pentecost (*CAO* III:4650). Text (adapted from 2 Sam. 18:33):

Rex autem David, cooperto capite incedens, lugebat filium suum, dicens:	But king David, as he went with his head covered, mourned his son, saying:
Absalon fili mi, fili mi Absalon, quis mihi det ut *ego moriar pro te*, fili mi Absalon?'	Absalom my son, my son Absalom, who would grant me that I might die for thee, Absalom my son?

Machaut probably manipulated the melody slightly and left off the words *ut* and *fili mi Absalon*. By this omission the possibility arises of a double translation, as an optative mood and as a future ("Might I die for thee"/ "I shall die for thee").

Quotations
The passage 2 Sam. 19:6: *diligis odientes te et odio habes diligentes te*, ("Thou lovest them that hate thee, and thou hatest them that love thee"), following on David's complaint quoted in the tenor, is relevant for the motet since the triplum text paraphrases it in ll. 2-3. The triplum also paraphrases some lines from Perrin d'Angicourt's *Chançon vueil fere de moy* (ed. Steffens, *Die Lieder*, Chanson 20, stanza ii). Exceptionally even the musical refrain of this chanson is quoted, in the triplum (see below).

Text structure
Triplum	a10a10a10b4 a10a10a10b4	a: -eü; b: -i; c: -er; d: -our
	b10b10b10a4 b10b10b10a4	
	c10c10c10d4 c10c10c10d4	
	d10d10d10c4 d10d10d10c4	
	c10c10c10	
Motetus	a8'a8'b8b8	
	a8'a8'b8b8	
	a8'a8'b8b8	
	a8'b8	
	b8a8'	
	b8a8'	a: -ure; b: -i

Tenor structure

Four colores of 21 notes; two colores taken together are divided by three taleae (2C=3T); the third and fourth color are diminished to one-half. The talea has a length of 19 imperfect longae, diminished to 19 imperfect breves; the first color measures 60 breves, the second 54, the third 30 and the fourth 25 (27 according to the planned form of the motet, if the last longa rest had not been left off). The first section thus lasts 114 breves, the second 55 (57 as planned). The whole motet is divided according to the same 10:9-proportion as in the colores (60:54, 30:27) by the rare coincidence of the word *amour* in both the upper voices in bb. 90-91 (taking the planned structure as determining the length, 171 imperfect breves which are then divided into 90:81); this point is emphasized in the music by an imitation, a cadence on D (the final of the motet), melodic parallels and a register exchange between triplum and motetus. Real length of the motet: 169 imperfect breves.

Mensuration

Imperfect maximodus, imperfect modus, imperfect tempus for the tenor, diminished to imperfect modus, imperfec tempus; for the upper voices imperfect modus, imperfect tempus, minor prolatio. Since the number 19 cannot be divided by 2 or 3, there will always be an excess measure. There is no reason, however, to suppose that the maximodus is perfect or changes to perfect (there is no coloration or any other indication); the final longa rest in the diminished talea cannot be divided over two mensurae, as transcribed in the editions by Ludwig and Schrade who suppose perfect modus; the same holds, by consequence, for the maxima rest closing the undiminished talea. I consider the rest before the central maxima to be the superfluous longa (bb. 17-18, 55-56 and 93-94 and, *mutatis mutandis*, at the corresponding places in diminution). The resulting syncopations are reflected by the hockets and syncopations in the upper voices. In its overall imperfection this motet is a counterpart to the all-perfect M1.

Variants and errors not marked in the score

Bar	Voice	MS	
1-3	Tr	all	*A, C* and *G* notate the mi-sign at the beginning of the staff; *Vg, B* and *E* before the first affected note.
4	Tr	*E*	the second minima is missing.
1-6	T	all	ternaria in *A* and *G*, very closely written longae in *Vg* and *B* (probably also meant as ternariae), no ligature in *C* and *E*.
17	Tr	*G*	mi-sign notated after the affected note.
22-25	Tr	*G*	the passage is a third too high; the fa-sign stands before the first note in b. 22 (g, correctly e).
35	Tr		♯ is recommended here since this a quoted melodic refrain from a chanson by Perrin d'Angicourt (see below) from which Machaut also quoted some text lines; likewise in b. 73 (same melody); in b. 101 the mi-sign is indeed given by all MSS. To be consistent one should perhaps also raise the f in b. 33, but this must be tried for its effect; the MSS give no indication.

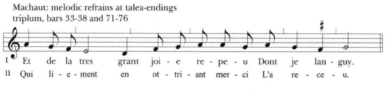

Machaut: melodic refrains at talea-endings
triplum, bars 33-38 and 71-76

I Et de la tres grant joi - e re - pe - u Dont je lan - guy.
II Qui li - e - ment en ot - tri - ant mer - ci L'a re - ce - u.

Perrin d'Angicourt: melodic refrain from *Chançon vueil fere de moy* (trouvère-MS X, fol. 108v)
(from stanza II, transposed one tone up for purpose of comparison)

Car je n'a - mai on - ques ce - lui qui m'a - moit.

37	Tr	*A*	two minimae instead of semibreves; one stem looks rather crooked; a later addition?
37	Mo	*G*	the second semibrevis is missing.
*40	Tr	*A*	the brevis aa is missing; emendation according to the other sources.
*42	Tr	*A*	the second minima is f only in *A*; all the other MSS have g which seems preferable.
44	Tr	*G*	the brevis shows traces of erasure of a stem.
45	Tr	*E*	erroneous mi-sign.
47	Tr	*C*	the second minima is an f.
50	Tr	*E*	the first semibrevis is a minima.
54	Tr	*Vg B*	in *Vg* the second minima looks like g, perhaps due to an unclear correction; *B* (but not *E*) copied g.
55	Tr	*E*	the first semibrevis is aa, not g.
70	T	*E*	maxima instead of longa.
72	Mo		raising to c♯ is recommended to make it conform with b. 34.
78	Mo	*A*	the brevis rest is missing.
81	Tr	*E*	three (wrong) notes instead of two (d e c ◆♦♦).
81	Mo	*Vg B*	up-stemmed longa.
89	Mo	*E*	mi-sign before c; all the other MSS have it in b. 90.
90	Mo	*C*	rhythm ◆♦◆ instead of ♦♦♦♦ (was the scribe for a moment thinking in major prolatio?).
98-99	Tr	*E*	the passage is a tone too low.
101	Mo	*E*	binaria of two breves (d-e) instead of the longa d.
107	Tr	*E*	e instead of g.
109	Tr	*E*	the second note is f instead of g.
123	Mo	*E*	four minimae (c♯ b c♯ a).
124	Mo	*G*	the mi-sign follows after the longa c to which it applies.
129	Mo	*C*	the semibrevis a originally was a minima; stem erased but still visible.
133-34	Mo	*E*	binaria extended to a ternaria c.o.p.
135	Mo	*E*	melisma d e d c (♦♦♦♦), instead of the plicated brevis b of *C*, *A* and *G*.
135	Mo	*A G*	left-tailed brevis.
137	Mo	*A G*	left-tailed brevis.
139-40	Mo	*E*	binaria extended to a ternaria c.o.p (as in bb. 133-34).
145	Mo	*G*	the two minimae are semibreves (or at least their stems are invisible; the first seems to have the beginning of a stem).
146	Mo	*G E*	the second note of the ligature is e, not d.
146-47	Tr	*Vg B*	*Vg* wrongly has the rhythm ◆♦◆; *B* took this over but then—exceptionally—corrected it into ♦♦♦♦; the erasure is visible.
150	Mo	*G*	the brevis rest is very vaguely visible.
152	Tr	*C*	longa instead of brevis.
154	Tr	*C*	rhythm ◆♦◆ instead of ♦♦♦♦ (cf. b. 90).
158-60	Mo	*E*	all four notes bound in a quaternaria.
167	Tr	*B*	*B* has four minimae (g g a a) instead of the two semibreves.
168	Mo	*G*	the mi-sign is very vague and stands before b.
169	T	*E*	two single breves instead of a binaria as in the other MSS.

Literature

Editions of text: Chichmaref, *Poésies lyriques*, pp. 495-96; Robertson, *Machaut and Reims*, pp. 304-5.

Editions of music: Ludwig, *Werke*, pp. 27-29; Schrade, *Works*, pp. 23-26; Turek, *Analytical Anthology*, pp. 33-41.

Tenor sources: Fuller, "Modal Tenors," p. 223; Clark, "Concordare cum materia," pp. 191, 241-42.

Discussions/interpretations (texts only): Brownlee, "La polyphonie textuelle;" Robertson, *Machaut and Reims*, pp. 129-32; Leach, *Machaut: Secretary*, pp. 249-52, 254, 260.

Analytical studies (text- and text/musical structure): Besseler, "Studien zur Musik II," p. 223; Machabey, *Guillaume de Machault 2*, pp. 79-80; Reichert, "Das Verhältnis," pp. 201, 206, 209, ex. 9, 210, 212-213; Reaney, *Guillaume de Machaut*, p. 52; Clarkson, "On the Nature," pp. 266-67; Sanders, "The Medieval Motet," p. 559n259; Ziino, "Isoritmia musicale," pp. 440, 447, 449; Maw, "Trespasser mesure," pp. 112-13; Zayaruznaya, "Hockets as Compositional and Scribal Practice," pp. 494-95.

Analytical studies (musical structure, counterpoint): Gombosi, "Machaut *Messe*," pp. 221-22; Günther, "The 14th-Century Motet," pp. 31-32 and ead., "Polymetric Rondeaux," pp. 83-84; Kühn, *Die Harmonik*, pp. 185-88; Dobrzańska, "Rola tenoru," p. 65; Fuller, "Modal Tenors," pp. 223-31; Clark, "Concordare cum materia," pp. 59-61.

Analysis and interpretation of text/music relationship: Boogaart,"O series," pp. 363-90; id., "Encompassing," pp. 26-31; id., "The Mirror of Love and Death;" Lavacek, "Contrapuntal Confrontation," pp. 57-67. See also Earp, *Guillaume de Machaut*, pp. 329.

M8   *Qui es promesses De Fortune se fie / Ha! Fortune, trop sui mis loing de port / Et non est qui adjuvat*

Musical concordances
C fols 212v-213r   *Vg* fols 267v-268r   *B* fols 265v-266r   *G* fols 109v-110r
E fol.133r   *Iv* fols 24v-25r   *CaB* fol.16v   *Trem* fol. 8 (triplum and tenor only)

M8 is the only motet for which a purely textual concordance also exists: *St* fol.138v, wich has the indication: *Tresble Guillaume de Marchant*; although music is lacking, the word *tresble* suggests the scribe was aware that the text belongs to a musical work.

Tenor source
Verse of the responsory for Passion Sunday *Circumdederunt me viri mendaces* (*Dom. de Passione*; *CAO* IV:6287). Text (for the text of the verse, see Ps. 21:12):

Circumdederunt me viri mendaces,	Liars have surrounded me,
sine causa flagellis ceciderunt me;	without cause they have struck me with scourges;
sed tu, Domine defensor, vindica me.	but You, Lord my defender, avenge me.
V. Quoniam tribulatio proxima est,	*V.* For tribulation is very near
et non est qui adiuvet.	and there is no one to help.

All the main MSS except *Vg* have *adiuvat*, and in *Vg* the *e* was emended from a former *a*; traces of the erasure are clearly visible. The literal translation of the tenor tag should thus be: "and there is no one who helps." Since the tenor of M21 derives from the same source (but with a larger fragment of the chant), it is interesting to note that in that work the text reads indeed *adiuvet*. It seems therefore likely that in M8 the change to the indicative mood (and thus the deviation from the chant text) is intentional.

Quotation: Hassell notes that the beginning of the triplum is a proverbial expression (*Middle French Proverbs*, no. F132). Chaucer apparently knew the motet since he quoted or paraphrased parts of the triplum text in his description of Fortune in *The Book of the Duchess* (ll. 620-35).

Text structure
Triplum (with internal rhyme in lines 1-4, a decasyllable divided into 4+6; from line 5 rhyme ostinato)

        a4'b6' a4'c6' d4b6'd4c6' (=b10'c10'b10'c10')10' c c c c c c c c c c c c c c c c c
        (with epic caesura at rhyme a in lines1-2)

        a: -esses; b:-ie; c: ure; d: -oit

Motetus   10 abab abab abab   a: -ort; b: -on

Tenor structure
Three colores of 16 notes, each divided by four taleae of 9 imperfect breves; the upper voices' isorhythmic patterns combine every three taleae into a "super-talea" of 27 breves (3 C=4T). Each color measures 36 breves. As a result color and super-talea coincide only at the end of the motet. Length of the motet: 108 imperfect breves.

Mensuration
Perfect modus for the tenor, perfect modus, imperfect tempus, minor prolatio for the upper voices. The tenor is notated once, with repeat sign, except in *Trem* where the tenor is written out in its entirety (and where the dot of perfection at the end of each third talea is omitted).

General remarks
To judge from the number of sources this is the most widely disseminated and thus perhaps Machaut's most popular motet. M8 is cited in a theoretical source, the St Victor version of *Ars nova*, as an example of tempus imperfectum, prolatio minor. Its tenor recalls the tenor of the probably earlier M12, which contains the talea of M8, but in alternation with a section of three perfect longae; M12's structure of three super-taleae each covering one color is simpler. Although the single taleae of M8 evoke the monotonous turning of Fortune's wheel, the stronger cadences of the super-taleae cause a contrary motion which gradually increases the contrapuntal tension; the first cadence is c-F (notes 11-12 of the color), the second G-c (notes 7-8), the third G-F♯ (notes 3-4) and only the fourth coincides with the color cadence G-F (notes 15-16); one can see this reverse movement in the taleae of color 1, the endings of taleae Ic, Ib, Ia and IIa. Machaut's subtle construction in M8 has an interesting iconographic parallel in the famous miniature in *Remede de Fortune* in C, fol. 30v: Fortune turns a crank on a secondary small wheel that runs in a contrary direction to her principal wheel. Alan Nelson has calculated that the construction with the double wheel in the miniature gives Fortune a mechanical advance of approximately 4:3, precisely the relationship between super-talea and color in this motet (Nelson, "Mechanical Wheels of Fortune," p. 227); the contrariwise motion of the main cadences in the motet can be likened to that of Fortune's two wheels.

Although generally the scribe of *E* tended to take over the mistakes in *B* he may well in this case have had another exemplar, since several mistakes of *B* are correct(ed?) in his version.

Variants and errors not marked in the score

Bar	Voice	MS	
5	Mo	A G	fa-sign at the beginning of the first and second staff.
		C Vg B E	a fa-sign at the beginning of the staff suffices for the whole phrase until b. 12.
5	Mo	B	semibrevis rest instead of the dot; the following a is a semibrevis. Curiously E has the correct version.
6	Mo	Iv	the second minima is a.
8-9	Tr	Iv Trem	the last two minimae of b. 8 and the first two minimae of b. 9 are a g a b.
11	Mo	Iv CaB	binaria c.o.p. instead of two single semibreves.
13	Mo	C G Vg B	up-stemmed longa. Since C and G generally write a longa in low position with a downward tail, I suppose that indeed a plica was meant in at least these two MSS, whereas for Vg and B it remains uncertain.
16	Tr	C	the first note is a.
18-19	Tr	CaB	the last note of b. 18 and the first of b. 19 are f♯ and g.
21	Mo	Iv CaB	the last two minimae are g f in Iv, the last minima is f in CaB.
22	Tr	Iv	the first note is d.
23	Mo	Iv	the second note is d.
25	T	Trem	the dot of perfection is missing.
28	Mo	CaB	downward plica brevis.

29	Te	*A*	Ludwig noted that *A* wrote b instead of a, but this is probably due to the difficulty of separating the notes of the ligature properly; all the MSS show this difficulty more or less.
31	Mo	*E*	the second note is b♭ only in this MS.
32	Mo	*CaB*	the second and third minimae are replaced by a semibrevis.
34	Tr	*Iv CaB*	the first two minimae are replaced by a semibrevis in both MSS and preceded by a mi-sign in *CaB*.
*34-35	Mo	*A*	emendation; these two bars are missing.
*36-38	Mo	*A*	the whole passage is a third too low, probably because the scribe confused the brevis f of b. 34 and the longa a of bb. 36-37. *A* originally also had *environ* like the other MSS, but "corrected" it to *aviron*.
37	Tr	*CaB*	up-stemmed longa.
40	Mo	*CaB*	b♭.
41	Tr	*CaB Trem*	c c.
42	Mo	*CaB*	the second and third minimae are replaced by a semibrevis.
44	Tr	*C*	mi-sign before g instead of f.
46	Tr	*Iv CaB*	the last note is e.
46	Mo	*E*	mi-sign before g instead of f.
48	Tr	*CaB*	up-tailed plica brevis.
48	Mo	*B*	signs of erasure of a minima after the minima e.
48-49	Mo	*B Iv CaB*	the last note of b. 48 and first note of b. 49 are a semibrevis f and a minima g in *B* (not followed up in *E*); the third and fourth note are aa bb in *Iv* and *CaB*.
49	Tr	*E Iv CaB Trem*	the first minima is g and the last one c.
49	Mo	*CaB*	the second note is a downward plica brevis.
51-52	Tr	*CaB Trem*	f e d e in *CaB*; the semibrevis g is replaced by two minimae in *Trem*.
54	Mo	*A*	erroneous imperfect longa rest.
55	Tr	*B*	the first note was a minima; the stem is incompletely erased.
55	Mo	all	all the main MSS have aa except *E* which has g; *CaB* has a downward plica brevis b. Leach's proposal to emend aa to f♯ makes sense; all the main MSS except *C* and *E* have a clef change here which may have been notated one note too early; with the old clef it would indeed be f (Leach, *Machaut: Secretary*, p. 213n32).
61	T	*Trem*	the dot of perfection is missing.
63	Tr	*Trem*	two minimae.
63	Mo	*CaB*	mimima rest instead of a dot after the first note.
72	Mo	*C*	fa-sign before the c; there is no b in that staff to which it could apply.
74	Mo	*E*	the last note is g.
76	Tr	*Iv Trem*	the first note is a semibrevis in *Trem*; the last note is g in *Iv*.
79	Mo	*Vg B*	up-stemmed longa. The fa-sign for the b is given only on the next staff, before the longa a.
81	Mo	*A*	erroneous imperfect longa rest.
85	Mo	*G*	fa-sign.
86	Tr	*E*	mi-sign before g (inspired by "fausse"?).
89	Mo	*Vg B CaB*	up-stemmed longa.
91	Mo	*CaB*	downward plica brevis.
92	Tr	*E*	again mi-sign before g (inspired by the word *point*?).
92	Mo	*Vg B*	mi-sign before b.
94	Tr	*Iv CaB*	the second note is aa.
97	T	*Trem*	dot of perfection is missing.
98-99	Mo	*Iv CaB*	these four notes are notated as two binariae c.o.p.
104-05	Tr	*Iv CaB*	the last note of b. 104 and the first of b. 105 are g aa.

Literature

Editions of text: Chichmaref, *Poésies lyriques*, pp. 497-98; Robertson, *Machaut and Reims*, pp. 306-7.

Editions of music: Ludwig, *Werke*, pp. 30-32; Schrade, *Works*, pp. 27-29; Lerner, *Study Scores*, pp. 45-46; Hoppin, *Anthology*, pp.134-39; Lerch, *Fragmente*, pp. 216-19; Brandt, *The Comprehensive Study*, pp. 62-66; Allorto, *Antologia*, pp. 33-34; Leach, *Machaut: Secretary*, pp. 214-15.

Tenor sources: Clark, "Concordare cum materia," pp. 192, 242-43.

Discussions/interpretations (texts only): Patch, *The goddess Fortuna*, pp. 50n2, 56n2, 65n1, 101n4, 119n1; Calin, *Poet at the Fountain*, p. 244; Kelly, *Medieval Imagination*, p. 284n50; Wimsatt, *Chaucer and His French Contemporaries*, pp. 130-31; Markstrom, "Machaut and the Wild Beast," p. 32n96; Brownlee, "Machaut's Motet 15," p. 14; id., "Textual Polyphony;" id., "La polyphonie textuelle;" Robertson, *Machaut and Reims*, pp. 132-37; Clark, "Concordare cum materia," pp. 88-92; ead., "Machaut Reading Machaut."

Analytical studies (text- and text/musical structure): Machabey, *Guillaume de Machault* 2, pp. 80-82; Reichert, "Das Verhältnis," p. 201; Clarkson, "On the Nature," pp. 239, 248; Sanders, "The Medieval Motet," p. 352; Ziino, "Isoritmia musicale," p. 447; Earp, "Declamatory Dissonance," pp. 114-16, exx. 9.12-13; Zaya-ruznaya, "Form and Idea," p. 61 and n115; ead., "Hockets as Compositional and Scribal Practice," pp. 494-95.

Analytical studies (musical structure, counterpoint): Lerner, *Study Scores*, pp. 45-46; Hoppin, *Medieval Music*, pp. 412-13; Dobrzańska, "Rola tenoru," pp. 52-54; Lerch, *Fragmente aus Cambrai*, I, pp. 115-18; Hughes, *Style and Symbol*, pp. 355-57; Fuller, "Modal Tenors," pp. 213-14, n33; Danckwardt, "Möglichkeiten dreistimmigen Komponierens," pp. 372-74, 381-82; Earp, "Machaut's Role," pp. 494-97; Clark, "Concordare cum materia," pp. 561-62; Zayaruznaya, "Form and Idea," pp. 123, 216-18.

Analysis and interpretation of text/music relationship: Boogaart, "O series," pp. 132-37; Leach, *Machaut: Secretary*, pp. 210-19, 254, 256n140, 260, 319; Lavacek, "Contrapuntal Confrontation," pp.174-79.

See also Earp, *Guillaume de Machaut*, pp. 366-68.

M9   *Fons totius Superbie / O Livoris feritas / Fera pessima*

Musical concordances

C fols 213v-214r   *Vg* fols 268v-269r   *B* fols 266v-267r   *G* fols 110v-111r
E fol.139v   *Trem* fol. 34 (index only)

Tenor source

Repetenda of the responsory *Videns Jacob vestimenta* for the third Sunday of Lent (*Dom. III Quadragesimae*; CAO IV:7858). Text (adapted from Genesis 37:20 and 33):

Videns Jacob vestimenta Joseph,	Jacob, seeing Joseph's garments,
scidit vestimenta sua cum fletu, et dixit:	tore his own clothes while weeping, and said:
Fera pessima devoravit filium meum Joseph.	a most evil wild beast hath devoured my son Joseph.

Quotations

The triplum text contains paraphrases of several biblical texts: Luke 10:18-19 and especially Isaiah 14:11-17 and 19-20. The image of the scorpion was, on its turn, borrowed by Chaucer, in the continuation of his description of Fortune in *The Book of the Duchess* (ll. 636-41). The combination with his borrowings from M8 make it seem possible that he had seen both motets in their proper order and had considered them to be related works.

Text structure

Triplum	a8a8a8b4 b8b8b8c4 c8c8c8d4 d8d8d8e4 e8e8e8f4	a: -ie; b: -atus; c: -ere; d: -imo
	f8f8f8g4 g8g8g8h4 h8h8h8i4 i8i8i8j4 i8i8i8j4	e: -atum; f: -ernis; g: -ibus;
		h: -eris; i: -itas; j: -avit
Motetus	7 aab aab bba bba	a: -itas; b: -ius

Tenor structure

After an introitus of the triplum, measuring 12 imperfect breves, plus a transitional longa measure (of three breves) during which motetus and tenor enter successively: six colores of 12 notes, every two colores being divided by three taleae of 15 imperfect breves (2C=3T); thus there are three such cycles (marked by A, B and C in bold) of which only one has been notated, with a double repeat sign. The talea begins with an "upbeat" semibrevis. Length of the motet: 150 imperfect breves.

Mensuration

Imperfect modus, imperfect tempus, major prolatio in the introitus; in the main body of the work perfect modus, imperfect tempus for the tenor; the same plus major prolatio for the upper voices. In the introitus the rest signs of both tenor and motetus, three pairs of imperfect longa rests, indicate the initial imperfect modus; this is no doubt symbolic, perhaps as a reference to Vitry's Trinity motet *Firmissime / Adesto Sancta Trinitas / Alleluya benedictus* which opens with the same constellation of rests in the triplum. In the triplum text Lucifer equals himself to the Most High; the three groups of imperfect longa rests could symbolize both a (diabolic) Trinity and Lucifer's imperfection, and, moreover, his deceitful character since the rests suggest the imperfect modus which is wrong for the main part of the motet.

Variants and errors not marked in the score

Bar	Voice	MS	
4	Tr	*A*	the first minima has a double stem.
5	Tr	*Vg B*	left-tailed brevis.
11	Tr	*A*	the first semibrevis has an incompletely erased stem; it was a minima.
13	Mo	*Vg*	the seventh longa rest is missing in all the MSS except *Vg*. Even there it could be a later correction since the stroke is thicker than the others. *B* apparently saw *Vg* before the addition of the seventh rest.
13	T	*C*	the longa rest is missing.
16	Mo	*B E*	◆⊤ instead of the other way round.
21	Mo	*C*	the second semibrevis is a minima.
25	Tr	*G*	the mi-sign is very vague.
22-27	T	*B E*	this passage is completely missing (as are the corresponding passages after 45 and 90 breves).
30	T	*C*	the dot after the semibrevis is missing in all the sources except *C*.
35	Mo	*Vg B*	downward plica.
38	Tr	*G*	the mi-sign was given in the previous staff.
47	Mo	*A G*	ternaria *cum* instead of *sine* proprietate (making the first note a brevis).
50	Tr	*A*	the mi-sign for b in b. 51 stands before and on the line of g.
60	Tr	*C*	the last minima is e.
62-63	Tr	*E*	the whole passage is notated a third too high.
67-72	T	*B E*	missing passage (see bb. 22-27).
68	Tr	*Vg B E*	the first note is f.
68	Mo	*E*	the mi-sign is notated a third too high.
77	Tr	*G*	an extra minima a is inserted after the first semibrevis a.
77-79	Mo	*E*	the two notes are bound in a binaria.
80	Tr	*A G*	the second note (minima) is a semibrevis.
84	Mo	*E*	the second minima is a semibrevis.
92	Tr	*BE*	the first note was at first a minima in *B* of which the stem is half erased; *E* took it over as a minima.
101	Mo	*G*	the mi-sign is given in the previous staff.
107-12	Tr	*B*	visible erasure in *B*; the scribe had first copied the staff below, then erased it and entered the correct notes.
108	Tr	*E*	mi-sign before the first note (a).

*109	Mo	A	emendation: the rhythm ♦♦♦ (g f e d) is in all the other MSS ♦ ♦♦ (g f e); the d (followed by another d) seems superfluous. The text *pungit* begins only in b. 110 which does not seem likely either.
111	Tr	E G	in *E* the first note is a brevis. In *G* the last minima is a semibrevis.
112	Mo	C G	up-stemmed longa in all the MSS except *C* and *G*; since these two MSS are clear in distinguishing plicae from up-stemmed longae it seems that in this case no plicae were meant.
112-17	T	B E	missing passage (see bb. 22-27).
145	Tr	E	the mi-sign is written before, and on the line of g.

Literature

Editions of text: Chichmaref, *Poésies lyriques*, pp. 499-500; Robertson, *Machaut and Reims*, pp. 307-9.

Editions of music: Ludwig, *Werke*, pp. 33-36; Schrade, *Works*, pp. 30-33; Lerner, *Study Scores*, pp. 45-46; Bent, "Words and Music in Machaut's Motet 9," pp. 368-71.

Tenor sources: Clark, "Concordare cum materia," pp. 193, 243-44.

Discussions/interpretations (texts only): Markstrom, "Machaut and the Wild Beast," pp. 17-26, 34; Wimsatt, *Chaucer and His French Contemporaries*, p. 130.

Analytical studies (text- and text/musical structure): Besseler, "Studien zur Musik II," p. 222; Machabey, *Guillaume de Machault* 2, pp. 82-84; Günther, "The 14th-Century Motet," p. 33; Reichert, "Das Verhältnis," pp. 201, 204 ex. 4, 211; Clarkson, "On the Nature," p. 266n93; Sanders, "The Medieval Motet," p. 563n390; Ziino, "Isoritmia musicale," pp. 440, 442-43; Zayaruznaya, "Form and Idea,"p. 61n115; ead., "Hockets as Compositional and Scribal Practice," pp. 494-95; ead., *The Monstrous New Art*, pp.34-35, 173.

Analytical studies (musical structure, counterpoint): Kühn, *Die Harmonik*, pp. 104-10; Fuller, "On sonority," pp. 36-37; ead., "Modal Tenors," 204-9.

Analysis and interpretation of text/music relationship: Eggebrecht, "Machauts Motette Nr. 9," (double article); Boogaart, "O series," pp. 153-60; id., "Encompassing," pp. 5-11; Robertson, *Machaut and Reims*, pp. 137-51; Bent, "Words and Music in Machaut's Motet 9;" Lavacek, "Contrapuntal Confrontation," pp. 96-103.

See also Earp, *Guillaume de Machaut*, pp. 321-22.

M10 *Hareu, hareu! Le feu, le feu, le feu / Helas! ou sera pris confors / Obediens usque ad mortem*

Musical concordances

C fols 214v-215r   *Vg* fols 269v-270r   *B* fols 267v-268r   *G* fols 111v-112r
E fols 140v-141   *Trem* fol. 3 (index only)

Tenor source

In the literature on this motet generally assumed to be the gradual *Christus factus est* from the Evening mass of Maundy Thursday; however, especially with regard to the fiery texts of the upper voices (in which the lover wishes that his amorous fire be extinguished), it seems more probable that it was the antiphon with the same text and melody, which is sung during the Tenebrae service, when all the candles are successively blown out (*Hebd. De Passione*; CAO III:1792). Text (from Philippians 2:8):

Christus factus est pro nobis	Christ became for us
obediens usque ad mortem,	obedient unto death,
mortem autem crucis.	even to the death of the cross.

Quotations

The texts playfully allude, and are in opposition, to the texts of Vitry's *Douce playsence / Garison / Neuma quinti toni* (ed. Schrade, *The Works of Philippe de Vitry*, pp. 16-19) whose talea is quoted in M5. Motets 5 and 10 have several elements in common, their relationship with Vitry's work being one of them: M10 refers to it in its texts and M5 in its music.

Text structure

Triplum	a10a10a10a10b10'b10'	a:-u; b: -ure; c: -ains; d: -aint; e: -iés
	c10c10c10c10b10'b10'	
	d10d10d10d10b10'b10'	
	e10e10e10e10b10'b10'	

Motetus	8 aab bcc dde ef fg gf	a: -ors; b: --uet; c: -us; d: -ir; e: -té; f: -oir; g: -ement

Tenor structure

Two colores of 30 notes, each divided by six taleae which are combined into three super-taleae by the upper voices' isorhythm; this is the same procedure as in M1 which moreover contains the same number of color notes. The second color is diminished to one-half. A large-scale syncopation is caused by the "upbeat" of a brevis which is completed at the end of each talea by a brevis and a brevis rest; the same construction features in the diminished talea. Length of the talea: 4 perfect longae (12 imperfect breves), diminished to 4 perfect breves (against 6 imperfect breves in the upper voices). Thus, in sheer numbers the tenor diminution would seem to be to one-third, but is in reality to one-half, by the shift from imperfect to perfect breves, the same procedure as in M5. Length of the motet: 108 imperfect breves or 72 perfect breves. The work is thus exactly twice as small as M1 with which it shares several other structural features (see above; but the diminution in M1 is really to one-third, not to one-half).

Mensuration

Perfect modus, imperfect tempus for the tenor, in diminution perfect tempus; for the upper voices imperfect modus, imperfect tempus, major prolatio. In the diminution section perfect tempus in the tenor and imperfect tempus in the upper voices are thus superimposed.

Variants and errors not marked in the score

Bar	Voice	MS	
1	Tr	*E*	the first note is a minima instead of semibrevis.
4	Mo	*B E*	the semibrevis c is erased in *B* and *E*; *E* moreover changed the minima b into c.
7-8	Tr	*A*	a superfluous semibrevis g with a vague stroke of erasure.
8-12	T	*B E*	binaria brevis-longa instead of longa-brevis.
16	Tr	*A*	erasure of a mi-sign which is then given on the next staff.
21-23	T	*E*	no ligature.
23	Tr	*G*	the last minima is a semibrevis.
27	Tr	all	all the sources wrote the mi-sign before and on the line of g.
30	Tr	*B*	semibrevis-minima instead of perfect semibrevis.
30	Mo	*A C G*	*A* wrongly has a plica longa, *G* had it too but stem and tail were erased; *C* has a plica brevis.
31	Mo	*G*	the mi-sign is clearly given only in this MS; in *C* it is at the beginning of the staff (before the word *chiere*, b. 27); the other MSS do not have it before b. 32.
32	Tr	*B E*	the first two notes are minima-semibrevis.
37-48	T	*B E*	the entire talea IIb is omitted; the confusion was probably due to the melodic similarity with talea IIa (although the mistake is not repeated in the diminution section).
40	Mo	*C*	semibrevis d.
*42	Tr	*A*	the last minima is g only in this MS; although this is possible, the motif should probably be identical to that in b. 13 and has been emended as such.
46	Tr	*B E*	all the notes are a tone too high.
47	Tr	*B E*	the semibrevis-minima e f are replaced by three minimae (f e f).

50	Mo	G	the semibreves were at first minimae; the stems are erased.
54	Mo	B E	brevis instead of longa.
56	Mo	B E	after the semibrevis follows a superfluous minima d.
57	Mo	C Vg B E	the second semibrevis (d) is a minima.
58	Mo	B	the stem of the last minima is erased but E copied a minima.
63	Mo	G	longa instead of brevis.
66	Mo	B E	mi-sign before the longa b.
75	Mo	B	the first note was a minima but the stem is half erased.
77	Tr	C	the second semibrevis is a minima.
81	Mo	B	the brevis has an erased stem (it was a longa).
*86	Tr	A	the second note (minima) is f♯ only in this ms; although possible, the three-fold repetition of this pitch is very unusual, hence the emendation to g.
91	Mo	B	mi-sign for b at the beginning of the staff.
*97	Tr	A	the fourth note is a semibrevis only in this MS and the minima rests are omitted; since this would destroy the isorhythmic structure it probably is a mistake and is emended according to the other MSS.
*99	Tr	all - C	A, G, Vg, B have a left-tailed brevis, G moreover a fa-sign and E a mi-sign. Some sound effect surely was meant, perhaps a plica to emphasize the word *desnature*? Apparently the exemplar was not clear.
104	Mo	B E	the first two notes are replaced by three minimae, f e f.
106 ff.	T	all	all the MSS have the tenor starting the final note later than the upper voices. This surely is an allusion to the texts: *morir malgré Nature* and *Ne puet longue durée avoir* against the tenor's *Obediens usque ad mortem*, but the singer of the tenor part can decide to begin his final note simultaneously with the upper voices.

Literature

Editions of text: Chichmaref, *Poésies lyriques*, pp. 501-2; Robertson, *Machaut and Reims*, pp. 309-10.

Editions of music: Ludwig, *Werke*, pp. 37-40; Schrade, *Works*, pp. 34-36; Wilkins, *Armes, Amours*, pp. 20-25; Kamien, *The Norton Scores*, pp. 4-7.

Tenor sources: Clark, "Concordare cum materia," pp. 194, 244.

Discussions/interpretations (texts only): Poirion, *Le Poète*, pp. 527-28; Sonnemann, "Die Ditdichtung," p. 63; Robertson, *Machaut and Reims*, pp. 152-54; Bétemps, *L'imaginaire*, pp. 126, 135; Huot, "Reading across Genres"; Brownlee, "Fire, Desire."

Analytical studies (text- and text/musical structure): Machabey, *Guillaume de Machault* 2, pp. 84-85; Reichert, "Das Verhältnis," pp. 201, 206; Hoppin, "Notational Licences, p. 25; Sanders, "The Medieval Motet," p. 558n257; Ziino, "Isoritmia musicale," pp. 444-45; Leech-Wilkinson, "Related Motets," p. 12; id., *Compositional Techniques* I, pp. 131-34, II, p. 24 ex. 38; Earp, "Declamatory Dissonance," pp. 116-17, ex. 9.11; Zayaruznaya, "Hockets as Compositional and Scribal Practice," pp. 494-95.

Analytical studies (musical structure, counterpoint): Günther, "The 14th-Century Motet," pp. 30, 32, 34; Dobrzańska, "Rola tenoru," pp. 66-67; Wilkins, *Armes, Amours*, p. 25; Clark, "Concordare cum materia," p. 62.

Analysis and interpretation of text/music relationship: Boogaart, "Love's Unstable Balance," II, pp. 24-33; id., "O series," pp. 241-69; id., "Encompassing," pp. 51-55.

See also Earp, *Guillaume de Machaut*, pp. 323-24.

M11 *Dame, je sui cils qui vueil endurer / Fins cuers dous, on me deffent / Fins cuers dous*

Musical concordances

C fols 215v-216r	Vg fols 270v-271r	B fols 268v-269r	G fols 112v-113r
E fol. 140r			

Tenor source

Unidentified chanson in irregular virelai-form.

Text structure

Triplum   a10a10 b10'b10' c10'c10' d10d10 e10'e10' f10'f10' g10g10 f10'g10f10'

a: -durer; b: -dure; c: -aie; d: -our; e: -aire; f: -voie; g: -ent

Motetus   a7b7'a7b7' c7c7b7' d7d7b7' e7e7b7' f7f7b7'

a: -ent; b: -oie; c: -ay; d: --r; e: -é; f: -oir

Musical structure

The tenor is divided into phrases A (a1+a2) B B b' a2' A (8+4+4+6+4+8 longae); b' is an extension of B; a2' is the second half (a2) of A, partly transposed but rhythmically identical.

Hockets in the upper voices intersect this structure by dividing the motet into three sections of 36+30+36 breves (12+10+12 longae, corresponding to the tenor's A B / B b' / a2' A). The upper voices have six phrases each, irregular in length: triplum 23+14+13+15+12+25; motetus 22+16+11+18+12+23 perfect breves. As a result the closing rests always occur in succession, with one bar difference in the three voices, but each time in different order. Length of the motet: 102 perfect breves.

Mensuration

Perfect modus, perfect tempus for all the voices, plus minor prolatio for the upper voices, although minimae are rare.[3] The motet is twice as long as M20 which has a length of 51 perfect breves (or 50; see its commentary) and is measured in perfect tempus, major prolatio and a single longa at the end; thus, they are a sort of complementary pieces with, in M11, perfect modus and tempus, and in M20 perfect tempus and prolatio. Both pieces are divided by three hockets in the upper voices.

Variants and errors not marked in the score

General remark: this is one of the most problematic motets with respect to musica ficta, not least because the indications in the tenor vary from manuscript to manuscript and are not always in accordance with those in the upper voices; hence the various question marks in the score. Moreover, due to rhythmical mistakes, several emendations were necessary, marked in the score with * and annotated below.

Bar	Voice	MS	
1	Tr	*B E*	B has an up-stemmed longa, E a down-stemmed longa without mi-sign.
4	Mo	*Vg B*	up-stemmed longa.
8	Mo	*G*	the mi-sign is given already at the end of the previous staff.
14-15	T	all	no MS has a fa-sign for c and b; G writes one on the b-line but only after the a in b. 15.
34	Mo	*A C G*	the descending plica in A and G may be in the wrong direction since the next note is higher. C has two semibreves of which the second strictly speaking could not be altered before a longa; the other MS have indeed a brevis here (in the two comparable cases, bb. 63 and 94, the semibreves stand before a brevis).
*36	Tr	all	emendation: the brevis in all the sources is clearly wrong and likewise is the

---

[3] Günther has suggested that the work might be read in *tempus perfectum diminutum* (Günther, "Der Gebrauch," p. 296).

longa in b. 48: the contrapuntal structure makes clear that it should be the other way round: in bb. 36-37 a longa and in b. 48 a brevis.

37-48	T	*B E*	this phrase is omitted. The omission possibly betrays some haste by the scribe of *B*: he may have overlooked that phrase B is repeated. *E* took it over. Curiously, *B*'s scribe had made the same mistake in M10, where also a (near-)identical phrase is omitted.
40-42	T	*C*	the longa is missing.
42	Tr	*C*	mi-sign.
42	Mo	*C G*	the fa-sign in b. 39 probably still applies to this note, but *C's* scribe may have understood it differently and hence have placed a mi-sign in the triplum. In *G* the fa-sign was given already in b. 40 on the previous staff at clef-change.
46	Tr	*E*	no ligature.
47	Tr	*A*	the second note (g) is missing.
*48	Tr	all	emendation; all the MSS except *G* have an e; it sounds strange at a phrase-end and cadence. I have transcribed the g of *G*, but another acceptable possibility would be to emend to d; the motif occurs several times in this manner (e.g. bb. 24-25 triplum, bb. 26-27 motetus, bb. 40-41 motetus).
47	Mo	all exc. *C*	emendation; the brevis should according to mensural conventions be altered, but the counterpoint shows that it cannot be.
48-49	Mo	*C*	brevis, not longa.
51	Tr	*B E*	*B* has an up-stemmed longa, *E* a down-stemmed longa.
53	T	all	a fa-sign is in all the MSS but does not accord with the f♯ in the triplum; only *E* does not have the mi-sign in the triplum.
55	Tr	*E*	a third too low (e e).
58	Tr	*E*	superfluous semibrevis rest after the aa.
63	Tr	*C E*	the first semibrevis is g in *C*; the second semibrevis is a brevis in *E*.
68	Tr	*Vg*	the brevis is a semibrevis only in *Vg*; in *B* something was erased before a brevis was copied in its place.
74	Mo	*G*	the second note (semibrevis a) possibly is b; it is not entirely clear which pitch the scribe meant.
77-80	Tr	*E*	the passage is a third too low (b b a).
79	T	*C*	fa-sign for b but the first b to which it could apply has a mi-sign before it (b. 93).
87	Mo	*C*	fa-sign for b and mi-sign for f; the b♭ could only apply to b. 95 where it would be wrong.
91	Mo	all	singing g♯ destroys the identity of this oft-ocurring motif, but singing g causes a severe dissonance with the tenor.
92	T	all	no MS has a fa-sign for the c.
93	T	all	*G, Vg* and *B* have a fa-sign for b; *C* and *A* on the other hand have a clear mi-sign which seems correct. Should this mean that in bb. 14-15 also c♯ and b should be sung (against the by now traditional way of singing c and b♭) or, the contrary, that this is a warning not to sing the same pitches as in that place?
95	Mo	*Vg*	Ludwig remarked that *Vg* has two semibreves here, but he misread it; the minimae have clear stems.
*96-98	Mo	all	emendation; all the MSS have a binaria ◄, but then a brevis' duration is missing in relation to the tenor; Ludwig's suggestion that a preceding brevis b was omitted (which can be tied to the next brevis) has been taken over.
*98	Tr	all	emendation; all the MSS have a brevis, which should then be altered; otherwise here too a brevis would be missing in comparison with the tenor.

Another way to solve the problem might be to sing the triplum and motetus as notated and to shorten the tenor's penultimate f♯ by one brevis. In both cases the less beautiful consonance E-a-e would result in b. 96.

Literature

Editions of text: Chichmaref, *Poésies lyriques*, pp. 503-4; Robertson, *Machaut and Reims*, pp. 310-11.

Editions of music: Ludwig, *Werke*, pp. 41-43; Schrade, *Works*, pp. 37-39.

Discussion/interpretation (texts only): Robertson, *Machaut and Reims*, pp. 154-56.

Analytical studies (text- and text/musical structure): Machabey, *Guillaume de Machault* 2, pp. 85-87; Günther, "The 14ᵗʰ-Century Motet," p. 29; Hoppin, "Notational Licences, pp. 19-20; Sanders, "The Medieval Motet," p. 564.

Analytical studies (musical structure, counterpoint): Reaney, *Guillaume de Machaut*, p. 55; Günther, "Der Gebrauch des tempus perfectum diminutum," p. 296; Kühn, *Die Harmonik*, pp. 144-51; Fuller, "Tendencies and Resolutions," pp. 243-44; Danckwardt, "Möglichkeiten dreistimmigen Komponierens," pp. 378-82; Hartt, "The Three Tenors;" Zayaruznaya, "Form and Idea," pp. 178-79; Lavacek, "Contrapuntal Confrontation," pp. 105-17; Rose-Steel, "French Ars Nova Motets," pp. 144-53.

Analysis and interpretation of text/music relationship: Boogaart, "O series," pp. 177-91.

See also Earp, *Guillaume de Machaut*, p. 304.

M12   *Helas! pour quoi virent onques mi oueil / Corde mesto / Libera me*

Musical concordances

C fols 216v-217r   *Vg* fols 271v-272r   *B* fols 269v-270r   *G* fols 113v-114r
E fols 141v-142r

Tenor source

Repetenda of the responsory *Minor sum cunctis* for the second Sunday of Lent (*Dom. II Quadragesimae*; *CAO* IV:7156). Text (adapted from Genesis 32: 9-11):

Minor sum cunctis miserationibus tuis,	I am not worthy of all Your mercies,
Domine Abraham;	Lord of Abraham;
in baculo meo transivi Jordanem istum,	with my staff I passed over this Jordan,
et nunc cum duabus turmis regredior.	and now I return with two companies.
Libera me, Domine, de manibus Esau,	Deliver me, Lord, from the hands of Esau,
quia valde contremit cor meum, illum timens.	for my heart trembles greatly in fear of him.

Quotations

Like in M5, the triplum text gives the impression that it is filled with quotations, but so far only one source chanson has been identified, for ll. 4 and 31-32: Gace Brulé's *Ire d'amour qui en mon cuer repaire* (ed. Huet, *Chansons de Gace Brulé*, no. 14, the endings of stanzas I and V).

Text structure

Triplum   a10a10 b8'b8' c10c10 d10d10 e8'e8' f10f10 g10'g10' h10h10 i10i10
                 j10j10 k8k8 d10d10 l10l10 m10'm10' n10'n10' o10o10 p10'p10'

                 a: -ueil; b: -ire; c: -ir; d: -er; e: -usse; f: -eüst; g: -euse; h: -i; i: -té;
                 j: -our; k: -ent; l: -ier; m: -oie; n: -uer; o: -ez; p: -ure

Motetus   a4b6a4b6a4b6 c4d6c4d6c4d6c4d6 e4f6e4f6e4f6e4f6
                 (which can be combined into 12 decasyllable lines with internal rhyme)
                 a: -esto; b: -eror; c: -risum; d: -onis; e: -ece; f: --ia

Tenor structure

Three colores of 21 notes, each divided by three taleae; although there is some upper voice isorhythm per single talea, repeating rhythmic patterns make clear that three taleae (marked a, b, and c in the score) combine to form one super-talea that coincides with one color (1C = 1 T). Length of the talea: 18 imperfect breves, of the super-talea/color 54 imperfect breves. Length of the motet: 162 imperfect breves.

Mensuration

Perfect modus for the tenor, perfect modus, imperfect tempus and major prolatio for the upper voices.

General remarks

The tenors of M12 and M8 are clearly related since the talea of M8 is almost identical to the second half of the talea of M12 (its first half consists of three perfect longae); the shared Fortune-theme, which in M12 appears only in the motetus, may well provide the explanation for this rhythmical relationship. Moreover, as in M8, the final of the tenor changes, here from F to D (in M8 from D to F). A particularity of this motet is that during the first half of the piece the motetus is generally higher than the triplum; exactly at the midpoint (b. 81) they exchange roles; the turning point is marked by a melodic imitation.

Variants and errors not marked in the score

General remark: the text underlay of the motetus is problematic in *A*; probably the text was entered first without taking account of the five *sine littera*-passages (such textless passages occur only in M1 and M12, and in M1 too the text scribe of *A* barely took account of the textless passages). The music scribe could not find room for most of them (once he entered it in the margin) and thus it mostly looks as if these passages are texted. Other sources, especially MS *G*, are much clearer in this respect and, while generally the transcription follows *A*, *G* has been consulted where in *A* the situation is unclear. The other MSS show the same difficulty; in *Vg* the scribe clarified the situation in some places by hairline strokes.

Bar	Voice	MS	
1	Mo	*Vg B*	left-tailed brevis.
8	Mo	*Vg B E*	f e instead of d c.
17	Tr	*E*	semibrevis instead of brevis.
21	Mo	*B*	note covered by a blot but still visible.
25	Tr	*A Vg*	superfluous semibrevis g at the end of the staff; on the next staff the stem was erased from a minima g (making it a semibrevis) and the minima g entered after it; thus the scribe may have overlooked that the semibrevis was already copied but on the previous staff (and without its text *me*). In *Vg* the stem of the minima g has almost disappeared under the capital H.
36-37	Mo	*Vg*	oblique strokes make clear that the melisma is not to be texted and to which notes the syllables *Et in-* belong.
44	Tr	*E*	the second note (c) is a semibrevis instead of a minima.
50	Tr	*C*	the second minima seems almost an a.
52	Tr	*C*	the last minima is an a.
53	Mo	*E*	semibrevis rest instead of brevis rest.
54	Mo	*Vg B*	left-tailed brevis. In *Vg* a small stroke clarifies the text underlay.
55	Tr	*E*	the last minima is a semibrevis.
71	Mo	*G*	the second semibrevis is missing.
78	Tr	*C*	the first two notes are clustered together.
86	Tr	*A E*	the third minima is e in *E*; the last minima is e only in *A*; the other MSS have d (transcribed as such in the older editions).
87	Tr	*Vg B E*	the last minima is f.
88	Tr	*C*	the last minima is d.
89	Tr	*C*	the second note (minima g) is a semibrevis.

91-92	Mo	*B E*	a tone too high after the brevis (a b instead of G a).
93	Mo	*E*	the first semibrevis is c instead of b.
94	Mo	*C G Vg B*	a clear plica in *C* and *G*; *Vg* has an up-stemmed longa which *B* indeed interpreted as a plica.
99	Mo	*E*	the first semibrevis is a minima.
103	Mo	*E*	the first note of the binaria is c instead of b.
112	Mo	*Vg B*	up-stemmed longa.
115	Tr	*G*	the last minima has an exceedingly thin hairline stem.
116	Mo	*B E*	a wrong clef-change is introduced by which the whole passage until the brevis e in b. 144 is a third too low.
123	Mo	*Vg B*	semibrevis instead of brevis.
132	Tr	*E*	brevis instead of semibrevis (c♯).
139	Mo	*C Vg B E*	*C* and *Vg* have an a instead of b as the first note of the binaria; *B* and *E* took this over but are moreover still a third too low at this point, as a result from the erroneous clef in b. 116.
140	Tr	*C*	the last minima is aa.
*147	Mo	all	emendation. These two notes are missing in all the sources; the isorhythmic structure makes clear that it should be a binaria c.o.p. similar to the one in bb. 39 and 93. Ludwig's emendation has been taken over.
151	Mo	*G*	the brevis was a longa; an incompletely erased stem is still visible.

Literature

Editions of text: Chichmaref, *Poésies lyriques*, pp. 505-6; Robertson, *Machaut and Reims*, pp. 311-13.

Editions of music: Ludwig, *Werke*, pp. 44-48; Schrade, *Works*, pp. 40-43.

Tenor sources: Anderson, "Responsory Chants," pp. 122, 126; Clark, "Concordare cum materia," pp. 195, 245.

Discussions/interpretations (texts only): Patch, *The Goddess Fortuna*, p. 81n2; Dömling, *Die mehrstimmigen Balladen*, p. 15; Huot, "Patience in Adversity," pp. 233-35; ead. "Reading across Genres;" Robertson, *Machaut and Reims*, pp. 156-59; Boogaart, "Encompassing," pp. 31-32.

Analytical studies (text- and text/musical structure): Machabey, *Guillaume de Machault* 2, pp. 87-89; Reichert, "Das Verhältnis," pp. 201-2; Clarkson, "On the Nature," pp. 211-12; Sanders, "The Medieval Motet," p. 558n257; Ziino, "Isoritmia musicale," p. 440; Zayaruznaya, *The Monstrous New Art*, pp. 119, 162, 174, 190-91, 220.

Analytical studies (musical structure, counterpoint): Leech-Wilkinson, *Compositional Techniques* I, p. 110n15; Clark, "Concordare cum materia," pp. 62-63.

Analysis and interpretation of text/music relationship: Boogaart, "O series," pp. 102-9, 111-14, 137-40; Zayaruznaya, "Form and Idea," pp. 181-98; ead., "She Has a Wheel," pp. 192-209; Lavacek, "Contrapuntal Confrontation," pp. 128-37; Rose-Steel, "French Ars Nova Motets," pp. 154-61.

See also Earp, *Guillaume de Machaut*, p. 326.

M13   *Tant doucement m'ont attrait / Eins que ma dame d'onnour / Ruina*

Musical concordances

C fols 217v-218r   *Vg* fols 272v-273r   *B* fols 270v-271r   *G* fols 114v-115r
E fol. 142v

Tenor source

Unidentified; the melisma was also used in the Fauvel-motet *Super cathedram Moysi / Presidentes in thronis / Ruina* (ed. Schrade, *Le Roman de Fauvel*, pp. 5-7) with which this motet moreover shares the theme of hypocrisy; Machaut may well have borrowed the tenor from that motet.

Quotation

Ll. 12-14 of the triplum paraphrase a metaphorical image of hypocrisy from the *Roman de la Rose*, ll. 7391-93 (ed. Lecoy, vol. I).

Text structure

Triplum	a7a7b5'a7a7a7b5'b5'	a: -trait; b: -(tr)aire; c: -i; d: -oit; e: -é
	c7c7b5'c7c7c7b5'b5'	
	d7d7b5'd7d7d7b5'b5'	
	e7e7b5'e7e7e7b5'b5'	

Motetus	a7b5a7b5 b7a5b7a5 a7b5b7a5 b7a5b7

Tenor structure

One color of 40 notes, divided by four taleae. Length of the talea: 28 imperfect breves. Length of the motet: 112 imperfect breves.

Mensuration

Imperfect maximodus and imperfect modus for the tenor; imperfect modus, imperfect tempus and major prolatio for the upper voices.

Variants and errors not marked in the score

General remark: the tenor is notated on three staves in *A, C* and *G*; only in *A* the third staff (that is: from b. 73) has no fa-sign. *Vg, B* and *E* have only one staff for the tenor, with fa-sign.

Bar	Voice	MS	
*1-4	Tr	*A*	emendation: the whole passage is written a third lower than in the other MSS; although this is not entirely impossible, the ensuing sixth (instead of octave) between triplum and tenor after the solo entrance of the triplum also suggests that it is a mistake (perhaps caused by an erroneous clef).
9-12	T	*C E*	no ligature.
11	Mo	*A C G*	up-stemmed longa in *A* and *C*; ascending plica longa in *G*.
14	Tr	*G B E*	superfluous minima g in *G*; the first minima (aa) is a semibrevis in *B* and *E*. In *E*, moreover, the minima rest is missing.
16-17	Mo	*A*	up-stemmed longa only in *A*; since a rest follows it seems that no plica was meant.
19	Mo	*C A G Vg B*	left-tailed brevis.
24-25	Mo		left-tailed brevis in *A*, descending plica brevis in *C, G, Vg* and *B*.
39	Tr	*B E*	the first note is bb.
47	Mo		descending plica brevis in *C*, left-tailed brevis in *A, G, Vg* and *B*.
49	T	*Vg B*	a curious descending plica brevis; surely a mistake since plicas otherwise never occur in the tenors.
51	Tr	*E*	the last minima is aa.
53-56	T	*E*	no ligature.
56	Mo	*C*	the first three notes (g f g) are missing.
61	Mo	*G*	the mi-sign is given before e; it applies only to the f on the next staff.
72	Tr	*B*	three minimae (bb aa bb).
75	Mo		left-tailed brevis in *A*, downward plica brevis in *C, G, Vg* and *B*.
76	Tr	*E*	the second note (minima aa) is bb.
78	Tr	*C G Vg B*	the first note is e (transcribed as such by Ludwig and Schrade).

*79	Tr	*A*	emendation; the second pair of minima rests and the minima aa were erased for unclear reasons; traces are visible.
81-85	T	*E*	no ligature.
89	Mo	*Vg B*	left-tailed brevis; perhaps a plica.
92	Mo	*A C G*	left-tailed brevis in *A*, plica brevis in *C* and *G*.
95	Mo	*A C G*	longa with both half-erased upward and downward stem in *A*; ascending plica longa in *C* and *G*.
97	Mo	*G*	both notes are a third too low (the scribe apparently was still for a moment thinking in the – changed – clef of the preceding staff).
98	Mo	*E*	all three notes are written a third too high.
*109	Tr	all	emendation; the second half of this bar is missing in all the sources. Two minima rests and a minima must be supplied; Ludwig and Schrade suggested f; here g is proposed but aa would be equally possible.
109	T	*A*	the scribe wrote a ligature brevis-longa but corrected it: the stem is crossed out.
110	Tr	all	mi-sign only before the last f.

Literature

Editions of text: Chichmaref, *Poésies lyriques*, pp. 507-8; Robertson, *Machaut and Reims*, pp. 313-14.

Editions of music: Ludwig, *Werke*, pp. 49-51; Schrade, *Works*, pp. 44-46.

Discussions/interpretations (texts only): Robertson, *Machaut and Reims*, pp. 159-61; Bétemps, *L'imaginaire*, p. 93; Boogaart, "Encompassing," pp. 32-33.

Analytical studies (text- and text/musical structure): Besseler, "Studien zur Musik II," p. 224; Machabey, *Guillaume de Machault* 2, pp. 89-90; Reichert, "Das Verhältnis," pp. 201, ex. 3, 206-7, 213; Clarkson, "On the Nature," p. 263; Ziino, "Isoritmia musicale," pp. 447, 449; Zayaruznaya, "Hockets as Compositional and Scribal Practice," pp. 494-95.

Analytical studies (musical structure, counterpoint): Hoppin, "Notational Licences," p. 25; Pelinski, "Zusammenhang und Aufbau," p. 68; Ziino, "Isoritmia musicale," pp. 447, 449; Dobrzańska, "Kszaltowanie," pp. 13-15.

Analysis and interpretation of text/music relationship: Boogaart, "O series," pp. 147-48; Clark, "Prope est ruina;" Lavacek, "Contrapuntal Confrontation," pp. 80-81, 168-74.

See also Earp, *Guillaume de Machaut*, p. 379.

M14 *Maugré mon cuer, contre mon sentement / De ma dolour / Quia amore langueo*

Musical concordances

C fols 218v-219r	*Vg* fols 273v-274r	*B* fols 271v-272r	*G* fols 115v-116r
E fol. 143r	*Trem* fol. 4 (index only)		

Tenor source

The antiphon *Anima mea liquefacta est* for the Vespers of the Assumption of the B. V. M. (*Assumptio S. Mariae*; *CAO* III:1418). Text (from Song of Songs 5:6-8):

Anima mea liquefacta est,	My soul melted
ut dilectus locutus est.	when my beloved spoke.
Quaesivi et non inveni;	I sought him, and found him not:
illum vocavi et non respondit mihi.	I called him, and he did not answer me.
Invenerunt me custodes civitatis;	The keepers that go about the city found me;
percusserunt me et vulneraverunt me;	they struck me and wounded me;
tulerunt pallium meum custodes murorum.	the keepers of the walls took away my veil from me.
Filiae Jerusalem, nuntiate dilecto	O daughters of Jerusalem, tell my beloved
quia amore langueo.	that I languish with love.

Quotation: Hassell identified the last line of the motetus as a proverbial expression (*Middle French Proverbs*, no. D37).

Text structure

Triplum	a10a10b4a10a10a10b4	b10b10c4b10b10b10c4	a: -ement; b: -our; c: -is;
	c10c10d4c10c10c10d4	d10d10d4d10d10d10	d: -i
Motetus	aa bb cc dd ee ff		a: -ment; b: -is; c: -é; d: -our; e: -ans (ens)
	(lines 1-4 and 7-8 have internal rhyme at the caesura, -our and -eus respectively)		

Tenor structure

Six colores of 10 notes, three together divided by two taleae (3C=2T); thus, the color appears in three different rhythmicizations. Length of the talea: 30 imperfect breves. Length of the motet: 120 imperfect breves.

Compared to the source melisma, the last three notes (F G G) are missing in the color, so that the piece ends on a surprising final G (one would expect F; if these three notes were added, the cadence on G would receive more emphasis). Curiously the missing notes are in fact present but sound right at the beginning of the motet, in three emphatic longae of the motetus (bb. 5-6, 10-12 and 17-18), which is extremely low only in this first part of the work. In the remainder of the piece the motetus is much higher and rises even sometimes above the triplum; hence the initial tenor clef, changing at b. 25.

Mensuration

Perfect modus for the tenor, perfect modus, imperfect tempus and major prolatio for the upper voices.

Variants and errors not marked in the score

General remark: dots of division to prevent mistakes in reading the prolation patterns in the triplum are mainly found in *Vg* and *B* but by far not in all the relevant places. All the MSS do have a dot, however, after the two semibreves of b. 105, in order to prevent a combination with the following minima (only in *E* it is wrongly placed after that minima).

Bar	Voice	MS	
3	Mo	*G*	the second note (mimima) seems a semibrevis (its stem is a hardly visible hairline).
5	Tr	*E*	the brevis is replaced by two semibreves.
5	Mo	*Vg B*	up-stemmed longa.
6	Tr	*B*	the first semibrevis has a curious oblique stem.
8	Tr	*Vg B*	dot of division after the minima.
*9	Tr	*A, E*	the second note (minima) is a semibrevis in *E*; the last minima is g only in *A*; this is probably a mistake and has been emended.
15	Tr	*C*	the second note (minima aa) is a semibrevis.
15	Mo	*A E*	emendation; the second note is g which seems less probable than the f of the other MSS. The last minima is d in *E*.
17	Mo	*Vg B*	up-stemmed longa.
21	Tr	*E*	the last minima is f.
26	Tr	*E*	mi-sign before g.
28	Tr	*Vg B E*	the last note (minima) is f in *Vg* and *B*, and is missing in *E*.
34	Mo	*G B E*	binaria obliqua worth ■■ instead of c.o.p. (worth ♦♦) in *G*. Its second note is e instead of d in *B* and *E*.

37	Mo	*A*	the second note of the binaria is d.
38	Tr	*B*	the last minima was at first a semibrevis; a corrector gave it a (thick) stem.
39	Tr	*B*	the first note was a minima instead of a semibrevis; the stem is erased.
43	Mo	*C*	longa rest instead of brevis rest.
45	Tr	*E*	the first two notes are e f (instead of c d).
52	Mo	*A*	the g was at first written as a semibrevis; it is covered with a (correct) brevis but the form is still recognizable.
58	Tr	*E*	the last note (minima) is aa.
58	Mo	*B*	longa instead of brevis (the mistake was not taken over in *E*).
60-61	Mo	*C*	brevis instead of longa.
62	Mo	*B*	the binaria has both an upward and a downward stem.
63	Mo	*E*	the third note (minima f) is d.
64	Mo	*Vg B*	perfect longa instead of brevis.
68	Tr	*E*	the third note (semibrevis) is c.
69	Tr	*G E*	the mi-sign stands before and on the line of g.
74	Tr	*E*	the second semibrevis is f.
75	Mo	*C Vg B*	the second note (minima) is e.
76	Tr	*G*	unusual change to gamma-clef until b. 82.
77	Mo	*E*	longa instead of brevis.
82	Tr	*B*	the last note was a minima instead of semibrevis; the stem is erased.
84	Tr	*C*	the first note is a semibrevis instead of a minima.
86	Tr	*E*	the last semibrevis is aa.
87	Tr	*E*	the last note (minima) is aa.
88	Mo	*E*	mi-sign before g.
90	Mo	*E*	mi-sign for g before the ligature.
95	Mo	*Vg B E*	no mi-sign; only before c in b. 96 in *Vg* and *B*.
99	Tr	*B*	the first note was a minima instead of semibrevis; the stem is erased.
105	Mo	*E*	the first note is a brevis instead of semibrevis.
106	Tr	*E*	erroneous dot after the first note.
117	Mo	*E*	curiously only *E* has a mi-sign here, but none in the triplum.

Literature

Editions of text: Chichmaref, *Poésies lyriques*, pp. 509-10; Robertson, *Machaut and Reims*, pp. 315-16.

Editions of music: Ludwig, *Werke*, pp. 52-54; Schrade, *Works*, pp. 47-49.

Tenor sources: Anderson, "Responsory Chants," p. 122; Clark, "Concordare cum materia," pp. 196, 246-47.

Discussions/interpretations (texts only): Patch, *The Goddess Fortuna*, p. 94n1; Clark, "Concordare cum materia," p. 83; Robertson, *Machaut and Reims*, pp. 161-63; Rose-Steel, "French Ars Nova Motets," pp. 162-67.

Analytical studies (text- and text/musical structure): Besseler, "Studien zur Musik II," p. 224; Machabey, *Guillaume de Machault* 2, pp. 90-92; Reichert, "Das Verhältnis," pp. 201, 208; Clarkson, "On the Nature," p. 256; Sanders, "The Medieval Motet," p. 563n286; Zayaruznaya, "Hockets as Compositional and Scribal Practice," pp. 494-95.

Analytical studies (musical structure): Hoppin, "Notational Licences," p. 25.

Analysis and interpretation of text/music relationship: Boogaart, "O series," pp. 140-44, 172-73; Sultan, "'Lyre—cette pratique;" Zayaruznaya, "Form and Idea," pp. 203-16; ead. "She Has a Wheel," pp. 209-20; Lavacek, "Contrapuntal Confrontation," pp. 137-44.

See also Earp, *Guillaume de Machaut*, p. 342-43.

M15 *Amours, qui a le pooir / Faus Samblant m'a deceü / Vidi Dominum*

Musical concordances

C fols 219v-220r   *Vg* fols 274v-275r   *B* fols 272v-273r   *G* fols 116v-117r
E fol. 143v   *Iv* fols 20v-21r   *Trem* fol. 8 (motetus and tenor only)

Tenor source

Responsory for the second Sunday of Lent (*Dom. II Quadragesimae; CAO* IV:7874). Text (from Genesis 32:30):

Vidi Dominum facie ad faciem;	I have seen God face to face;
et salva facta est anima mea.	and my soul has been saved.

Quotations

The concluding lines of both upper voice texts are well-known topoi in trouvère poetry, but they could be quotations from Thibaut de Champagne's *Qui plus aime plus endure* since this chanson is quoted more extensively in M5 (ed. Wallensköld, *Les chansons*, Chanson 35).

Text structure

Triplum	a7a7b5'a7a7b5'c7c7c7b5'c7c7b5'c7b5'c7c7c7b5'	a: -oir; b: -ure; c: -ment;
	d7d7b5'd7d7b5'e7e7e7b5'e7e7b5'e7b5'e7e7e7b5'	d: -iés; e: -é
Motetus	a7b7c7' a7b7c7' a7b7c7' a7b7c7'	a: eü; b: -ance (-ence); c: -oir

Tenor structure

One color of 40 notes, divided by four taleae. The isorhythmic patterns of the upper voices combine two pairs of taleae into two super-taleae. Length of the talea: 30 imperfect breves, of the super-talea 60 breves (the longest talea in the entire corpus, corresponding with the exceptionally long text strophes of the triplum). Length of the motet: 120 imperfect breves.

Mensuration

Perfect modus for the tenor, perfect modus, imperfect tempus and major prolatio for the upper voices.

Variants and errors not marked in the score

Bar	Voice	MS	
1-2	Tr	*Iv*	the first five notes are a third too high.
1	Mo	*Iv*	c (almost b) instead of d.
1-3	T	*C*	imperfect longa rest.
7-9	Tr	*C A Vg B*	dots of division before the semibrevis and after the longa;
		G E Iv	dot only after the longa.
5	Mo	*Trem*	the first two notes are written as a binaria c.o.p.
8	T	*Trem*	single longa (followed by a binaria).
16	Mo	*Trem*	up-stemmed longa.
19	Tr	*Vg B*	mi-sign before and on the line of aa (third note).
20	Tr	*A Iv*	although it seems probable that the first f should be raised, a fixed motif f e f♯ g occurs more often in the motets and chansons, so *A* could well be correct in giving the mi-sign only for the second f. No mi-sign at all in *Iv*.
22	Mo	*Trem*	up-stemmed longa; no mi-sign.
25-30	T	*C B Iv*	both *C* and *B* had a binaria brevis-longa but the tail is erased; no ligature in *Iv*.
26	Mo	*G Vg B E Iv*	the third note (minima) is e.
27	Mo	*A*	the third note is e only in this ms; d in all the others.
28	Mo	*Trem*	up-stemmed longa.

38	Tr	*Iv*	the first minima is g.
38	T	*Trem*	single longa (followed by a binaria).
49	Tr	*Iv*	the first note is f.
50	Mo	*A*	the brevis has two very short tails; perhaps a plica was meant.
55	T	*G*	brevis instead of longa.
55	Mo	*Trem*	the third note is b.
57	Mo	*C*	the notes are written in the margin and are placed a little too low.
58-59	Mo	*Iv*	e instead of g.
60-63	Tr	*Iv*	the passage is a third too low; the last two notes of b. 63 are again correct.
63-64	Tr	*G*	the three semibreves are a third too low caused by a brief clef-change (to gamma-clef) in b. 60 which is not repeated on the new staff, while the scribe probably continued momentarily to think in it; from the minima f onward the pitches are correct.
64	Tr	*C; Iv*	the last note (minima b) is c in *C*; no mi-sign before c in *Iv*.
65	Mo	*Trem*	the first two notes are written as a binaria c.o.p.
67-69	Tr	*C A G Vg B* *E Iv*	dots of division before the semibrevis and after the longa; dot only after the longa.
68	T	*Trem*	single longa (followed by a binaria).
72	Mo	*Vg B*	the mi-sign is repeated at staff-change.
73	T	*B E*	perfect longa rest instead of brevis rest.
75	Mo	*Trem*	the last two notes (semibrevis minima) are g f.
79-81	T	*B E*	the perfect longa rest is missing.
81	Tr	*Iv*	the second note (minima) is d.
82-90	T	*Trem*	ternaria.
85	Mo	*B*	the second note was a minima, but the stem is crossed out.
87	Mo	*Trem*	the third note (minima) is f.
97	T	*Trem*	single longa (followed by a binaria).
99	Tr	*A E*	the first minima (e) almost seems f in *A*; *E* omits the second pair of minima rests.
115-20	T	*Trem*	binaria.
116	Mo	*Iv Trem*	the third note (minima) is aa.

Literature

Editions of text: Chichmaref, *Poésies lyriques*, pp. 511-12; Robertson, *Machaut and Reims*, pp. 316-18.

Editions of music: Ludwig, *Werke*, pp. 55-57; Schrade, *Works*, pp. 50-52; Bent, "Deception, Exegesis," pp. 16-19.

Tenor sources: Clark, "Concordare cum materia," pp. 197, 247.

Discussions/interpretations (texts only): Badel, *Le Roman de la Rose*, p. 210; Brownlee, "Machaut's Motet 15;" Robertson, *Machaut and Reims*, pp. 163-65; Huot, "Reading across Genres."

Analytical studies (text- and text/musical structure): Besseler, "Studien zur Musik II," p. 223; Machabey, *Guillaume de Machault* 2, pp. 92-94; Reichert, "Das Verhältnis," pp. 202, 213 ex. 8; Günther, "The 14th-Century Motet," p. 32; Clarkson, "On the Nature," pp. 267, 271, 286-87, 291; Sanders, "The Medieval Motet," p. 558n257; Ziino, "Isoritmia musicale," pp. 444-45, 450; Lühmann, *Versdeklamation*, pp. 163-65; Kügle, "Die Musik des 14. Jahrhunderts," p. 370; Earp, "Declamatory Dissonance," pp. 114-16, exx. 9.12-13; Zayaruznaya, "Hockets as Compositional and Scribal Practice," pp. 494-95.

Analytical studies (musical structure, counterpoint): Pelinski, "Zusammenhang und Aufbau," p. 69; Fuller, "On Sonority," pp. 57-59; Leech-Wilkinson, *Compositional Techniques* I, pp. 110n15; Kügle, *The Manuscript Ivrea*, pp. 24-25, 51, 85, 146; Clark, "Concordare cum materia," p. 63.

Analysis and interpretation of text/music relationship: Bent, "Deception, Exegesis;" Boogaart, "O series," pp. 94-102, 111-14, 144-46; Zayaruznaya, "Form and Idea," pp. 198-203; ead., "She Has a Wheel," pp. 206-9; ead., *The Monstrous New Art*, p. 201; Lavacek, "Contrapuntal Confrontation," pp. 83-85.

See also Earp, *Guillaume de Machaut*, pp. 291-92.

M16 *Lasse! Comment oublieray / Se j'aim mon loial amy / Pour quoi me bat mes maris?*

Musical concordances
C fols 220v-221r   *Vg* fols 275v-276r   *B* fols 273v-274r   *G* fols 117v-118r
E fol. 137v-138r   *Trem* fol. 5 (index only)

Tenor source
Irregular virelai of which the text has a concordance in the pastourelles of MS *Oxford Bodleian Douce 308* fol. 197r (207r; ed. Atchinson, p. 328; Raynaud-Spanke, no. 1564; Van den Boogaard, no. 1515). Machaut quoted only the first stanza and changed the originally farcical *maumariee* text slightly in order to give his subject matter a more serious and elevated character.

Quotation: Hassell identified ll. 19-22 of the motetus as a proverbial expression (*Middle French Proverbs*, no. M54).

Text structure

Triplum	a8a8a8b4 b8b8b8c4 c8c8c8d4 d8d8d8e4 e8e8e8f4 f8f8f8g4	a: -ay; b: -i; c: -ent;
	g8g8g8h4 h8h8h8i4 i8i8i8j4 j8j8j8k4 k8k8k8l4 l8l8l8	d: -vuet; e: -oi; f: -uis;
		g: -ien; h: -is; i: -ui;
		j: -ort; k: -our; l: eins
Motetus	a7a3b4 a7a3b4 b7b3a4 b7b3a4 a7a3b4 a7a3b4 b7b3a4 b7b3a4 a7a3b4 a7a3b4	
		a: -i; b: -ent
Tenor	a7b2'c3 a7b2 d7d7 e7b2'c3 e7b2' a7b2'c3 a7b2'	
(music: A	A' B B' A A' A A')	

Musical structure
In the tenor phrases A24 A'18 B12 B'12 A24 A'18 A24 A'18 imperfect breves. A consists of three subphrases (12+6+6 breves), A' of two (12+6), corresponding with the structure of the chanson text.
Triplum: six phrases, of 25 + 25 + 26 + 25 + 25 + 24 imperfect breves; motetus: ten phrases of 15 imperfect breves. The lengthening of the triplum's third phrase serves to avoid a simultaneous rest and phrase-end with the motetus in b. 75. Length of the motet: 150 imperfect breves.

Mensuration
Perfect modus, imperfect tempus for the tenor; the same plus minor prolatio for the upper voices.

Variants and errors not marked in the score
General remark: like M11 this work is complex in the application of musica ficta, especially where the choice is between f-fa and f-mi; the MSS are fairly clear about g-mi but give only once, in motetus bb. 85-86, an indication that f should be fa and g mi. Since the question is open, f-mi is recommended only where it sounds together with b; elsewhere alterations are suggested between brackets.

Bar	Voice	MS	
5	Mo	*Vg B*	up-stemmed longa.
8	Tr	*E*	mi-sign before the g.
14	Tr	*E*	the second minima is f.
16	Mo	*Vg B*	left-tailed brevis.

20	Tr	E	the minima is a.
24	Mo	G	clef-change between the two e's.
25	Mo	E	the third minima is e.
29	Tr	C	signs of erasure before the c; was it a mi-sign?
36	Tr	E	the last minima is f.
37	Tr	E	the first semibrevis is g.
39	Tr	E	the first minima is f.
41	Tr	all -E	up-stemmed longa; since especially G always writes low longae with the stem Downward, a plica must be meant.
46	Mo	E	the mi-sign is written above the note.
52	Tr	E	the last minima is d.
53-54	Mo	E	the passage is a third too high; correct pitches from b. 55.
55	Tr	B	this MS initially had a semibrevis, later covered by a brevis.
56-59	Tr	Vg B	the whole passage is a third too low, probably because of the omission of a clef change; halfway through b. 60 these MSS begin a new staff with the right clef. Curiously the mistake was not taken over in E.
60	Mo	B	longa rest instead of brevis rest (also not taken over in E).
64	Mo	A	the minima d seems an accident in copying (an e that descended too much); all the other MSS have e.
65	Mo	E	fa-sign before c.
66	Tr	E	the last three minimae are f e d.
67	Tr	A	the second note was a minima; the stem is crossed through.
70	T	E	mi-sign before F.
71	Tr	C	the second minima is e.
76	T	A	the dot is missing.
*80-81	Tr	A	A deviates in rhythm from all the other MSS which have ♩♩♩♩♩♦♦ but A's version reinforces the expressive monotony and repetitiveness in this part of the motet.
80	Mo	all minus E	up-stemmed longa; like in b. 41 probably a plica was meant.
83	T	C	D instead of C♯.
88	Mo	E	fa-sign before b.
94	Mo	E	the last minima is f.
94	T	E	mi-sign before F.
97	Mo	E	deviating rhythm ♩♦♩
101	Mo	Vg B	up-stemmed longa.
107	Tr	A	no up-stemmed longa as in C, G, Vg, B and E.
107	Mo	E	deviating rhythm ♩♦♩
118	T	Vg B	the dot is missing.
123	Mo	C	the two minimae are semibreves.
125	Mo	Vg B	up-stemmed longa in Vg, possibly a plica longa in B.
128	Mo	C E	no up-stemmed longa as in A, G, Vg and B; brevis in E.
131	Tr	E B	mi-sign before c in E; the minima has a blotted stem in B.
136	T	E	mi-sign before F.
137	Mo	E	brevis instead of longa.
142	Mo	C E	no dot of perfection after the longa.
145	Tr	A	erroneous brevis rest.

Literature

Editions of text: Chichmaref, *Poésies lyriques*, pp. 513-15; Robertson, *Machaut and Reims*, pp. 318-20.
Editions of music: Ludwig, *Werke*, pp. 58-61; Schrade, *Works*, pp. 53-56.

Discussions/interpretations (texts only): Imbs, *Le Voir Dit*, p. 94; Robertson, *Machaut and Reims*, pp. 165-68.

Analytical studies (text- and text/musical structure): Machabey, *Guillaume de Machault 2*, pp. 94-96; Clarkson, "On the Nature," pp. 266, 268, 317n106, 315-18; Sanders, "The Medieval Motet," p. 564; Ziino, "Isoritmia musicale," p. 443n11; Rose-Steel, "French Ars Nova Motets," pp. 168-73; Zayaruznaya, "Hockets as Compositional and Scribal Practice," pp. 494-95.

Analytical studies (musical structure/counterpoint): Reaney, *Guillaume de Machaut*, p. 55; Hartt, "The Three Tenors."

Analysis and interpretation of text/music relationship: Boogaart, "O series," pp. 72-79; id., "Encompassing," pp. 35-41; Lavacek, "Contrapuntal Confrontation," pp. 118-27.

See also Earp, *Guillaume de Machaut*, p. 336.

M17   *Quant Vraie Amour enflamee / O Series summe rata / Super omnes speciosa*

Musical concordances
C fols 221v-222r   *Vg* fols 276v-277r   *B* fols 274v-275r   *G* fols 118v-119r
E fols 136v-137r

Tenor source
The Marian antiphon *Ave regina celorum* (*De beata*; *CAO* III:1542). Text:

Ave regina celorum, ave, Domina angelorum;	Hail, Queen of heavens, hail, Lady of angels;
salve, radix sancta ex qua mundo lux est orta.	hail, holy root from whom light for the world was [born.
Gaude, Virgo gloriosa, *super omnes speciosa*;	Rejoice, glorious Virgin, fair above all;
vale, valde decora,	fare well, most beautiful one,
et pro nobis semper exora Christum, alleluia.	and pray Christ for us always, alleluia.

Textual models
The source for the tenor words in the antiphon probably is Sapientia 7:29, a eulogy of Divine Wisdom: "Est enim haec *speciosior* sole et *super omnem* stellarum dispositionem" (For she is more beautiful than the sun, and above all the order of the stars.) The triplum text possibly refers by its rhetorical structure to one of the most famous Boethian poems (*De consolatione philosophiae* II, metrum 8: *Quod mundus stabili fide*; ed. Tester, pp. 226-27). The motetus text similarly may well refer to Alain de Lille's equally famous poem from *De planctu naturae*, metrum 4 (*O Dei proles genitrixque rerum*; ed. Häring, p. 842).

Text structure
Triplum	a7'a7'b6'a7'b6' a7'a7'b6'a7'b6' a7'a7'b6'a7'b6'	a: -ee; b: -ie
	a7'a7'b6'a7'b6' a7'a7'b6'a7'b6' a7'a7'b6'a7'b5'	
Motetus	a8b6a8b6 a8b6a8b6 a8b6a8b6 a8b6a8b6	a: -ata; b: -uram

Tenor structure
The same tenor, but with a larger fragment, was used by Philippe de Vitry in his motet *Vos quid admiramini / Gratissima / Gaude gloriosa / Contratenor* (*The Works of Philippe de Vitry*, ed. Schrade, pp. 20-25). Compared to the original antiphon and to the tenor of Vitry's motet, Machaut transposed the melisma a fifth higher. Two colores of 18 notes, each divided by three taleae. The tenor is notated only once, with repeat sign. Length of the talea: 22 imperfect breves. The color has a length of 66 breves but at its second iteration the upper voices end earlier than the tenor; the complete length of the tenor would be 132 imperfect breves but the upper voices already end in bb. 128-29. This shortening clearly is be a playful allusion to the message of the triplum text, paraphrased: "goods cannot be had twice without cheating," i.e. the tenor cannot be repeated fully "without cheating" of the upper voices (see also below).

Mensuration

Perfect modus, imperfect tempus for the tenor; imperfect modus, imperfect tempus and major prolatio for the upper voices. The existing editions assume perfect modus also for the upper voices, but this would imply that Machaut ignored or chose to ignore the first rule of perfection (*similis ante similem perfecta*; even the otherwise very precise Ludwig made no remark about this): the motetus begins with two longae of which the first would then necessarily be perfect. On the other hand the tenor would seem to be measured according to imperfect modus on the ground of the many imperfect longa rests between its longae; not before bb. 15-17 does it become clear that the modus is perfect. The six imperfect longa rests in each color (two per talea) add up to form a long-term syncopation (illustrating the 'series summe rata', the 'well-calculated chain' with which the motetus text begins). Machaut seems to be trying his hand at the possibilities of syncopation in this probably early work; the upper voices also have many longae in syncopated position throughout the whole motet. In order to avoid many ties, the modus bar-lines in the upper voices, from b. 15 on, have been shifted for one bar. The work is special, moreover, in its sound effects: long-sounding perfect or imperfect sonorities, chains of parallel fifths, a very unruly motetus melody that sometimes dips far below the other voices (adorned with many plicae in the plaintive talea V) but in the last talea rises far above them.

Variants and errors not marked in the score

Bar	Voice	MS	
3	Tr	*B E*	rhythm ♩♩♩♦
4	T	*E*	longa rest instead of brevis rest.
5	Mo	*G*	superfluous semibrevis d after the third note.
17	Tr	*B E*	an extra minima f♯ is added after the second semibrevis.
20	Tr	*A C G*	a clear mi-sign before f, but in the following taleae this melodic refrain appears without it; *Vg*, *B* and *E* are less explicit. Perhaps all the refrains should be identical, either with or without f♯.
28	Mo	*B E*	a minima d is added after the semibrevis.
29	Tr	*B E*	the brevis is replaced by two semibreves.
32	T	*C*	brevis rest instead of longa rest.
35	Mo	*A*	up-stemmed longa only in *A*; since this scribe did not hesitate to write down-stemmed longae in low position, a plica surely was meant.
36	Tr	*C G*	up-stemmed longa; since the note is in the middle of the staff this can hardly be anything other than a plica longa.
40	Mo	*E*	e instead of c.
59-63	Mo	*E*	from the second note (G) the whole passage is a third too high.
59-60	T	*C*	the longa rest is missing.
61	Tr	*G*	the last note (f) is a semibrevis.
64	Tr	*A*	the scribe initially forgot to copy the passage bb. 64-72 but later wrote it at the bottom of the page, put a reference mark in the staff and the right clef for the omitted passage. However, the clef does not apply to the notes following it in the staff itself (which would then be a and e); the main clef (the one at the beginning of the staff) still applies here.
64	Tr	*G*	the last note (e) is a semibrevis.
76	Tr	*B*	the last note (aa) is bb.
*77-78	Tr	*A*	the last note of b. 77 and the following longa are d and c; a curling line seems to draw attention to this place and it probably is a mistake; hence the emendation in accordance with the other MSS.
77	Mo	*A*	the last note (e) is a semibrevis.
94	Tr	*Vg B E*	g g instead of aa aa.
96	Mo	*Vg B*	the sign is a little unclear in *Vg* but the scribe of *B* interpreted it as a plica.
98	T	*C*	brevis rest instead of longa rest (as in b. 32).

99	Mo	*C G*	left-tailed brevis.
100	Mo	*Vg B*	up-stemmed longa.
114	Mo	*A*	the second half of this bar (♦ ♪ bb cc) is missing.
122	Mo	*E*	brevis instead of longa.
125	T	*C*	the longa rest is missing (as in b. 59).
126	Tr Mo	all	the upper voices end a brevis earlier than the tenor. Performers who prefer not to end on a dissonance may take over Ludwig's and Schrade's solution to make the longa rest of bb. 125-26 a brevis rest, so that the tenor's d will coincide with the penultimate bar of the upper voices and the voices will end together.

Literature

Editions of text: Chichmaref, *Poésies lyriques*, pp. 516-17; Robertson, *Machaut and Reims*, pp. 320-21.

Editions of music: Ludwig, *Werke*, pp. 62-64; Schrade, *Works*, pp. 57-59.

Tenor sources: Clark, "Concordare cum materia," pp. 204, 251.

Discussions/interpretations (texts only): Clark, "Concordare cum materia," pp. 83-84; Robertson, *Machaut and Reims*, pp. 174-77; Rose-Steel, "The Ars Nova Motet," pp. 156-58.

Analytical studies (text- and text/musical structure): Besseler, "Studien zur Musik II," p. 224; Machabey, *Guillaume de Machault* 2, pp. 96-98; Reichert, "Das Verhältnis," pp. 201, 212, ex. 11; Reaney, *Guillaume de Machaut*, p. 53; Clarkson, "On the Nature," p. 240; Sanders, "The Medieval Motet," p. 564; Ziino, "Isoritmia musicale," pp. 444, 446-47; Lavacek, "Contrapuntal Confrontation," pp. 67-70, 152-68; Zayaruznaya, "Hockets as Compositional and Scribal Practice," pp. 494-95.

Analytical studies (musical structure/counterpoint): Günther, "The 14ᵗʰ-Century Motet," pp. 32, 34; Hoppin, "Notational Licences," p. 25; Reaney, *Guillaume de Machaut*, p. 53; Pelinski, "Zusammenhang und Aufbau," p. 69; Wernli, "La percettibilità," pp. 18-19; Fuller, "On Sonority," pp. 45-46; ead., "Modal Tenors," pp. 215-43; Clark, "Listening," pp. 492-93; ead., "Machaut Reading Machaut," p. 95.

Analysis and interpretation of text/music relationship: Boogaart, "O series," pp. 79-92 and pp. 148-51; id., "Encompassing," pp. 41-50.

See also Earp, *Guillaume de Machaut*, pp. 364-65.

M18   *Bone pastor Guillerme / Bone pastor, qui pastores / Bone pastor*

Musical concordances

C fols 222v-223r   *Vg* fols 277v-278r   *B* fols 275v-276r   *G* fols 119v-120r
E fol. 144v

Tenor source

Not identified. Robertson suggests that the melody could stem from the responsory *Ego pro te rogavi* for the feast of SS Peter and Paul (*CAO* IV:6630), from which it would be the melisma *Fratres*. Machaut would then have changed the text and part of the melody (which is itself extremely unstable in the sources). Text of this responsory (adapted from Luke 22:32):

Ego pro te rogavi, Petre,	But I have prayed for thee, Peter,
ut non deficiat fides tua,	that thy faith fail not;
et tu, aliquando conversus,	and thou, being once converted,
confirma fratres tuos.	confirm thy brethren.

Text structure

Triplum   a7a7b6c7c7b6   d7d7e6f7f7e6   g7g7h6i7i7h6   j7j7k6l7l7k8
            m7m7i6m7i4   n7n7i6n7i4   o7o7p6o7p4   q7q7p6q7p4

a: -erme; b: -atum; c: -erva; d: -ostes; e:-entur; f: -aro; g: -ingit; h: -amenta;
i: -ere; j: -uius; k:-atis; l: -igna; m: -uli; n: ia; o: -amine; p: -ili; q: -ium

Motetus   a8a8b4c8c8b4   d8d8e4f8f8e4   g8h4g8h4   i8j4i8j4
a: -ores; b: -enus; c: -iorum; d: -enter; e: -egit; f: -orem; g: -estum; h: -igne;
i: -ale; j: -egi

Tenor structure

Four colores of 16 notes, each divided by two taleae, color 3 and 4 in diminution to one-half. The tenor is notated in integer valor and in diminution, both with repeat sign. Length of the talea: 24 imperfect breves, 12 in diminution. The color has a length of 48 imperfect breves, 24 in diminution. Length of the motet: 144 imperfect breves.

Mensuration

Imperfect maximodus, perfect modus, imperfect tempus for the tenor, diminished to imperfect modus, perfect tempus; imperfect modus, imperfect tempus and major prolatio for the upper voices. Thus, the upper voices and the tenor are in continuous mensural contrast. The Ludwig and Schrade editions assume perfect modus also for the upper voices, but, as in M17, this supposes a breach of the first rule of perfection (*similis ante similem perfecta*; also in this case Ludwig made no remark about it). The motetus sometimes may give the impression of perfect modus (e.g. in bb. 31-36) but then, according to the rule, the first of the two longae would be perfect.

Variants and errors not marked in the score

General: only *C* repeats the fa-sign for the tenor on each staff. *A* and *G* have the fa-sign for the tenor only at the beginning of the first staff but not further. *Vg* and *B* repeat the clef before the diminished tenor part (which is on the same staff) but then omit the fa-sign. Since the clef is the same as before, and thus actually superfluous, this could (but must not necessarily) mean that, according to these manuscripts, in diminution b should be sung as mi, not fa. *E* has the fa-sign at the beginning of its only staff.

Bar	Voice	MS	
7	Mo	*B E*	rhythm ♦♩ ♦ instead of ♦ ♦♩
9	Mo	*B E*	rhythm ♦♩♩ instead of ♦ ♦♩ although it seems that in *B* an attempt was made to erase the stem.
10	Mo	*Vg B*	left-tailed brevis.
11	Mo	*Vg B*	up-stemmed longa.
15	Tr	*E*	the brevis rest is missing.
15-19	Mo	*E*	the whole passage is written a third too high.
18-20	Tr	*E*	the last note of b. 18 is c, the longa is d.
31	Tr	*A*	only *A* has the mi-sign, placed before the g; it was probably meant to apply to the following f and then forms a motif that occurs more often in Machaut's melodies: a descending half-tone, followed by ascending tone and half-tone (f e f♯ g), here in ornamented form; see e.g. the motetus parts of M2 and M4 and the triplum of M15 (but it occurs also in the tenors of some chansons).
33	Tr	*B E*	rhythm ♦♩ ♦ instead of ♦ ♦♩
34	Tr	*C*	the last note (minima) is f.
36-37	Tr	*Vg B E*	the last note of b. 36 and the first note of b. 37 are c and d.
45	Tr	*C G*	the last note (minima) is a semibrevis.
48	Mo	*B*	the second minima is a semibrevis.
52-53	Tr	*C*	brevis instead of longa.
52-53	Mo	*C*	brevis instead of longa.
56	Mo	*C*	*C* is the only MS not to have this curious g♯, which is strongly dissonant against the tenor's b♭. Perhaps the mi-sign was unclearly placed in the exemplar and was intended for the following longa f♯.

59-60	Tr	*Vg B E*	up-stemmed longa. The mi-sign is very vague in *A*.
76-77	Mo	*C*	brevis instead of longa.
79-90	Tr	*G*	from the second semibrevis in b. 79 the whole passage is a third too high; the scribe even erased the right clef at page change (before *cervix*); at b. 91 a new (and correct) clef is placed. An unusual dot at the beginning of the passage (at *imbutus*) seems to ask for attention, perhaps a sign that some problem was noticed?
86-87	Mo	*C*	brevis instead of longa.
*92	Tr	all	emendation; the longa is a brevis in all the MSS.
96	Mo	*E*	the second semibrevis is a minima.
98	Tr	*B*	the scribe wrote a semibrevis but covered it with a brevis.
101	Tr	*E*	one minima rest is missing.
102	Tr	*E*	the second note (minima) is e.
118	Tr	*Vg B*	up-stemmed longa.
121-24	Tr	*C*	the whole passage is a third too low (wrong clef).
125	Tr	*C*	the second note (minima) is g.
125	Mo	*A*	the semibrevis e is missing.
126	Tr	*C*	the first semibrevis had a stem, erased but still visible.
133	Tr	*E*	the first note is e.

Literature

Editions of text: Chichmaref, *Poésies lyriques*, pp. 518-20; Robertson, *Machaut and Reims*, pp. 321-23.

Editions of music: Ludwig, *Werke*, pp. 65-67; Schrade, *Works*, pp. 60-63.

Discussion/interpretation (texts only): Robertson, *Machaut and Reims*, pp. 55-69; Leach, *Machaut: Secretary*, pp. 28-29.

Analytical studies (text- and text/musical structure): Besseler, "Studien zur Musik II," p. 222; Machabey, *Guillaume de Machault* 2, pp. 98-101; Reichert, "Das Verhältnis," pp. 201, 205-9, 211-12; Clarkson, "On the Nature," p. 255; Ziino, "Isoritmia musicale," pp. 442, 444, 446, 449, 451.

Analytical studies (musical structure/counterpoint): Günther, "The 14th-Century Motet," p. 34; Dömling, *Die mehrstimmigen Balladen*, pp. 68-69; Hoppin, "Notational Licences," p. 26; Bank, *Tactus, tempo*, pp. 39, 43; Sanders, "The Medieval Motet," p. 563n286; Kühn, *Die Harmonik*, pp. 131-37; Wernli, "La percettibilità," pp. 19-21; Pelinski, "Zusammenhang und Aufbau," pp. 69-70; Wernli, "La percettibilità," pp. 19-21; Fuller, "On Sonority," pp. 47-55, 61-62; ead., "Modal Tenors," pp. 202-03; Leech-Wilkinson, "Related motets," pp. 4, 14-15; Boogaart, "O series," pp. 170-72.

See also Earp, *Guillaume de Machaut*, pp. 296-97.

M19   *Martyrum gemma latria / Diligenter inquiramus / A Christo honoratus*

Musical concordances

C fols 223v-224r	*Vg* fols 278v-279r	*B* fols 276v-277r	*G* fols 120v-121r
E fol. 144r	*Iv* fols 10v-11r	*Trem* fol. 23 (index only)	

Tenor source

Repetenda of the responsory *Sanctus namque Quintinus* for the feast of St Quintinus (31st October). Text (cited from MS Paris, BnF lat. 15182, fols 413r-414v):

Sanctus namque Quintinus urbe Roma genitus	For Saint Quintinus, born in the city of Rome,
Domino ducente Gallias venit	came, God leading him, to Gaul,
insignis et virtutibus	excellent, and for his virtues
gloriose *a Christo honoratus*.	gloriously honored by Christ.

Text structure

Triplum	8 aaaa aaaaaa aaaaaa aaaaaa aaaaaa aaaaaa a: -ia
Motetus	a8b7a8b7 c8b7c8b7 d8c7d8c7 e8f7e8f7 a: -amus; b: -ia; c: -abilis; d: -erat; e: -issime; f: -iter

The text structure was probably inspired by, or even borrowed from, the motets *Virtutibus / Impudenter / Tenor [Alma redemptoris mater] / Contratenor* and *Flos ortus / Celsa cedrus / Quam magnus pontifex*, both ascribed to Vitry (Kügle, *The Manuscript Ivrea*, pp. 119-25).

Tenor structure

After a solo introitus of the triplum of 12 perfect breves: two colores of 30 notes, together divided by five taleae (2C=5T). Length of the talea: 21 perfect breves. Color 1 has a length of 53 breves, color 2 of 52 breves. Length of the motet: 117 perfect breves.

Mensuration

Perfect modus, perfect tempus for the tenor; the same with minor prolatio for the upper voices.

Variants and errors not marked in the score

General remark: the MSS do not show an entirely consistent use of the dot of perfection but it is usually clear how the perfections are composed. The notation of the tenor is uniform except in *Iv* whose scribe wrote the eleventh note as a single semibrevis (and thus not as a brevis forming part of a binaria ◄) which then apparently is supposed to be altered (against the convention that alteration only can take place before a note of the next higher value; here the semibrevis stands before a longa). Although usually *E* took over the mistakes of *B*, it seems not to be the case with this work; perhaps *E* had another exemplar.

Bar	Voice	MS	
1	Tr	*Vg B*	left-tailed brevis.
1	Mo, T	all	the perfect modus is indicated by four perfect longa rests in *A*, *C* and *G*. *Vg*, *B*, *E* and *Iv* have this only for the tenor, but write six imperfect longa rests for the motetus, in *Vg* and *B* all between the same lines; in *Vg* perhaps on calligraphic grounds as Ludwig suggested (Ludwig, *Werke* III, p. 70).
2	Tr	*E*	the last note is g.
4	Tr	*E*	rhythm ♩♩♩♩♦ with pitches bb aa aa g aa.
5	Tr	*E*	a minima bb is interpolated after the the semibrevis cc.
*17	Tr	*A*	the second and third note are c d only in *A*; the other MSS have d e, which would, however, result in three consecutive f-e dissonances. That may be correct but so may be *A*'s alternative.
19	Tr	all	Ludwig and Schrade remark that only *Iv* has aa as the third note (instead of bb), but all the MSS have aa.
22	Mo	*Vg B*	left-tailed brevis.
23	Tr	*E B*	the first note (aa) is missing in *E*; the last note was a minima in *B* but its stem was erased.
28	Tr	*Iv*	the minima rest after the first note (g) is very vague.
31	Mo	*A*	signs of erasure.
35	Tr	*C B*	the mi-sign is placed very clearly before the g.
36	Tr	*E*	the last note (aa) is g.
37	Tr	*E*	the last note (g) is missing.
38	Tr	*Vg B*	left-tailed brevis.
39	Tr	*E Iv*	the first note (minima) is a semibrevis in *E*; the second note is bb, not cc in *Iv*.
42	Tr	*C*	the first note (bb) is missing.

43	Mo	*A*	first a semibrevis was written but it was covered with a brevis.
49	Tr	*A C G E Iv*	the first note (g) looks like aa in *C*, *G*, *E* and *Iv*; in *A* it is unclear whether g or aa is meant; g seems likely. The last note (semibrevis g) is aa in *E*.
50	Tr	*B*	the first note (bb) is missing.
50	Mo	*Iv*	the two semibreves are d e (instead of e f♯).
52	Mo	*G Vg B*	*Vg* and *B* have a mi-sign before g but it must refer to f in bb. 56-57; *G* has it also at that position but on the correct line.
53	Mo	*Vg B*	the brevis rest is missing.
58	Mo	*B*	brevis instead of longa
64	Tr	*B*	the second note (dd) is cc.
65	Mo	*B*	the fourth note (e) is f.
68-70	Mo	*E*	the passage is a third too high until the rest in b. 70.
69	Tr	*B*	the last note (minima) is a semibrevis.
71	Tr	*E*	the last note (minima) is a semibrevis.
72-73	Tr	*B*	the last note of b. 72 (minima f) and the first of b. 73 (brevis g) are missing.
73	Tr	*Vg E*	left-tailed brevis in *Vg*. The second note (g) is f in *E*.
74	Mo	*C*	the brevis rest is missing.
78	Tr	*E*	the first note (d) is e.
82	Mo	*A*	first a semibrevis was written but it then was covered with a brevis.
84	Mo	*A*	the fourth note (minima bb) is aa in all the other MSS.
86	Mo	*E*	the last two notes (f e) are g f.
91	Tr	*E*	the last note (aa) is g.
91	T	*B Iv*	c, not b (or it was very negligently written).
92	Tr	*E*	the last note (aa) is g.
93	Mo	*C*	the first and last note (both f♯) are g's.
98	Mo	*E Iv*	the fourth note (g) is bb.
99	Tr	*E*	the mi-sign is very clearly placed after f and before g.
99	Mo	*E*	the last three notes (♩♩♦) are replaced by four minimae g f e f.
100	Mo	*Vg B*	up-stemmed longa.
102	Tr	*Iv*	the first note (f) is d.
106	Tr	*A*	first a semibrevis was written, later covered by a brevis.
108	Tr	*E Iv*	the second and third note (e g) are f aa in *E*, g aa in *Iv*.
111	Mo	*G*	mi-sign before e; the f to which it applies is on the next staff.
113	Tr	*E*	the first note (bb) is cc.
114	Tr, Mo	*A C G E*	curiously neither of these MSS has a mi-sign before the penultimate note in either of the two upper voices.
115	Mo	*Vg B*	an up-stemmed maxima, five semibreves (referring to Quintinus) and a down-stemmed maxima serve as a symbolic decoration of the final.

Literature

Editions of text: Chichmaref, *Poésies lyriques*, pp. 521-23; Robertson, *Machaut and Reims*, pp. 323-25.

Editions of music: Ludwig, *Werke*, pp. 68-70; Schrade, *Works*, pp. 64-66.

Tenor sources: Fuller, "Modal Tenors," p. 231n43; Clark, "Concordare cum materia," pp. 198, 248.

Discussion/interpretation (texts only): Günther, "Chronologie und Stil," p. 100; ead., "Sinnbezüge," p. 267; Clark, "Concordare cum materia," p. 78; Robertson, *Machaut and Reims*, pp. 69-75; Fiala, "La collégiale royale," pp. 195-205.

Analytical studies (text- and text/musical structure): Besseler, "Studien zur Musik II," p. 222; Machabey, *Guillaume de Machault* 2, pp. 101-3; Reichert, "Das Verhältnis," pp. 201; Ziino, "Isoritmia musicale," p., 444n13; Kügle, *The Manuscript Ivrea*, pp. 119-24; Zayaruznaya, "Hockets as Compositional and Scribal Practice," pp. 494-95.

Analytical studies (musical structure/counterpoint): Günther, "The 14th-Century Motet," p. 34; Sanders, "The Medieval Motet," p. 563; Fuller, "Modal Tenors," pp. 231-43; Clark, "Concordare cum materia," pp. 63-64.
See also Earp, *Guillaume de Machaut*, p. 342.

M20   *Trop plus est bele que Biauté / Biauté paree de valour / Je ne sui mie certeins d'avoir amie*

Musical concordances

C fols 224v-225r	*Vg* fols 279v-280r	*B* fols 277v-278r	*G* fols 121v-122r
E fol. 131r	*Trem* fol. 12 (index only)		

Tenor source
Unidentified rondeau. Only the refrain is given, with the instruction to sing it in the way of a rondeau ("dicitur ad modum rondelli" in *A*, "Rondel" in *C*, *G*, *Vg*, and *B*; no indication in *E*). Since no other text is extant the singer can either repeat the two text lines or vocalize the untexted phrases.

Text structure

Triplum	8 aa bb cc dd ee ff gg hh ii jj	a: -té; b: --oir; c: desir; d: -uis; e: -on; f: -chiés;
		g: -ien; h: -ient; i: -ort; j: -i
Motetus	8 aaaa aaaa aaaa	a: -our

Both texts end with *Amen*

Musical structure
The tenor's rondeau phrase A has a length of 7 perfect breves, phrase B of 5 breves. Thus, the complete form (ABaAabAB) would have a length of 50 perfect breves, ending on an imperfect longa. However, the upper voices have three phrases of 17 breves, marked by isorhythmic figures in bb. 8-10, 25-27 and 42-44; in accordance with these, the complete form would extend to 51 perfect breves, precisely twice as short as M11 with which the work shares also the division by isorhythmic hocket passages. The final longa might then be considered as perfect, worth three perfect breves, which would accord also with the final word *Amen*. Length of the motet: 51 or 50 perfect breves.

Mensuration
Perfect tempus for the tenor, perfect tempus and major prolatio for the upper voices. For this motet, with its syncopations on the prolation level, it proved more practical to transcribe in 9/8 rather than in 3/4 as in the other motets.

Variants and errors not marked in the score:
General remark: *A* has no fa-sign for the tenor; *C* on all of its tenor staves, *G* on the first two staves (of three); *Vg*, *B*, and *E* have only one staff for the tenor, with fa-sign.

Bar	Voice	MS	
3	Tr	*C*	the second note (minima) is a semibrevis.
6	Tr	*B E*	the first note was a correct minima in *B* but the stem is erased. *E* has the rhythm ♦♩ ♦ ♦ for the first four notes. Schrade remarks that the second note (d) is a minima in *C* only, but it is, correctly, an (altered) minima in all the MSS except *E*.
8	Tr	*C*	the second minima (a) is a semibrevis.
9	Tr	*C*	the second minima (e) is a semibrevis.
11-12	Mo	*C*	the second semibrevis (f) is a minima, the following minima a semibrevis, and the following two notes are minimae followed by a brevis.

16	Tr	*B E*	the first note (semibrevis f) is missing. In *B* the sixth, seventh and eighth minimae have very vague stems, if at all; they became ♦♪♦ in *E*.
18	Mo	*B E*	the last four notes have the rhythm ♦♪ ♦♪
*18	Mo	*A G*	although both prescribe b♭, yet it seems that the version in the other MSS – not applying it before b. 19 – is more plausible.
19	Tr	*C E*	*C* has a brevis instead of semibrevis. In *E* the second and third note are semibreves.
19	Mo	*B E*	the last four notes have again the rhythm ♦♪ ♦♪
29	Tr	*E*	the second note (minima d) is missing.
30	Tr	*E*	the fourth note (minima d) is a semibrevis.
33	Tr	*C*	the second note (e) is a minima which would result in a iambic rhythm (as found in many places in this motet).
34	Tr	*G*	the second note (d) is a semibrevis. The dot that Ludwig observed (with consequences for the interpretation of the rhythm) is so strangely displaced (above the staff) that it probably has no signification other than being a blot or a slip of the pen.
40	Tr	*G*	the semibrevis aa is followed by four minimae instead of ♪♦ ♪♪
40	Mo	*C*	the brevis (a) is c.
41	Mo	*C E*	the last note (minima b) is a semibrevis in *C*. The second note is a minima in *E*.
42	Tr	*E*	the last note (minima g) is aa.
44	Mo	*C E*	the two minima rests are missing in *C*. The last note (semibrevis b) is a minima in *E*.
48	Tr	*A*	emendation; *A* has ♪♦ instead of ♪♪, which would imply the syncopation occuring in many places (see e.g. motetus b. 3), but since the other MSS do not have this, it probably is a mistake; one would expect the two voices coming together at last in this penultimate measure.
48	Mo	*E*	the third note (semibrevis a) is a curious longa c.
49-51		*G*	the final notes of the upper voices are drawn as maximae suggesting that the final note may be held very long.

Literature

Editions of text: Chichmaref, *Poésies lyriques*, pp. 524-25; Robertson, *Machaut and Reims*, pp. 325-26.

Editions of music: Ludwig, *Werke*, pp. 68-70; Schrade, *Works*, pp. 64-66; Hüschen, *The Motet*, pp. 31-32.

Discussion/interpretation (texts only): Sonnemann, *Die Ditdichtung*, p. 62; Wright, "Verbal Counterpoint;" Earp, *Guillaume de Machaut*, pp. 25-26; id., *The Ferrell-Vogüé Manuscript* I, p. 31, 31n17; Robertson, *Machaut and Reims*, pp. 184-85.

Analytical studies (text- and text/musical structure): Machabey, *Guillaume de Machault* 2, pp. 103-4; Reichert, "Das Verhältnis," pp. 201; Günther, "The 14th-Century Motet," pp. 29, 35n28; Hoppin, "Notational Licences," pp. 15-16; Clarkson, "On the Nature," pp. 245n74, 315-18; Bank, *Tactus, Tempo*, pp. 39, 43; Sanders, "The Medieval Motet," p. 564.

Analytical studies (musical structure/counterpoint): Günther, "The 14th-Century Motet," p. 35n28; Reaney, *Guillaume de Machaut*, pp. 54-55; Sanders, "The Medieval Motet," p. 564; Hartt, "The Three Tenors."

Analysis and interpretation of text/music relationship: Boogaart, "O series," pp. 192-203; id., "L'accomplissement," pp. 54-60; Earp, *The Ferrell-Vogüé Manuscript* I, p. 34.

See also Earp, *Guillaume de Machaut*, pp. 382-83.

M21 *Christe, qui lux es et dies / Veni, Creator Spiritus / Tribulatio proxima est et non est qui adjuvet / Ct*

Musical concordances

Vg fols 280v-281r   *B* fols 278v-279r   *G* fols 122v-123r   *E* fols 145v-146r

Manuscript appearance

This is an intriguing motet with respect to the relationship between the manuscripts. *A* has the introitus and first talea of both tenor and contratenor written at the bottom of fol. 435r, in what seems to be a different (and clumsier) scribal hand that was also responsible for the deviating fa-sign (as a round b) in both the added part and in the main staff of the tenor, at the beginning of the diminution section and a little further after the ternaria and rest, where it almost seems a second imperfect longa rest. He also may have written the (initially forgotten) thick brevis rest above the b-mi, the eighth note before the diminution section. The folio was severely trimmed, so that parts of the tenor's first and last talea have disappeared, part of the word *tribula[tio]*, and also part of the contratenor. *G*, on the other hand, has the introitus of the triplum at the bottom of fol. 122v, and that of the motetus at the bottom of fol. 123r but those of tenor and contratenor at their proper place. Leech-Wilkinson (*Compositional Techniques* I, pp. 242-43) supposed that all the introits were composed after the main body of the work and for that reason were added later. This does not explain, however, why the earlier *Vg* would have had access to a complete version and the arguably later *A* and *G* not. Earp ("Interpreting the deluxe manuscript," p. 236) suggests that the scribe of *G* had entered the text at the usual place, at the beginning, without taking account of the melismatic introitus, and that the music scribe therefore had to give the opening melismas at the bottom of the pages.

Clear links between *A* and *G* are the absence of an opening syllable for the introitus of the upper voices (as found in the other MSS) and the curious notation of the final note of the motetus introitus, as a maxima with two downward stems, a longa with two downward stems and a maxima drawn like the first, which clearly make no musical sense but form a symbolic decoration of which the signification is not apparent. In *G* the capital V for the motetus text is missing, although space has been left for it, the only such instance in the motets.

In *Vg*, *B* and *E* the voice parts are notated consecutively with the introits at their proper places; *B*'s scribe uncharacteristically could not cope with *Vg*'s economic script and had to copy the last part of the triplum's introitus on a new staff, whereas *Vg*'s scribe managed to compress it onto one staff.

Tenor source

Verse of the responsory *Circumdederunt me viri mendaces* for Passion Sunday (*Dom. de Passione*; *CAO* IV:6287), as in M8, but with a larger fragment of the chant. Text (source: partly Psalm 21:12; the verses 5 and 6 of this psalm are paraphrased in the triplum text while other verses seem to have influenced the imagery of both the upper voice texts):

Circumdederunt me viri mendaces,	Lying men have surrounded me,
sine causa flagellis ceciderunt me;	without cause they have struck me with scourges;
sed tu, Domine defensor, vindica me.	but You, Lord my defender, avenge me.
V. Quoniam *tribulatio proxima est,*	*V.* For tribulation is very near
et non est qui adjuvet.	and there is no one to help.

MS *A* has only the word *proxima* while another hand added the word *tribula[tio]* at the bottom of the page where the introitus and first talea of the tenor are notated; the word is cut off by the trimming of the folio. The complete text appears in the other MSS.

Quotations

In the triplum text ll. 11-14 recall Ps. 21:5-6; in the motetus text the beasts of ll. 16-18 probably are a reference to Habakkuk 1:8 and 14.

Text structure

Triplum	a8a8b4a8a8b4	b8b8c4b8b8c4	c8c8d4c8c8d4	d8d8e4d8d8e4
	e8e8f4e8e8f4	f8f8g4f8f8g4	a: -ies; b: -ita; c: -erant; d: -ortis; e: -egas;	
			f: -ator; g: -ace	

Motetus   8 aa bb cc dd ee ff gg hh ii jj kjk   a: -itus; b: -era; c: -ficit; d: -ia; e: -itas; f: -amus; g: -ici; h: -ones; i: -ile; j: -uli; k: -acem

Tenor structure

After an introitus of the triplum, which is joined by the motetus after 24 imperfect breves, and by tenor and contratenor after 38 breves: two colores of 40 notes, each divided by four taleae, the second color in diminution to one-half. The contratenor melody has 48 notes, also divided by four taleae; in diminution its melody is repeated but the last two notes (which formed a transition) are omitted. Length of the introitus: 50 imperfect breves; length of the talea: 30 imperfect breves, diminished to 15 imperfect breves. Length of the motet: 230 imperfect breves.

Mensuration

The introitus is measured in imperfect maximodus and modus as indicated by the rest signs (groups of paired imperfect longa rests) and one bar of perfect maximodus before the entry of the the lower voices; the same with imperfect tempus, major prolatio for the upper voices. In the main body of the work perfect maximodus, imperfect modus for the tenor, diminished to perfect modus, imperfect tempus. The contratenor's mensuration is confusing: the notation of the "perfect" longa rests in all the MSS (always as a brevis rest plus imperfect longa rest and, in diminution,the same in twice smaller values) suggests imperfect modus (imperfect tempus in diminution) like the tenor,[4] but the dots of perfection cause alterations that can only take place in perfect modus. The actual result, then, is imperfect maximodus, perfect modus, diminished to imperfect modus, perfect tempus, the reverse (or complement) of the tenor's mensuration; the transcription is according to this mensuration but with exact transcription of the notation of the rests. The upper voices are measured in imperfect modus, imperfect tempus, major prolatio.

It is not clear why Machaut should have notated the contratenor in such a complex and laborious way; he apparently wanted to suggest imperfect modus. Could it be a playful allusion to the tenor words: "trouble is very near and there is no one to help"? Or could the combination of words "est et non est" ("it is and is not") have triggered it? Neither Ludwig nor Schrade made any remark about this. Nor is it clear why the introitus is measured in imperfect maximodus (in all the voices) whereas the tenor taleae have perfect maximodus.

Variants and errors not marked in the score

Notation of the introitus: *B* and *E* have for tenor and contratenor each 18 imperfect longa rests (grouped in nine pairs) instead of 19; *E* has for the motetus three pairs of imperfect longa rests, one pair of perfect longa rests and two pairs of imperfect longa rests: one longa worth too much; probably the perfect rests were a scribal accident. The other MSS notate the imperfect longa rests in tenor and contratenor as eight pairs plus one group of three (= bb. 33-38), those of the motetus as six pairs.

Bar	Voice	MS	
1	Tr, Mo	*A G*	no text, and only in *A* the indication Introitus. *Vg*, *B* and *E* give the first syllable of both texts which serves to vocalize the introitus.
26	Tr	*E*	the dot is missing.
29	Tr	*B E*	the first note (semibrevis) is a minima.
37-40	Tr	*Vg B E*	the longae are written as a binaria.
43-50	Tr	*Vg B E*	a binaria followed by a longa in *Vg*, a ternaria of longae in *B* and *E*; the final longa should have been a maxima, as in the other voices.
50	Tr, Mo	*A*	(superfluous) perfect longa rest at the end of both introits, perhaps meant as (incomplete) *finis* strokes.
51-56	T	*G Vg B*	no ligature.
51-54	Ct	*G Vg B E*	no ligature between the first two notes.

---

[4] The same notation for the rests of three breves is used in the upper voices of M5.

65	Tr	*A*	the second note (minima g) is aa only in *A*; g seems more plausible.
69-72	T	*E*	binaria.
73-76	T	*E*	binaria.
75	Tr	*B*	the last note (minima aa) seems almost bb (not taken over in *E*).
73-80	T	*A*	the note b is halved by the trimming of the folio; the following bars (until b. 81) are missing.
81-86	T	*E*	binaria.
81-86	Ct	*Vg B E*	up-stemmed longa in *Vg* and *B*.
83	Tr	*A E*	longa in *E*; all the other MSS have this curious ascending plica followed by a lower note; its right tail is half erased in *A*.
91-94	T	*E*	binaria.
93-98	Ct	*G Vg B*	no ligature.
94	Tr	*B*	traces of erasure of a mi-sign.
95	T	*A*	vague fa-sign at the beginning of the staff.
96	Ct	*E*	the dot is missing.
97-100	T	*E*	binaria.
99-102	T	*G Vg B E*	no ligature.
103-06	T	*E*	binaria.
1050-8	Mo	*Vg B*	no ligature.
196	Tr	*B*	the fourth note (semibrevis f) seems almost g (not taken over in *E*).
107	Mo	*Vg B*	up-stemmed longa.
111	Tr	*A*	signs of erasure, perhaps of plica tails. Some signs of erasure of a rest also appear a little further on.
111-4	T	*E*	binaria.
114	Tr	*G*	the mi-sign stands before g; the f to which it belongs is on the next staff.
116	Ct	*G*	an a instead of G. Schrade noted this, incorrectly, also for *A*.
119-20	Tr	*B E*	the semibrevis g is changed into two minima rests and a minima b; the rest of bb. 119 and 120 is missing in both MSS.
121-24	T	*E*	binaria.
123	T	*Vg B*	up-stemmed longa.
127	T	*Vg* B	up-stemmed longa.
127-30	T	*E*	binaria.
131-32	Tr, Mo	*A G Vg B*	the plica in Tr could also be an up-stemmed longa, but in Mo it is a clear plica longa. No plicae in *G*; up-stemmed longae in *Vg* and *B*.
131-34	T	*E*	binaria.
137	Mo	*Vg B*	up-stemmed longa.
141	Tr	*B E*	the longa rest is missing.
141-46	T	*Vg B E*	binaria.
147	T	*A*	the scribe apparently forgot the rest; another hand put it above b.
155-56	Mo	*B E*	the last note of b. 155 and the first of b. 156 are g f.
156-59	T	*E*	binaria.
160	Tr	*E*	the last note (minima f) is a semibrevis.
161	Mo	*Vg B*	up-stemmed longa.
163-6	T	*E*	binaria.
167	Mo	*Vg B*	up-stemmed longa.
168-69	Ct	*Vg B E*	binaria.
171	Mo	*B E*	a semibrevis rest is inserted after the c.
171	Ct	*G*	instead of the note c which is omitted, the MS has a semibrevis rest at its place.
173	Tr	*B E*	the semibrevis rest is missing.
178	Ct	*E*	the dot is missing.
180	Tr	*A*	the first note was a minima; the stem has been erased.

181	Tr	*B E*	the first note (semibrevis) is a minima.
184	T	*A*	two longa rests instead of one.
186	T	*Vg*	the downward stem of the binaria was erased.
199	Tr	*Vg*	erroneous dot after the second semibrevis.
199	Mo		Schrade emended the second and third note to g and f, which is incorrect.
200	Mo	*E*	the second note (semibrevis) is a minima.
204	T	*E*	a instead of g.
205	Mo	*A*	the stem of the minima c is hardly visible; the mimima rests are right above the note.
207-09	Ct	*A E*	the note D is halved and the note a has disappeared by the trimming of the folio. Binaria in *E*.
*209	Mo	*A G*	emendation: the semibrevis is e; the other MSS have d which seems preferable.
216-18	T	*E*	no ligature.
225-30	T	*A*	the g is halved, the rest of the tenor notes have disappeared by the trimming of the page.
228	Tr, Mo	*G Vg B*	the final longa is drawn as a maxima, in *Vg* and *B* only in the triplum.

Literature

Editions of text: Chichmaref, *Poésies lyriques*, pp. 526-28; Robertson, *Machaut and Reims*, pp. 326-28.

Editions of music: Ludwig, *Werke* III, pp. 73-78; Schrade, *Works*, pp. 69-77; Leech-Wilkinson, *Compositional Techniques* II, pp. 67-70.

Tenor sources: Clark, "Concordare cum materia," pp. 199, 242-43.

Discussions/interpretations (texts only): Yudkin, *Music in Medieval Europe*, pp. 476-82; Robertson, *Machaut and Reims*, pp. 192-206; Clark, "Machaut Reading Machaut"; Earp, "Interpreting the deluxe manuscript," p. 236.

Analytical studies (text- and text/musical structure): Machabey, *Guillaume de Machault* 2, pp. 104-7; Reichert, "Das Verhältnis," pp. 201, 203, 206, ex. 7; Günther, "The 14th-Century Motet," pp. 33-34; Sanders, "The Medieval Motet," p. 565; Wernli, "La percettibilità," pp. 23-24; Ziino, "Isoritmia musicale," pp. 440, 448; Leech-Wilkinson, *Compositional Techniques* I, pp. 108-13, 138-41; Lavacek, "Contrapuntal Confrontation," pp. 174-79; Zayaruznaya, "Hockets as Compositional and Scribal Practice," pp. 494-95.

Analytical studies (musical structure, counterpoint): Kühn, *Die Harmonik*, pp. 93-97; Leech-Wilkinson, "Related Motets," pp. 3-4; id., *Compositional Techniques* I, pp. 114-18, 124-26; Clark, "Concordare cum materia," pp. 61-62.

See also Earp, *Guillaume de Machaut*, pp. 298-99.

M22 *Tu qui gregem tuum ducis / Plange, regni res publica / Apprehenda arma et scutum et exurge / Ct*

Musical concordances

Vg fols 281v-282r   *B* fols 279v-280r   *G* fols 123v-124r   *E* fol. 145r

Tenor source

Verse of the responsory *Posuit coronam capiti meo* for the Common of One Martyr (*Commune unius martyris*; *CAO* IV:7415). Text (paraphrase of Ps. 20:4 and Isaiah 61:10; for the verse text Ps. 34:1-2):

Posuit coronam capiti meo,	He has set a crown upon my head,
et circumdedit me vestimento salutis,	and has surrounded me with the garment of salvation,
ad expugnandas gentes et omnes inimicos.	to overthrow peoples and all enemies.
V. Judica, Domine, nocentes me,	*V*. Judge thou, O Lord, them that wrong me:
expugna impugnantes me;	overthrow them that fight against me;
apprehende arma et scutum et exurge	take hold of arms and shield
in adiutorium mihi.	and rise up to help me.

Text structure

Triplum	8 aa bb cc dd ee ff gg hh ii jj	a: -ducis; b: -duci; c: -io; d: -ire; e: -iter; f: --uce;
		g: -ucem; h: -ducitur; i: -ores; j: -ducas

Motetus	a8a8b4a8a8b4 b8b8c4b8b8c4	a: -ica; b: -atur; c: -enter; d: -ari
	c8c8d4c8c8d4	

Tenor structure

After an introitus of the motetus, joined by the triplum after 12 breves: two colores of 24 notes, together divided by three taleae, and followed by a partial third color of 11 notes. This third color is, however, not notated, but only indicated in *A* and *G* by a partial text repeat; the other MSS do not even provide this clue. The contratenor melody is not repeated but differs for colores 1 and 2; only in combination with the third color the contratenor melody must also be partially repeated (like the tenor melody it is not notated). Length of the introitus: 24 imperfect breves; of the talea: 36 imperfect breves; of the additional partial talea 24 breves. Color 1 and 2 measure 54 breves each, color 3 24 breves. Thus, the introitus of 24 breves and the shortened third color surround the two complete colores in a symmetrical structure. Length of the motet: 156 imperfect breves.

Mensuration

Perfect modus, imperfect tempus for tenor and contratenor, the same, with major prolatio for the upper voices. *G*, *Vg*, *B* and *E* have dots of division in most (but not all) of the syncopated passages of the motetus (the first is in bb. 39-43, with the dot after the semibrevis in b. 41); it might suggest that these passages were thought of by the scribes as being read in perfect tempus (in which the dots would prevent alteration), but they are not necessary, and *A* has the dots nowhere.

Variants and errors not marked in the score

Bar	Voice	MS	
13-18	Tr	*E*	binaria instead of single longae.
15	Mo	*G*	an interesting difference between *G* and the other MSS: only *G* splits the word *regni* as *reg-ni*; the other MSS follow the French pronunciation: *re-gni*.
29	Ct	*A*	the same hand as in the additions to M21 drew a round b here instead of the usual fa-sign.
32-42	Ct	*E*	the whole passage is a third too low.
42	Tr	*E*	the second pair of minima rests is missing.
44	Tr	*Vg*	dot after the last note (semibrevis d).
45-46	Mo	*G Vg B E*	binaria and a single brevis instead of ternaria.
47	Mo	*B E*	the three minimae are g f g (instead of aa g aa).
55	Mo	*B*	signs of erasure between the brevis b and the semibrevis d.
56	Tr	*A*	the semibrevis could be c as well as d (Ludwig and Schrade transcribed c); since all the other MSS have d, this seems the best reading.
56-57	T	*A*	the note looks like a G; possibly caused by a difficulty in drawing the ligature properly.
57	Mo	*A G*	the two semibreves were minimae in *A* but the stems have been erased; the last note (semibrevis c) is a minima in *G*.
59-60	Mo	*B*	brevis rest instead of longa rest.
60	Tr	*A*	the second note (minima d) is e in all the other MSS.
65	Ct	*G E*	the note f♯ is not part of the ligature.
66	Tr	*B*	the second note (semibrevis aa) is a minima.
67	Tr	*B E*	the last note (semibrevis aa) is a minima.
68	Tr	*B E*	g g f e instead of g f e d.
78	Tr	*E*	the first note (should be a minima b) is an a; in *B* it looks indeed like an a.

79	Tr	*B E*	dot after the first note and omission of the two minima rests (Schrade suggested it could be a different version).
82	Tr	*B*	dot above the brevis.
82	Mo	*B*	the brevis was at first a semibrevis.
92	T	*G*	the second note is D.
97	T	*E*	the note G forms part of a quaternaria with the three preceding notes.
101-02	T	*A*	like in bb. 56-57, the note looks like G; possibly caused by the difficulty of drawing the ligature properly.
107	Mo	*G Vg B E*	the brevis rest is missing.
116	Tr	*B*	the semibrevis b was corrected to an a.
*117	Tr	*A*	the last minima b is a; since b seems more correct it has been emended.
127	Tr	*Vg*	the last note (minima d) is a semibrevis.
127	Mo	*Vg B*	the semibrevis is an a.
128	Tr	*E*	the minima rest is missing; thus, the last semibrevis would become perfect.
131	Tr	*E*	brevis rest after the first note.
138	Tr	*B*	the first note was a minima; the stem is crossed through.
146	Tr	*G*	the stem of the last note (minima c) is (almost) invisible.
*148	Tr	*A*	emendation; only in this MS the two minimae are bb's; in all the other MSS they are cc's which contrapuntally also seems more probable.
150-51	Mo	*A*	the brevis a looks as if it had been a plica of which the tails were erased.
151	Tr	*G*	the semibrevis was g, but the lower half of the note was erased so that it is now aa.
153	Tr	*B*	the last note (semibrevis e) was a minima; the stem is visibly erased.

Literature

Editions of text: Chichmaref, *Poésies lyriques*, pp. 529-30; Robertson, *Machaut and Reims*, pp. 328-29.

Editions of music: Ludwig, *Werke* III, pp. 79-81; Schrade, *Works*, pp. 78-81; Kühn, "Guillaume de Machaut, Motette Nr. 22"; Leech-Wilkinson, *Compositional Techniques* II, pp. 71-73.

Tenor sources: Clark, "Concordare cum materia," pp. 200, 248-49.

Discussions/interpretations (texts only): Clarkson,"On the Nature," p. 222; Markstrom, "Machaut and the Wild Beast," p. 35; Clark, "Concordare cum materia," pp. 78-81; Robertson, *Machaut and Reims*, pp. 206-15.

Analytical studies (text- and text/musical structure): Machabey, *Guillaume de Machault* 2, pp. 107-8; Reichert, "Das Verhältnis," pp. 201; Wernli, "La percettibilità," pp. 21-23; Ziino, "Isoritmia musicale," pp. 440, 443-44; Leech-Wilkinson, *Compositional Techniques* I, p. 120n31; Zayaruznaya, "Hockets as Compositional and Scribal Practice," pp. 494-95.

Analytical studies (musical structure, counterpoint): Gombosi, "Machaut's *Messe*," p. 222; Pelinski, "Zusammenhang und Aufbau," p. 70; Kühn, *Die Harmonik*, pp. 91-92, 138-44; id., "Guillaume de Machaut, Motette Nr. 22;" Leech-Wilkinson, "Related Motets," pp. 3-4; id., *Compositional Techniques* I, pp. 119-28, 138-41; Finscher, "Arten der Motette," pp. 285-86; Clark, "Concordare cum materia," p. 64.

Analysis and interpretation of text/music relationship: Busse-Berger, *Medieval Music*, pp. 212-13; Fiala, "Le prince au miroir des musiques," pp. 15-29.

See also Earp, *Guillaume de Machaut*, pp. 383-84.

M23 *Felix virgo, mater Christi / Inviolata genitrix / Ad te suspiramus gementes et flentes / Ct*

Musical concordances:

Vg fols 282v-283r *B* fols 280v-281r *G* fols 124v-125r *Trem* fol. 32 (? index only, with the text *Inviolant*))

Tenor source

The Marian antiphon *Salve regina*. Text:

Salve, regina mater misericordiae:	Hail, queen, mother of mercy;
Vita, dulcedo, et spes nostra, salve.	life, sweetness and our hope, hail.
Ad te clamamus, exsules, filii Hevae.	To you we cry, exiles, sons of Eve.
Ad te suspiramus, gementes et flentes	To you we sigh, groaning and weeping
in hac lacrimarum valle.	in this vale of tears.
Eya ergo, advocata nostra,	Well then, you, our advocate,
illos tuos misericordes oculos ad nos converte.	Turn your merciful eyes toward us.
Et Jesum, benedictum fructum ventris tui,	And after this exile show us Jesus,
nobis post hoc exsilium ostende.	the blessed fruit of thy womb.
O clemens, o pia, o dulcis Virgo Maria.	O clement, o pious, o sweet Virgin Mary.

Text structure

Triplum	a8a8a8b4a8a8a8b4 b8b8b8c4b8b8b8c4 c8c8c8d4c8c8c8d4	a: -isti; b: -ima;
	d8d8d8e4d8d8d8e4	c: -imur; d: -utis; e: -io
Motetus	a8a8b4a8a8b4 b8b8c4b8b8c4 c8c8d4c8c8d4	a: -trix; b: -aris;
	d8d8e4d8d8e4	c: iter; d: -imus; e: -ere

Tenor structure

After an introitus of the triplum, joined by the motetus after 10 breves and by tenor and contratenor after 24 breves: two colores of 48 notes, each divided by three taleae, the second color diminished to one-half. Length of the introitus: 42 imperfect breves, of the talea: 36 imperfect breves, in diminution 18 imperfect breves. Color 1 measures 108 breves, color 2 54 breves. Length of the motet: 204 imperfect breves.

This is the only motet in *A* where a page-turn is needed; the diminution section is written on the next verso for all the voices, clearly with respect to the performance situation.

Mensuration

In the introitus perfect modus, imperfect tempus for tenor and contratenor, imperfect modus, imperfect tempus with major prolatio for the upper voices; both mensurations are indicated by the different longa rest-strokes in motetus, tenor and contratenor. Two perfect longae (bb. 31-33 and 40-42) form exceptional perfections in the upper voices. In the main part: perfect modus, imperfect tempus in the tenor versus imperfect modus, imperfect tempus in the contratenor, the contrast being indicated by red coloration for the imperfect modus; halfway through each talea the voices exchange mensuration and coloration. In diminution this becomes perfect versus imperfect tempus with the same regular exchange. The canon *Nigre sunt perfecte et rubee imperfecte* appears in all four manuscripts. Contrary to M5 where *B* used white notation with the remark *rouge clef*, it here has the normal contrast of black and red color. The upper voices have imperfect modus, imperfect tempus, major prolatio.

Variants and errors not marked in the score

Bar	Voice	MS	
1	Mo	*G B*	the five imperfect longa rest-strokes are notated correctly in *A* and *Vg*; *G* has four perfect longa rests, followed by one imperfect longa rest (or an incompletely drawn perfect longa rest); *B* has six imperfect longa rests.
10	Tr	*G*	the last note (minima) is a semibrevis.
11	Tr	*G*	mi-sign on the previous staff.
22	Tr	*B*	the last note (d) is a brevis.

28-33	Ct	*G Vg B*	no ligature.
31	Tr	*G B*	the mi-sign is very vague in *G* but visible (cf. Leech-Wilkinson, *Compositional Techniques* I, p. 247 who notes that it is absent). No dot in *B*.
38	Ct	*G*	Ludwig notes that the penultimate note is too low in all the MSS, but this is only slightly the case in *G*.
40-42	Tr, Mo	all	no MS has the dots of perfection needed for the longae to correspond with the perfect longae of tenor and contratenor.
43	Tr	*Vg B*	left-tailed brevis.
53-58	Mo	*G*	after the semibrevis g in b. 53 the whole passage is a third too high.
64	Tr	*B*	a longa stem was incompletely erased.
66	Mo	*A*	erroneous dot (or a blot?).
75	Tr	*G*	Schrade noted that the last note is a semibrevis in *G* but he misread it; it correctly is a minima.
101-02	Tr	*G*	the rest stroke is drawn very long, through almost three spaces.
103	Mo	*B*	the stem of the longa is very short; it seems almost a brevis.
110-14	T	*A*	clear signs of erasure within the ligature which at first was a quinaria; after the scribe had noticed that there was one note too much and had erased it, he forgot to restore the connection between d and f; as a result the f in b. 111 is now a longa, not a brevis as it should be. The other MSS have a quaternaria.
123*	Tr	all	all the MSS have *virgo*. Nevertheless I follow Ludwig and Schrade in this emendation since the genitive *servitutis* must depend on something while *subicimur* takes no genitive. The word *jugo* has in this script but one leg less and in the context of this motet a scribal mistake to *virgo* would easily be made. Especially in *G* it is visible how close they are.
127	Tr	*B*	left-tailed brevis (but plica in *Vg*).
142	Mo	*G*	plica longa instead of brevis.
149	Ct	all	the second brevis is not followed by a longa and could thus, strictly speaking, not be altered. However, the rhythmic identity with the other taleae appears to overrule this.
151	Tr	all	in all four MSS the text *Gracie* begins only at *c.* b. 154, which seems strange; perhaps the exemplar was unclear. Performers may prefer to put the syllable *Gra-* at the beginning of the diminution section (b. 151).
154	Mo	*B*	the semibrevis d is replaced by a semibrevis rest.
159	T	*B*	the second note of the binaria (g) is a.
173-74	Tr	*G*	from the second semibrevis (f) in b. 173 on, in *G* the passage is a third lower than the other MSS, which is equally well possible; this was taken over by Ludwig who notes that in *A* it is a third too high. Interestingly, *Vg* apparently had at first the same version but corrected it; the signs of erasure and correction are clearly visible.
185	Ct	*A*	the first note of the binaria (semibrevis a) looks like g.
193	T	*A*	the dot is missing.
199	Tr	*G Vg B*	the first minima (d) is e.
204	Tr	*Vg B*	abundantly ornamented nota finalis.

Literature

Editions of text: Chichmaref, *Poésies lyriques*, pp. 531-33; Robertson, *Machaut and Reims*, pp. 329-31.

Editions of music: Wolf, *Geschichte* 2, pp. 24-27 (diplomatic transcription); id., *Geschichte* 3, pp. 41-49; Ludwig, *Werke* III, pp. 82-86; Schrade, *Works*, pp. 82-89; Leech-Wilkinson, *Compositional Techniques* II, pp. 74-76.

Tenor sources: Clark, "Concordare cum materia," pp. 201, 249.

Discussions/interpretations (texts only): Cerquiglini, "Un engin si soutil," pp. 81-82; Brownlee, "Machaut's Motet 15," p. 14; Robertson, *Machaut and Reims*, pp. 215-21.

Analytical studies (text- and text/musical structure): Machabey, *Guillaume de Machault* 2, pp. 108-11 Reichert, "Das Verhältnis," pp. 201, 206; Günther, "The 14th-Century Motet," pp. 33-34; Hoppin, "Notational Licences," p. 25; Bank, *Tactus, Tempo*, pp. 41, 43; Reaney, *Guillaume de Machaut*, p. 58; Clarkson, "On the Nature," pp. 214-15; Ziino, "Isoritmia musicale," pp. 441, 443, 445; Hoppin, *Medieval Music*, pp. 413-14; Leech-Wilkinson, *Compositional Techniques* I, pp. 131-34; ib. II, p. 24 ex. 38;; Koehler, *Pythagoreisch-platonische Proportionen*, pp. 102-5; Zayaruznaya, "Hockets as Compositional and Scribal Practice," pp. 494-95.

Analytical studies (musical structure, counterpoint): Gombosi, "Machaut's *Messe*," p. 222; Leech-Wilkinson, "Related Motets," pp. 3-4; id., *Compositional Techniques* I, pp. 129-37, 138-41; Cross, "Chromatic Alteration," pp. 230-31, 266-67, 271.

See also Earp, *Guillaume de Machaut*, pp. 320-21.

 # BIBLIOGRAPHY

EDITIONS OF MACHAUT'S WORKS

Musical Works

The Ferrell-Vogüé Machaut Manuscript. Volume I: *Introductory Study* by Lawrence Earp, with Domenic Leo and Carla Shapreau. Volume II: *Facsimile*. Oxford: Digital Image Archive of Medieval Music, 2014 (DIAMM facsimiles).

Complete Editions

Ludwig, Friedrich, ed. *Guillaume de Machaut, Musikalische Werke. Erster Band: Balladen, Rondeaux und Virelais*. Publikationen älterer Musik 1/1. Leipzig: Breitkopf & Härtel, 1926; *Zweiter Band: Einleitung*. Leipzig: Breitkopf & Härtel, 1928; *Dritter Band: Motetten*. Publikationen älterer Musik 4/2. Leipzig: Breitkopf & Härtel, 1929; *Vierter Band: Messe und Lais*. Ed. Heinrich Besseler. Leipzig: Breitkopf & Härtel, 1943. Rpt. of Band I-IV: Leipzig: Breitkopf & Härtel, 1954.

Schrade, Leo, ed. *The Works of Guillaume de Machaut*. Polyphonic Music of the Fourteenth Century, Vols II & III. Monaco: L'Oiseau-Lyre, 1956. Rpt. in 5 vols, 1977.

———. *Commentary to the Volumes II & III*. (PMFC). Monaco: L'Oiseau-Lyre, 1956.

Editions of the Messe de Nostre Dame

Chailley, Jacques, ed. *Guillaume de Machaut (1300-1377): Messe Nostre Dame dite du Sacre de Charles V (1364) à 4 voix égales*. Paris: Rouart & Lerolle, 1948.

Cross, Lucy, ed. *Machaut: Messe de Nostre Dame*. New York [etc.]: Peters, 1998.

De Van, Guillaume, ed. *Guglielmi de Mascaudio: Opera I, La Messe de Nostre Dame*. Corpus Mensurabilis Musicae 2. Rome: American Institute of Musicology, 1949.

Leech-Wilkinson, Daniel, ed. *Guillaume de Machaut: La Messe de Nostre Dame*. Oxford Choral Music. Oxford: Clarendon, 1990.

Machabey, Armand, ed. *Messe Nostre Dame à quatre voix de Guillaume de Machault (130?–1377) transcrite en notation moderne*. Liège: Aelberts, 1948.

Pérès, Marcel, ed. *Guillaume de Machaut: La Messe*. Moissac: Editio Scriptorium CIRMA, 2005. [Diplomatic transcription from MS *A*.]

Stevens, Dennis. *Guillaume de Machaut: La Messe de Nostre Dame*. London: Oxford University Press, 1973.

Literary Works

Bétemps, Isabelle, ed. and trans. *Guillaume de Machaut: Quatre dits*. Traductions des classiques du Moyen Âge 82. Paris: Champion, 2008.

Cerquiglini-Toulet, ed. and trans. *Guillaume de Machaut: La Fontaine amoureuse*. Moyen Age. Paris: Stock, 1993.

Chichmaref, Vladimir, ed. *Guillaume de Machaut: Poésies lyriques*. Édition complète en deux parties. Paris: Champion, 1909. Rpt. Genève: Slatkine, 1973.

Gaudet, Minnette and Constance B. Hieatt, trans. *Guillaume de Machaut: The Tale of the Alerion*. Toronto [etc.]: University of Toronto Press, 1994.

Hoepffner, Ernest, ed. *Œuvres de Guillaume de Machaut*. Société des Anciens Textes Français 57. 3 vols. Paris: Firmin-Didot, 1908–1911, Champion, 1921. Rpt. New York: Johnson, 1965.

Imbs, Paul and Jacqueline Cerquiglini-Toulet, eds and rev. *Guillaume de Machaut: Le Livre du Voir Dit*. Lettres gothiques. Paris: Librairie Générale Française, 1999.

Leech-Wilkinson, Daniel, ed. and R. Barton Palmer, trans. *Guillaume de Machaut: Le Livre dou Voir Dit (The Book of the True Poem)*. New York: Garland Publishing, 1998.

Mas Latrie, M. Louis de, ed. *La Prise d'Alexandrie; ou, Chronique du roi Pierre Ier de Lusignan, par Guillaume de Machaut*. Publications de la Société de l'Orient latin, série historique 1. Genève: Fick, 1877. Rpt. Osnabrück: Zeller, 1968.

Palmer, R. Barton, ed. and trans. *Guillaume de Machaut: The Judgment of the King of Bohemia (Le Jugement dou Roy de Behaingne)*. New York: Garland Publishing, 1984.

———, ed. and trans. *Guillaume de Machaut: The Judgment of the King of Navarre*. New York: Garland Publishing, 1988.

———, ed. and trans. *Guillaume de Machaut: Le Confort d'ami (Comfort for a Friend)*. New York: Garland Publishing, 1992.

———, ed. and trans. *Guillaume de Machaut: The Fountain of Love (La Fonteinne Amoureuse) and Two Other Love Vision Poems*. New York: Garland, 1993.

———, ed. and trans. *Guillaume de Machaut: La Prise d'Alixandre (The Taking of Alexandria)*. New York: Routledge, 2002.

———, ed. and trans. *Guillaume de Machaut, The Complete Poetry and Music, Volume 1: The Debate Poems*. Kalamazoo: Medieval Text Publications, 2016.

Paris, Paulin, ed. *Le Livre du Voir-Dit de Guillaume de Machaut, [...] publié sur trois manuscrits du XIVe siècle*. Paris: Société des Bibliophiles François, 1875. Rpt. Genève: Slatkine, 1969.

Shirley, Janet, ed. and Peter W. Edbury, trans. *Guillaume de Machaut, The Capture of Alexandria*. Burlington, VT: Ashgate, 2001.

Wilkins, Nigel, ed. *La Louange des Dames, by Guillaume de Machaut*. Edinburgh: Scottish Academic Press, 1972.

Wimsatt, James I. *The Marguerite Poetry of Guillaume de Machaut*. Chapel Hill, NC: University of North Carolina Press, 1970.

Wimsatt, James I., William W. Kibler and Rebecca A. Baltzer, eds. *Guillaume de Machaut: Le Jugement du roy de Behaigne* and *Remede de Fortune*. The Chaucer Library. Athens and London: University of Georgia Press, 1988.

Young, Karl, ed. "The *Dit de la Harpe* of Guillaume de Machaut." In *Essays in Honor of Albert Feuillerat*. Ed. Henri M. Peyre. New Haven, CT: Yale University Press, 1943. Pp. 1–20.

CITED STUDIES AND EDITIONS

Alanus ab Insulis. "Alan of Lille, «De Planctu naturae»." Ed. Nikolaus M. Häring. In *Studi medievali*, serie terza, 19 (1978), 797–879. Trans. in James J. Sheridan, *Alan of Lille, The Plaint of Nature*. Toronto: Pontifical Institute of Mediaeval Studies, 1980.

Allorto, Riccardo, ed. *Antologia storica della musica (dai Greci al Rinascimento)*. Milan: Ricordi, 1983.

Anderson, Gordon A. "Responsory Chants in the Tenors of Some Fourteenth-Century Continental Motets." *Journal of the American Musicological Society* 29 (1976), 19–27.

Apel, Willi. *The Notation of Polyphonic Music*. Cambridge, MA: The Mediaeval Academy of America, fifth rev. edn, 1961.

———. "Remarks about the Isorhythmic Motet." In *Les colloques de Wégimont. II. 1955. L'Ars Nova: Recueil d'études sur la musique du XIVe siècle*. Bibliothèque de la Faculté de Philosophie et Lettres de l'Université de Liège 149. Paris: Les belles Lettres, 1959. Pp.139–44.

———. "The Development of French Secular Music During the Fourteenth Century." *Musica Disciplina* 27 (1973), 41–59.

Apfel, Ernst. *Beiträge zu einer Geschichte der Satztechnik von der frühen Motette bis Bach*. 2 vols. Munich: Fink, 1964–1965.

Atchison, Mary, ed. *The Chansonnier of Oxford Bodleian MS Douce 308: Essays and Complete Edition of Texts*. Aldershot and Burlington, VT: Ashgate, 2005.

Aubry, Pierre, ed. *Le chansonnier de l'Arsenal: Réproduction phototypique du manuscrit 5198 de la bibliothèque de l'Arsenal*. Trouvères du XIIe-XIIIe siècle. Paris: Geuthner, 1909–1910.

Aubry, Pierre and A. Gastoué. *Recherches sur les 'ténors' français du treizième siècle*. Paris: Champion, 1907.

Avril, François. *Manuscript Painting at the Court of France: The Fourteenth Century (1310–1380)*. Trans. Ursula Molinaro and Bruce Benderson. New York: George Braziller, 1978.

———."Les manuscrits enluminés de Guillaume de Machaut." In *Guillaume de Machaut, Poète et compositeur*. Pp. 117–33.

Bain, Jennifer. "Theorizing the Cadence in the Music of Machaut." *Journal of Music Theory* 47 (2003), 325–62.

———."Tonal Structure and the Melodic Role of Chromatic Inflections in the Music of Machaut." *Plainsong and Medieval Music* 14 (2005), 59–88.

Bank, Joannes Antonius. *Tactus, Tempo and Notation in Mensural Music from the 13th to the 17th Century*. Amsterdam: Annie Bank, 1972.

Bent, Margaret. "Musica recta and musica ficta." *Musica Disciplina* 26 (1972), 73–100.

———. "The Machaut Manuscripts Vg, B and E." *Musica Disciplina* 37 (1983), 83–112.

———. "A Note on the Dating of the Trémoïlle Manuscript." In *Beyond the Moon. Festschrift Luther Dittmer*. Ed. Bryan Gillingham and Paul Merkley. Ottawa: Institute of Medieval Music, 1990. Pp. 217–42.

———. "Deception, Exegesis and Sounding Number in Machaut's Motet 15." *Early Music History* 10 (1991), 15–27.

———. "The Late-Medieval Motet." In *Companion to Medieval & Renaissance Music*. Ed. Tess Knighton and David Fallows. London: Dent, 1992. Pp. 114–19.

———. "Editing Early Music: The Dilemma of Translation." *Early Music* 12 (1994), 373–92.

———. "The Grammar of Early Music: Preconditions for Analysis." In *Tonal Structures*. Ed. Cristle Collins Judd. New York and London: Garland, 1998. Pp. 15–59.

———. "Words and Music in Machaut's Motet 9." *Early Music* 31 (2003), 363–88.

———. "What is Isorhythm?" In *Quomodo cantabimus canticum? Studies in Honor of Edward H. Roesner*. Ed. David Cannata [et al.]. Middleton, WI: American Institute of Musicology, 2008. Pp. 121–43.

———. *Magister Jacobus de Ispania, Author of the Speculum musicae*. Farnham: Ashgate, 2015.

Bent, Margaret and Andrew Wathey, eds. *Fauvel Studies: Allegory, Chronicle, and Image in Paris, Bibliothèque Nationale de France, MS Français 146*. Oxford: Oxford University Press, 1998.

Berger, Karol. "Musica ficta." In *Performance Practice. Music before 1600*. Ed. Howard Mayer Brown and Stanley Sadie. London: Macmillan, 1989. Pp. 107–25.

Besseler, Heinrich. "Studien zur Musik des Mittelalters. I. Neue Quellen des 14. und beginnenden 15. Jahrhunderts." *Archiv für Musikwissenschaft* 7 (1925), 167–252.

———."Studien zur Musik des Mittelalters. II. Die Motette von Franko von Köln bis Philipp von Vitry." *Archiv für Musikwissenschaft* 8 (1926), 137–258.

Bétemps, Isabelle. *L'Imaginaire dans l'œuvre de Guillaume de Machaut*. Bibliothèque du XVe siècle 59. Paris: Champion, 1998.

Boer, Cornelis de. "Guillaume de Machaut et *l'Ovide moralisé*." *Romania* 43 (1914), 335–52.

Boer, Cornelis de, ed. *L'Ovide moralisé*. Verhandelingen der koninklijke Akademie van Wetenschappen te Amsterdam. Afdeeling Letterkunde, nos 15, 21, 30.3, 37, 43. Amsterdam: Müller [etc.], 1915–1938. 5 vols.

Boethius. *Anicius Manlius Severinus Boethius, Philosophiae Consolationis libri quinque*. Ed. Karl Büchner. Heidelberg: Carl Winter Universitätsverlag, 3rd edn, 1977.

———. *Boethius, The Theological Tractates, De consolatione philosophiae*. Trans. H. F. Stewart, E. K. Rand, and S. J. Tester. Loeb Classical Library. London-Cambridge, MA: Harvard University Press, 1918. New edn 1973, rpt. 1978.

Boogaard, Nico H. J. van den. *Rondeaux et refrains du XIIe siècle au début du XIVe. Collationnement, introduction et notes*. Paris: Klincksieck, 1969.

Boogaart, Jacques. "Love's Unstable Balance. Part I: Analogy of Ideas in Text and Music of Machaut's Motet 6. Part II: More Balance Problems and the Order of Machaut's Motets." *Muziek & Wetenschap* 3 (1993), 3–33.

———. "O series summe rata: De motetten van Guillaume de Machaut; de ordening van het corpus en de samenhang van tekst en muziek." With a Summary in English. PhD diss. Utrecht University, 2001.

———. "Encompassing Past and Present: Quotations and Their Function in Machaut's Motets." *Early Music History* 20 (2001), 1–86.

———. "Speculum Mortis: Structure and Signification in Machaut's Motet *Hé Mors/ Fine Amour/ Quare non sum mortuus* (M3)." In *Machaut's Music: New Interpretations*. Pp. 13–30.

———. "L'accomplissement du cercle: observations analytiques sur l'ordre des motets de Guillaume de Machaut." *Analyse musicale* 50 (2004), 45–63.

———. Review of Anne Walters Robertson, *Guillaume de Machaut and Reims: Context and Meaning in His Musical Works*" (Cambridge, 2002). *Early Music* 32 (2004), 603–6.

———. "Thought-Provoking Dissonances. Remarks about Machaut's Compositional Licences in Relation to His Texts." *Dutch Journal of Music Theory* 12 (2007), 273–92.

———. "Playing with the Performer in Medieval Music: Machaut's Ideas on Love and Order in *Quant vraie Amour / O series summe rata / Super omnes speciosa* (Motet 17)." *Dutch Journal of Music Theory* 14 (2009), 32–41.

———. "*Folie couvient avoir*: Citation and Transformation in Machaut's Musical Works — Gender Change and Transgression." In *Citation, Intertextuality and Memory*, 2011. Pp. 15–40.

———. "L'amant confus: interprétation du motet 2, *Tous corps / De souspirant cuer / Suspiro* de Guillaume de Machaut." In *La chanson de trouvères. Formes, registres, genres*. Ed. Marie-Geneviève Grossel. Valenciennes: Presses Universitaires de Valenciennes, 2012. Pp. 29–48.

———. Review of Elizabeth Eva Leach, *Guillaume de Machaut: Secretary, Poet, Musician* (Ithaca and London, 2011). *Music & Letters* 93/3 (2012), 397–99.

———. "The Mirror of Love and Death. Multiplicity of Voices in an Ars nova Motet." In *Liber plurium vocum, voor Rokus de Groot*. Ed. Sander van Maas [et al.]. Amsterdam: Amsterdam University Press, 2012. Pp. 62–71.

Boone, Graeme. "Marking Mensural Time." *Music Theory Spectrum* 22 (2000), 1–43.

Bourciez, Édouard et Jean. *Phonétique française: Étude historique*. Paris, Klincksieck, 1974.

Bowers, Roger. "Guillaume de Machaut and His Canonry of Reims, 1338–1377." *Early Music History* 23 (2004), 1–48.

Brandt, William [et al.], eds. *The Comprehensive Study of Music. Vol. 1, Anthology of Music from Plainsong through Gabrieli*. New York: Harper's College Press, 1980.

Brejon de la Vergnée, Marie-Edith. "Note sur la maison de Guillaume de Machaut à Reims. " In *Guillaume de Machaut, Poète et Compositeur*, 1982. Pp. 149–53 and Pl. I, II.

Brothers, Thomas. *Chromatic Beauty in the Late Medieval Chanson: An Interpretation of Manuscript Accidentals*. Cambridge: Cambridge University Press, 1997.

Brown, Thomas. "Another Mirror of Lovers? — Order, Structure and Allusion in Machaut's Motets." *Plainsong and Medieval Music* 10 (2001), 121–33.

———. "*Flos/Celsa* and Machaut's Motets: Emulation – and Error?" In *Machaut's Music: New Interpretations*, 2003. Pp. 37–52.

Brownlee, Kevin. "Machaut's Motet 15 and the *Roman de la Rose*: The Literary Context of *Amours qui a le pouoir/ Faus Samblant m'a deceü/Vidi Dominum*." *Early Music History* 10 (1991), 1–14.

———. "Textual Polyphony in Machaut's Motets 8 and 4." *Revista de musicologia* 16/3 (1993),1554–1558 (20–24).

———. "Polyphonie et intertextualité dans les motets 8 et 4 de Guillaume de Machaut." In *L'hostellerie de pensée: études sur l'art littéraire au Moyen Âge offertes à Daniel Poirion par ses anciens élèves*. Ed. Michel Zink and Danielle Bohler. Paris: Presses de l'Université de Paris-Sorbonne, 1995. Pp. 97–104.

———. "La polyphonie textuelle dans le Motet 7 de Machaut: Narcisse, la *Rose* et la voix féminine." In *Guillaume de Machaut 1300-2000*, 2000. Pp. 137–46.

———. "Fire, Desire, Duration, Death: Machaut's Motet 10." In *Citation and Authority*, 2005. Pp. 79–93.

Brunetto Latini. *Brunetto Latini, Li Livres dou Tresor*. Ed. Francis J. Carmody. Berkeley-Los Angeles, 1948, rpt. Genève: Slatkine, 1975.

Burkhart, Charles, ed. *Anthology for Music Analysis*. Fifth edn. New York: Harcourt Brace, 1994.

Busse Berger, Anna Maria. *Medieval Music and the Art of Memory*. Berkeley: University of California Press, 2005.

Butterfield, Ardis. "*Enté*: A Survey and Reassessment of the Term in Thirteenth- and Fourteenth-Century Music and Poetry." *Early Music History* 22 (2003), 67–101.

CAO See Hesbert, *Corpus Antiphonalium Officii*.

Calligraphy of Medieval Music, The. Ed. John Haines. Musicalia Medii Aevi 1. Turnhout: Brepols, 2011.

Cerquiglini [-Toulet], Jacqueline. «*Un engin si soutil*». *Guillaume de Machaut et l'écriture au XIVe siècle*. Paris: Champion, 1985.

———. "Écrire le temps: Le lyrisme de la durée au XIVe et XVe siècles." In *Le temps et la durée dans la littérature au Moyen Âge et à la Renaissance*. Actes du colloque organisé par le Centre de Recherche sur la Littérature du Moyen Âge et de la Renaissance de l'université de Reims (1984). Ed. Yvonne Bellenger. Reims: Nizet, 1986. Pp. 103–14.

Cerquiglini-Toulet, Jacqueline and Nigel Wilkins, eds. *Guillaume de Machaut 1300-2000. Actes du Colloque international*. Collection Musiques/Écritures. Paris: Presses de l'Université de Paris-Sorbonne, 2001.

Chanson d'Aubery le Bourgoin. Ed. Adolf Tobler. *Mittheilungen aus altfranzösischen Handschriften I: Aus der Chanson de Geste von Auberi, nach einer vaticanischen Handschrift*. Leipzig: Hirzel, 1870.

Chantilly. Ed. Yolanda Plumley and Anne Stone. *Codex Chantilly, Bibliothèque du château de Chantilly, Ms. 564*. Facsimile and Introduction. Collection "Épitome musical." Turnhout: Brepols, 2008.

Chatelain, Henri. *Recherches sur le vers français au XVe siècle. Rimes, mètres et strophes*. Paris, 1908. Rpt. Genève: Slatkine, 1974.

Citation, Intertextuality and Memory in the Middle Ages and Renaissance, Vol. I: Text, Music and Image from Machaut to Ariosto. Ed. Yolanda Plumley, Giuliano Di Bacco, and Stefano Jossa. Exeter: Exeter University Press, 2011.

Clark, Alice V. "Concordare cum materia: The Tenor in the Fourteenth-Century Motet." PhD diss. Princeton University, 1996 (UMI 9622648).

———. "New Tenor Sources for Fourteenth-Century Motets." *Plainsong and Medieval Music* 8 (1999), 107–31.

———. "Listening to Machaut's Motets." *The Journal of Musicology* 21 (2005), 487–513.

———. "Observations on Machaut's Motet *He! Mors, com tu es haie/ Fine Amour, qui me vint Navrer/ Quare non sum mortuus* (M3)." In *Machaut's Music: New Interpretations*, 2003. Pp. 32–35.

———. "Machaut Reading Machaut: Self-Borrowing and Reinterpretation in Motets 8 and 21." In *Citation and Authority*, 2005. Pp. 94–101.

———. "*Prope est ruina*: The Transformation of a Medieval Tenor." In *Music, Dance and Society: Medieval and Renaissance Studies in Memory of Ingrid G. Brainard*. Ed. Ann Buckley and Cynthia J. Cyrus. Kalamazoo, MI: Medieval Institute Publications, 2011. Pp. 129–42.

———. "The Motets Read and Heard." In *Companion to Guillaume de Machaut*, 2012. Pp. 185–208.

Clark, Suzannah and Elizabeth Eva Leach, eds. *Citation and Authority in Medieval and Renaissance Musical Culture: Learning from the Learned*. Woodbridge: Boydell Press, 2005.

Clarkson, George A. "On the Nature of Medieval Song: The Declamation of Plainchant and the Lyric Structure of the Fourteenth- Century Motet." PhD diss. Columbia University, 1970 (UMI 7117475).

Coleman, Joyce. "The Text Recontextualized in Performance: Deschamps' Prelection of Machaut's *Voir Dit* to the Count of Flanders." *Viator* 31 (2000), 233–48.

Companion to Guillaume de Machaut, A. Ed. Deborah McGrady and Jennifer Bain. Brill's Companions to the Christian Tradition 33. Leiden and Boston: Brill, 2012.

Cosman, Madeleine Pelner and Bruce Chandler, eds. *Machaut's World: Science and Art in the Fourteenth Century*. New York: Academy of Sciences, 1978.

Coussemaker, Edmond de. *Scriptores de musica medii aevi. Novam Seriem a Gerbertina alteram, collegit nuncque primum edidit E. de Coussemaker*. 4 vols. Paris: Durand, 1864–1876. Rpt. Hildesheim [etc.]: Olms, 1987.

Cowell, Andrew. *At Play in the Tavern: Signs, Coins and Bodies in the Middle Ages*. Stylus: Studies in Medieval Culture. Detroit: University of Michigan Press, 1999.

Cross, Lucy. "Chromatic Alteration and Extrahexachordal Intervals in Fourteenth-Century Polyphonic Repertories." PhD diss. Columbia University, 1990 (UMI 9118548).

Danckwardt, Marianne. "Möglichkeiten dreistimmigen Komponierens bei Guillaume de Machaut." In *De musica et cantu: Studien zur Geschichte der Kirchenmusik und der Oper; Helmut Hucke zum 60. Geburtstag*. Ed. Peter Cahn and Ann-Katrin Heimer. Musikwissenschaftliche Publikationen, Hochschule für Musik und darstellende Kunst Frankfurt/Main 2. Hildesheim [etc.]: Olms, 1993. Pp. 371–83.

Davison, Archibald T. and Willi Apel, eds. *Historical Anthology of Music. Vol. 1, Oriental, Medieval and Renaissance Music.* Cambridge, MA: Harvard University Press, 1946, rev. edn 1949.

De Boer. See Boer, Cornelis de.

Dedeck-Hery, V.L. 'Boethius' *De Consolatione* by Jean de Meun.' In: *Medieval Studies* 14 (1952), 165–275.

De Muris. See Johannes de Muris.

Deschamps, Eustache. *Œuvres complètes de Eustache Deschamps.* Ed. A. de Queux de Saint-Hilaire and Gaston Raynaud. 11 vols. Paris: Firmin Didot, 1878–1903.

———. *L'Art de Dictier.* Ed. and trans. Deborah M. Sinnreich-Levi. East Lansing, MI: Colleagues Press, 1994.

Desmond, Karen. "New Light on Jacobus, Author of *Speculum musicae*." *Plainsong and Medieval Music* 9 (2000), 19–40.

Di Stefano. See Stefano, Giuseppe di.

Dillon, Emma. *The Sense of Sound.* New York: Oxford University Press, 2012.

Dobrzańska, Zofia. "Kształtowanie tenoru w motetach Guillaume'a de Machaut." *Muzyka* 24/2 (1979), 3–18.

———. "Rola tenoru w kształtowaniu motetu izorytmicznego."*Muzyka* 24/3 (1979), 45–75.

Dömling, Wolfgang. *Die mehrstimmigen Balladen, Rondeaux und Virelais von Guillaume de Machaut.* Tutzing: Schneider, 1970.

———. "Isorhythmie und Variation. Über Kompositionstechniken in der Messe Guillaume de Machauts."*Archiv für Musikwissenschaft* 28 (1971), 24–32.

———. "Aspekte der Sprachvertonung in den Balladen Guillaume de Machauts." *Die Musikforschung* 25 (1972), 301–07.

Doss-Quinby, Eglal. "*Rolan, de ceu ke m'avez / parti dirai mon samblant:* The Feminine Voice in the Old French *Jeu-Parti*." *Neophilologus* 83 (1999), 497–516.

Doss-Quinby, Eglal. [et al.], eds. *Songs of the Women Trouvères.* New Haven & London: Yale University Press, 2001.

Earp, Lawrence. "Scribal Practice, Manuscript Production and the Transmission of Music in Late Medieval France." PhD diss. Princeton University, 1983 (UMI 8318466).

———. "Machaut's Role in the Production of Manuscripts of His Works." *Journal of the American Musicological Society* 42 (1989), 461–503.

———. *Guillaume de Machaut. A Guide to Research.* New York and London: Garland, 1995.

———. Review of Anne W. Robertson, *Guillaume de Machaut and Reims: Context and Meaning in His Musical Works* (Cambridge, 2002.). *Journal of the American Musicological Society* 57/2 (2004), 384–93.

———. "Declamatory Dissonance in Machaut." In *Citation and Authority*, 2011. Pp. 102–22.

———. "Interpreting the Deluxe Manuscript: Exigencies of Scribal Practice and Manuscript Production in Machaut." In *Calligraphy of Medieval Music*, 2012. Pp. 223–40.

———. "Declamation as Expression in Machaut's Music." In *Companion to Guillaume de Machaut*, 2014. Pp. 209–40.

———. *The Ferrell-Vogüé Machaut Manuscript, Vol. I: Introductory Study*, Chs 1–4. 2014. Pp.1–80.

Eggebrecht, Hans-Heinrich. "Musik als Tonsprache." *Archiv für Musikwissenschaft* 18 (1961), 73–100.

———. "Machauts Motette Nr. 9." *Archiv für Musikwissenschaft* 19–20 (1962–1963), 281–93.

———. "Machauts Motette Nr. 9." (Cont.) *Archiv für Musikwissenschaft* 25 (1968), 173–95.

Egidius de Murino. *Magistri Aegidii de Murino Tractatus cantus mensurabilis.* In *Coussemaker* III, 1864–1876. Pp. 124–28. Partly ed. and trans. in Leech-Wilkinson, *Compositional Techniques*, 1989. Pp. 18–23.

Ellsworth, Oliver, ed. *The Berkeley Manuscript. University of California Music Library, MS. 744 (olim Phillipps 4450).* Ed. and trans. Oliver B. Ellsworth. Greek and Latin Music Theory 2. Lincoln and London: University of Nebraska Press, 1984.

Everist, Mark. "The Horse, the Clerk and the Lyric: The Musicography of the Thirteenth and Fourteenth Centuries." *Journal of the Royal Musical Association* 130 (2005), 136–53.

———. "Machaut's Musical Heritage." In *Companion to Guillaume de Machaut*. 2012. Pp. 143–58.

Fast, Susan. "God, Desire, and Musical Narrative in the Isorhythmic Motet." *Canadian University Music Review/ Revue de musique des universités canadiennes* 18 (1997), 19–37.

Fauvel Studies: Allegory, Chronicle, Music and Image in Paris, Bibliothèque nationale de France, MS français 146. Ed. Margaret Bent and Andrew Wathey. Oxford: Clarendon Press, 1998.

Fiala, David. "Le prince au miroir des musiques politiques des XIVe et XVe siècles." In *Le Prince au miroir de la littérature politique de l'Antiquité aux Lumières*. Ed. Frédérique Lachaud and Lydwine Scordia. Mont-Saint-Aignan: Publications des Universités de Rouen et du Havre, 2007. Pp. 319–50.

————. "La collégiale royale de Saint-Quentin et la musique." In *La Musique en Picardie du XIVe au XVIIe siècle*. Ed. Camilla Cavicchi, Marie-A. Colin, and Philippe Vendrix. Turnhout: Brepols, 2012. Pp.189–230.

Finscher, Ludwig."Arten der Motette im 15. und 16. Jahrhundert." In *Die Musik des 15. und 16. Jahrhunderts*. Ed. Ludwig Finscher. Neues Handbuch der Musikwissenschaft 3, 2. Laaber: Laaber, 1990. Pp. 277–324.

Franco of Cologne. *Franconis de Colonia Ars cantus mensurabilis*. Ed. Gilbert Reyney and André Gilles. Corpus Scriptorum de Musica 18. Rome: American Institute of Musicology, 1974.

Froissart, Jean. *Chroniques, Livres I et II*. Ed. and comm. Peter F. Ainsworth and George T. Diller. Lettres gothiques. Paris: Librairie Générale Française, 2001.

Fuller, Sarah. "On Sonority in Fourteenth-Century Polyphony: Some Preliminary Reflections." *Journal of Music Theory* 30 (1986), 35–71.

————. "Modal Tenors and Tonal Orientation in Motets of Guillaume de Machaut." In *Studies in Medieval Music. Festschrift for Ernest H. Sanders: Current Musicology* 45–47 (1990), 199–245.

————. "Tendencies and Resolutions: The Directed Progression in *Ars Nova* Music." *Journal of Music Theory* 36 (1992), 229–58.

————. "*Contrapunctus*, Dissonance Regulation, and French Polyphony of the Fourteenth Century." In *Medieval Music in Practice*. 2013. Pp. 113–52.

Gace Brulé. *Chansons de Gace Brulé*. Ed. Gédéon Huet. Société des Anciens Textes Français. Paris: Firmin Didot, 1902.

Gallo, Alberto F. *Music in the Castle: Troubadours, Books & Orators in Italian Courts of the Thirteenth, Fourteenth, and Fifteenth Centuries*. Trans. Anna Herklotz. Chicago: University of Chicago Press, 1995.

Gennrich, Friedrich. *Rondeaux, Virelais und Balladen aus dem Ende des XII., des XIII. und dem ersten Drittel des XIV. Jahrhunderts mit den überlieferten Melodien*. Vol. 1, Texte. Dresden: Gesellschaft für romanische Literatur, 1921. Vol. 2, *Materialien, Literaturnachweise, Refrainverzeichnis*. Göttingen: Gesellschaft für romanische Literatur, 1927. Vol. 3, *Das altfranzösische Rondeau und Virelai im 12. und 13. Jahrhundert*. Summa Musica Medii Aevi 10. Langen bei Erfurt: n.p., 1963.

————. "Trouvèrelieder und Motettenrepertoire." *Zeitschrift für Musikwissenschaft* 9 (1926–1927), 8–39, 65–85.

Gilles Li Muisis. *Poésies de Gilles Li Muisis*. Vol. I. Ed. M. le Baron J.M.B.C. Kervyn de Lettenhove. Louvain: Lefever, 1882.

Gombosi, Otto. "Machaut's *Messe Notre-Dame*." *The Musical Quarterly* 36 (1950), 204–24.

Guillaume de Machaut, Poète et compositeur. Colloque-table ronde, organisé par l'université de Reims, 1978. Ed. Jacques Chailley [et al.]. Actes et colloques 23. Paris: Klincksieck 1982.

Guillaume de Machaut 1300–2000. Ed. Jacqueline Cerquiglini-Toulet and Nigel Wilkins (Actes du Colloque de la Sorbonne Sept. 2000). Collection Musique/Écritures. Paris: Presses de l'Université de Paris-Sorbonne, 2002.

Günther, Ursula. "The 14th-Century Motet and Its Development." *Musica Disciplina* 12 (1958), 27–58.

————. "Der Gebrauch des tempus perfectum diminutum in der Handschrift Chantilly 1047."*Archiv für Musikwissenschaft* 17 (1960), 277–97.

————. "Chronologie und Stil der Kompositionen Guillaume de Machauts." *Acta Musicologica* 35 (1963), 96–114.

————. "Zitate in französischen Liedsätzen der Ars Nova und Ars Subtilior." *Musica Disciplina* 26 (1972), 55–68.

————. "Contribution de la musicologie à la chronologie de Guillaume de Machaut." In *Guillaume de Machaut, Poète et compositeur*, 1982. Pp. 95–115.

————. "Sinnbezüge zwischen Text und Musik in Ars Nova und Ars Subtilior." In *Musik und Text in der Mehrstimmigkeit*. 1984. Pp. 229–68.

Günther, Ursula and Ludwig Finscher, eds. *Musik und Text in der Mehrstimmigkeit des 14. und 15. Jahrhunderts*. Basel-London: Bärenreiter, 1984.

Gushee, Lawrence. "Jehan des Murs and His Milieu." In *Musik – und die Geschichte der Philosophie und Naturwissenschaften in Mittelalter: Fragen zur Wechselwirkung von 'Musica' und 'Philosophia' im Mittelalter*. Ed. Frank Hentschel. Leiden [etc.]: Brill, 1998. Pp. 339–71.

Guthrie, Steven R. "Machaut and the *Octosyllabe*." In *Chaucer's French Contemporaries*, 1999. Pp. 111–36.

Haines, John. "Lambertus's *Epiglotus*." *The Journal of Medieval Latin* 16 (2006), 142–63.

————. "On Ligaturae and Their Properties: Medieval Music Notation as Esoteric Writing." In *Calligraphy of Medieval Music*, 2011. Pp. 203–22.

Hamburg, Otto and Margaretha Landwehr von Pragenau, eds. *Musikgeschichte in Beispielen, von der Antike bis Johann Sebastian Bach*. Taschenbücher zur Musikwissenschaft 39. Wilhelmshaven: Heinrichshofen, 1976.

Harden, Jean. "Musica Ficta in Machaut." *Early Music* 5 (1977), 473–77.

———. "Sharps, Flats, and Scribes: Musica ficta in the Machaut Manuscripts." 2 vols. PhD diss. Cornell University, 1983 (UMI 8328707).

Harman, Alec, ed. *Mediaeval and Early Renaissance Music (up to c. 1525)*. Man and His Music 1. Fair Lawn, NJ: Essential Books, 1958.

Harrison, Frank Ll., ed. *Motets of French Provenance*. Polyphonic Music of the Fourteenth Century, vol. V. Monaco: L'Oiseau-Lyre, 1968.

Hartt, Jared C. "Sonority, Syntax, and Line in the Three-Voice Motets of Guillaume de Machaut." PhD diss. Washington University, St Louis, 2007 (UMI 3268033).

———. "The Three Tenors. Machaut's Secular Trio." *Studi Musicali* 38 (2009), 237–71.

———. "Rehearing Machaut's Motets: Taking the Next Step in Understanding Sonority." *Journal of Music Theory* 54 (2010), 179–93.

———. "Tonal and Structural Implications of Isorhythmic Design in Guillaume de Machaut's Tenors." *Theory and Practice* 35 (2010), 57–94.

———. "*Les doubles hoqués et les motés*: Guillaume de Machaut's *Hoquetus David*." *Plainsong and Medieval Music* 21 (2012), 137–73.

Hasenohr, Geneviève. *Introduction à l'ancien français, de Guy Raynaud de Lage*. Paris: SEDES, rev. edn 1993.

Hassell, James W. *Middle French Proverbs, Sentences and Proverbial Expressions*. Subsidia Mediaevalia 12. Toronto: Pontifical Institute of Medieval Studies. Leiden: Brill, 1982.

Hearing the Motet: Essays on the Motet of the Middle Ages and Renaissance. Ed. Dolores Pesce. New York & Oxford: Oxford University Press, 1996.

Hesbert, R.-J., ed. *Corpus Antiphonalium Officii (CAO)*, 6 vols. Vol. 3: *Invitatoria et antiphonae*; vol.4: *Versus, hymni, responsoria et varia*. Rerum Ecclesiasticarum Documenta, Series Maior, Fontes X. Rome: Herder, 1968–1970.

Hiley, David. "The Plica and Liquescence." In *Gordon Athol Anderson (1929–1981): in memoriam von seinen Studenten, Freunden und Kollegen*. Henryville, PA: Institute of Mediaeval Music, 1984. Pp. 379–91.

Holy Bible. *Holy Bible, Translated from the Latin Vulgate; Diligently Compared with the Hebrew,Greek and Other Editions in Divers Languages. The Old Testament First Published by the English College at Douay, A. D. 1609, and the New Testament First Published by the English College at Rheims, A. D. 1582; with Annotations, References and an Historical and Chronological Table*. Baltimore, MD: John Murphy Company, 1914.

Hoppin, Richard H. "Notational Licences of Guillaume de Machaut." *Musica Disciplina* 14 (1960), 13–27.

———. *Medieval Music*. The Norton Introduction to Music History. New York: Norton, 1978.

———. *Anthology of Medieval Music*. Ed. Richard H. Hoppin. New York: Norton, 1978.

Howlett, David. "*Apollinis eclipsatur*: Foundation of the Collegium Musicorum." In *Citation and Authority*. 2005. Pp. 152–59.

Hughes, Andrew. *Style and Symbol: Medieval Music: 800–1453*. Musicological Studies 51. Ottawa: Institute of Mediaeval Music, 1989.

Huot, Sylvia. *From Song to Book: The Poetics of Writing in Old French Lyric and Lyrical Narrative Poetry*. Ithaca-London: Cornell University Press, 1987.

———. "Patience in Adversity: The Courtly Lover and Job in Machaut's Motets 2 and 3." *Medium Aevum* 63 (1994), 222–38.

———. *Allegorical Play in the Old French Motet: The Sacred and Profane in Thirteenth-Century Polyphony*. Stanford: Stanford University Press, 1997.

———. "Guillaume de Machaut and the Consolation of Poetry." *Modern Philology* 100 (2002), 169–95.

———. "Reading Across Genres: Froissart's *Joli Buisson de Jonece* and Machaut's Motets." *French Studies* 57 (2003), 1–10.

Hüschen, Heinrich. *The Motet*. Trans. A.C. Howie. Anthology of Music 47. Cologne: Volk, 1975.

Jacques de Liège. *Jacobi Leodiensis Speculum musicae Libri VII*. Ed. R. Bragard. Corpus Scriptorum de Musica 3, 1–7. Rome: American Institute of Musicology 1955–1973.

Jackson, Roland. "Guillaume de Machaut and Dissonance in Fourteenth Century French Music." *Musica Disciplina* 53 (2003–2008), 7–49.

Jaeger, C. Stephen. *Ennobling Love: In Search of a Lost Sensibility*. Philadelphia: University of Pennsylvania Press, 1999.

Jeanroy, Alfred and Arthur Långfors, eds. *Chanson satyriques et bachiques du XIIIe siècle*, Paris: Champion, 1921.

Jerome of Moravia. *Hieronymus de Moravia O.P.: Tractatus de Musica*. Ed. S.M. Cserba. Freiburger Studien zur Musikwissenschaft 2. Regensburg: Pustet, 1935.

Johannes Boen. *Johannes Boens Musica und seine Konsonanzenlehre*. Ed. Wolf Frobenius. Freiburger Schriften zur Musikwissenschaft 11. Stuttgart: Musikwissenschaftliche Verlags-Gesellschaft, 1971.

———. *Ars (musicae) Johannis Boen*. Ed. F.A. Gallo. Corpus Scriptorum de Musica 19. Rome: American Institute of Musicology, 1972.

Johannes de Grocheio. *Die Quellenhandschriften zum Musiktraktat des Johannes de Grocheio*. Facsimile, ed. and German trans. Ernst Rohloff. Leipzig: Deutscher Verlag für Musik, 1972.

———. *Ars musice*. Ed. and trans. Constant J. Mews [et al.]. Kalamazoo, MI: Medieval Institute Publications, 2011.

Johannes de Muris. *Johannis de Muris, Notitia artis musicae et Compendium musicae practicae*; *Petrus de Sancto Dionysio, Tractatus de musica*. Ed. Ulrich Michels. Corpus Scriptorum de Musica 17. Rome: American Institute of Musicology, 1972.

———. *Die musica speculativa des Johannes de Muris*. Kommentar zur Überlieferung und kritische Edition von Christoph Falkenroth. Beihefte zum Archiv für Musikwissenschaft 34. Stuttgart: Steiner, 1992.

———. *Ars practica mensurabilis cantus secundum Iohannem de Muris. Die Recensio maior des sogenannten "Libellus practice cantus mensurabilis."* Ed. Christian Berktold. Veröffentlichungen der Musikhistorischen Kommission 14. München: Verlag der bayerischen Akademie der Wissenschaften, 1999.

———. *Jean de Murs, Écrits sur la musique*. Trans. and commentary by Christian Meyer. Sciences de la Musique. Paris: CNRS Editions, 2000.

Kamien, Roger, ed. *The Norton Scores. An Anthology for Listening*. Vol. 1, *Gregorian Chant to Beethoven*. Fourth rev. edn. New York and London: Norton, 1984.

Kelly, Douglas. *Machaut and the Medieval Apprenticeship Tradition: Truth, Fiction and Poetic Craft*. Gallica 35. Cambridge: Brewer, 2014.

Kibler, W. William and James I. Wimsatt. "Machaut's Text and the Question of His Personal Supervision." In *Chaucer's French Contemporaries*. 1999. Pp. 93–110.

Koehler, Laurie. *Pythagoreisch-platonische Proportionen in Werken der ars nova und ars subtilior*. Göttinger musikwissenschaftliche Arbeiten 12. Kassel-Basel [etc.]: Bärenreiter, 1990.

Kügle, Karl. "Die Musik des 14. Jahrhunderts: Frankreich und sein direkter Einflußbereich." In *Die Musik des Mittelalters*. Ed. Hartmut Möller and Rudolf Stephan. Neues Handbuch der Musikwissenschaft 2. Laaber: Laaber, 1991. Pp. 335–84.

———. *The Manuscript Ivrea, Biblioteca capitolare 115: Studies in the Transmission and Composition of Ars Nova Polyphony*. Ottawa: The Institute of Mediaeval Music, 1997.

Kühn, Helmuth. *Die Harmonik der Ars Nova*. München: Katzbichler, 1973.

———. "Guillaume de Machaut, Motette Nr. 22." In *Chormusik und Analyse: Beiträge zur Formanalyse und Interpretation mehrstimmiger Vokalmusik*. Ed. Heinrich Poos. Vol. 1, *Texte*, pp. 29–42; Vol. 2, *Noten*, pp. 11–16.

Långfors, Arthur [et al.] *Recueil général des jeux-partis français*. Société des Anciens Textes Français 69. Paris: Champion 1926.

Langlois, M. Ernest. *Recueil d'arts de seconde rhétorique*. Paris: Imprimerie Nationale, 1902.

Lavacek, Justin. "Contrapuntal Confrontation and Expressive Signification in the Motets of Guillaume de Machaut." PhD diss. Indiana University, 2011 (UMI 3488417).

Leach, Elizabeth Eva. "Counterpoint and Analysis in Fourteenth-Century Song." *Journal of Music Theory* 44 (2000), 45–79.

———. "Gendering the Semitone, Sexing the Leading Tone: Fourteenth-Century Music Theory and the Directed Progression." *Music Theory Spectrum* 28 (2006), 1–21.

———. *Guillaume de Machaut: Secretary, Poet, Musician*. Ithaca & London: Cornell University Press, 2011.

Leach, Elizabeth Eva, ed. *Machaut's Music: New Interpretations*. Woodbridge: Boydell & Brewer, 2003.

Leech-Wilkinson, Daniel. "Related Motets from Fourteenth-Century France." *Proceedings of the Royal Musical Association* 109 (1982–1983), 1–22.

———. *Compositional Techniques in the Four-Part Isorhythmic Motets of Philippe de Vitry and His Contemporaries*. New York: Garland, 1989.

———. *Machaut's Mass: An Introduction*. Oxford: Clarendon Press, 1990.

———. "The Emergence of *ars nova*." *The Journal of Musicology* 13 (1995), 285–317.

Leo, Domenic. "The Program of Miniatures in Manuscript A." In *Guillaume de Machaut: Le Livre dou Voir Dit (The Book of the True Poem)*. Ed. Daniel Leech-Wilkinson, trans. R. Barton Palmer. New York: Garland, 1998. Pp. xci–xciii.

———. "Authorial Presence in the Illuminated Machaut Manuscripts." PhD diss. New York University, Institute of Fine Arts, 2005.

———. "The Beginning is the End: Guillaume de Machaut's Illuminated *Prologue*." In *Citation, Intertextuality and Memory*. 2011. Pp. 96–112.

———. *The Ferrell-Vogüé Machaut Manuscript, Vol. I: Introductory Study*, Ch. 6. 2014. Pp. 95–126.

Lerch, Irmgard. *Fragmente aus Cambrai: Ein Beitrag zur Rekonstruktion einer Handschrift mit spätmittelalterlicher Polyphonie*. 2 vols. Göttinger musikwissenschaftliche Arbeiten 11. Kassel [etc.]: Bärenreiter, 1987.

Lerner, Edward R. *Study Scores of Musical Styles*. New York: McGraw-Hill, 1968.

Lorris, Guillaume de, and Jean de Meun. *Le Roman de la Rose*. Ed. Félix Lecoy. 3 vols. Paris: Champion, 1965.

Ludwig, Friedrich. "Die mehrstimmige Musik des 14. Jahrhunderts." *Sammelbände der internationalen Musikgesellschaft* 4 (1902–1903), 16–69.

———. "Die französischen Balladen, Virelais und Rondeaux des 14. Jahrhunderts; die isorhythmische Motette des 14. und beginnenden 15. Jahrhunderts; die italienische Madrigale, Balladen und Cacce; die mehrstimmige Messe des 14. Jahrhunderts. Etwa 1300–1430." In *Handbuch der Musikgeschichte*. Ed. Guido Adler. Frankfurt a/M: Frankfurter Verlags- Anstalt, 1924. Pp. 228–48.

Lühmann, Rose. *Versdeklamation bei Guillaume de Machaut*. Inaugural-Dissertation: Ludwig Maximilians-Universität München, 1975, ed. 1978.

Machabey, Armand. *Guillaume de Machault, La vie et l'oeuvre musical*. 2 vols. Bibliothèque d'études musicales. Paris: Richard-Masse, 1955.

Markstrom, Kurt. "Machaut and the Wild Beast." *Acta Musicologica* 61 (1989), 12–39.

Maury, Yossi. "A Courtly Lover and an Earthly Knight Turned Soldiers of Christ in Machaut's Motet 5." *Early Music History* 24 (2005), 170–211.

Maw, David. "'Trespasser mesure': Meter in Machaut's Polyphonic Songs." *Journal of Musicology* 21 (2004), 46–126.

———. "Machaut and the 'Critical' Phase of Medieval Polyphony." *Music & Letters* 87 (2006), 262–94.

McGrady, Deborah. "Machaut and His Material Legacy." In *Companion to Guillaume de Machaut*. 2012. Pp. 361–86.

McGrady, Deborah and Jennifer Bain, eds. *A Companion to Guillaume de Machaut*. Brill's Companions to the Christian Tradition 33. Leiden and Boston: Brill, 2012.

Medieval Music in Practice: Studies in Honor of Richard Crocker. Ed. Judith A. Peraino. Publications of the American Institute of Musicology 8. Middleton, WI: American Institute of Musicology, 2013.

Meiss, Millard, and Edith W. Kirsch. *The Visconti Hours*. New York: Braziller, 1972.

Melander, Johan. "Les poésies de Robert de Castel." *Studia Neophilologica* 3 (1930), 17–43.

Meyer, Christian, ed. and trans. *Jean de Murs, Écrits sur la musique*. Sciences de la Musique. Paris: CNRS Editions, 2000.

Meyer, Heinz and Rudolf Suntrup. *Lexikon der mittelalterlichen Zahlenbedeutungen*. Münstersche Mittelalter-Schriften 56. München: Fink, 1987.

Michels, Ulrich. *Die Musiktraktate des Johannes de Muris*. Beihefte zum Archiv für Musikwissenschaft 8. Wiesbaden: Steiner, 1970.

Moll, Kevin N. "Paradigms of Four-voice Composition in the Machaut Era." *Journal of Musicological Research* 22 (2003), 349–86.

Morawski, Joseph. *Proverbes français antérieurs au XVe siècle*. Paris: Champion, 1925, rpt. 2007.

Mulder, Etty. Guillaume de Machaut, een grensbewoner. Samenhang van allegorie en muziek bij een laat-middeleeuws dichter-componist. Amsterdam: Musicater, 1978.

Musik und Text in der Mehrstimmigkeit des 14. und 15. Jahrhunderts. Ed. Ursula Günther and Ludwig Finscher. Basel-London: Bärenreiter, 1984.

Nelson, Alan H. "Mechanical Wheels of Fortune, 1100–1547." *Journal of the Warburg and Courtauld Institutes* 43 (1980), 227–33.

Newes, Virginia. "Imitation in the Ars nova and Ars Subtilior." *Revue belge de musicologie* 31 (1977), 38–59.

———. "The Relationship of Text to Imitative Techniques in 14ᵗʰ-Century Polyphony." In *Musik und Text in der Mehrstimmigkeit*, 1984. Pp. 121–54.

———. "Writing, Reading and Memorizing: The Transmission and Resolution of Retrograde Canons from the 14ᵗʰ and Early 15ᵗʰ Centuries." *Early Music* 18 (1990), 218–34.

———. "Turning Fortune's Wheel: Musical and Textual Design in Machaut's Canonic Lais." *Musica Disciplina* 45 (1991), 95–121.

———. "'Qui bien aimme a tart oublie': Guillaume de Machaut's *Lay de plour* in context." In *Citation and Authority*. 2005. Pp. 123–40.

North, John. "The Quadrivium." In Ridder-Symoens, ed. *History of the University in Europe*. 2005. Pp. 337–59.

Page, Christopher. "Machaut's 'Pupil' Deschamps on the Performance of Music: Voices or Instruments?" *Early Music* 5 (1977), 484–92.

———. "A Treatise on Musicians from c. 1400: The *Tractatulus de differentiis et gradibus cantorum* by Arnulf de St Ghislain." *Journal of the Royal Musical Association* 117 (1992), 1–21.

———. "Johannes de Grocheio on Secular Music: A Corrected Text and a New Translation." *Plainsong and Medieval Music* 2 (1993), 17–41.

———. "An English Motet of the Fourteenth Century in Performance: Two Contemporary Images." *Early Music* 25 (1997), pp. 7–32.

———. "Around the Performance of a Thirteenth-Century Motet." *Early Music* 28 (2000), 343–57.

Palmer, R. Barton. "Guillaume de Machaut and the Classical Tradition: Individual Talent and (Un)Communal Tradition." In *Companion to Guillaume de Machaut*. 2012. Pp. 241–60.

Palmer, R. Barton, ed. *Chaucer's French Contemporaries: The Poetry/Poetics of Self and Tradition*. New York: AMS Press, 1999.

Patch, Howard Rolin. "Fortuna in Old French Literature." In *Smith College Studies in Modern Languages* 4/4 (1923). Pp. 1–45.

———. *The Goddess Fortuna in Mediaeval Literature*. Cambridge, MA: Harvard University Press, 1927. Rpt. New York: Octagon Books, 1967.

Pelinski, Ramon A. "Zusammenklang und Aufbau in den Motetten Machauts." *Die Musikforschung* 28 (1975), 62–71.

Perrin d'Angicourt. *Die Lieder des troveors Perrin von Angicourt*. Ed. Georg Steffens. Halle a.d. S.: Niemeyer, 1905.

Pesce, Dolores, ed. *Hearing the Motet: Essays on the Motet of the Middle Ages and Renaissance*. NewYork-Oxford: Oxford University Press, 1996.

Petrus dictus Palma ociosa. Ed. Johannes Wolf: "Ein Beitrag zur Diskantlehre des 14. Jahrhunderts." *Sammelbände der Internationalen Musikgesellschaft* 15 (1913–1914), 505–34.

Philippe de Vitry. *The Works of Philippe de Vitry*. Ed. Leo Schrade. Polyphonic Music of the Fourteenth Century, vol. I. Monaco: L'Oiseau-Lyre, 1956. Rpt., with a new introduction by Edward H. Roesner, 1984.

———. *Philippi de Vitriaco Ars nova*. Ed. Gilbert Reaney [et al.]. Corpus Scriptorum de Musica 8. Rome: American Institute of Musicology, 1964.

Plumley, Yolanda. *The Art of Grafted Song, Citation and Allusion in the Age of Machaut*. New York & London: Oxford University Press, 2013.

———. and Uri Smilansky. "A Courtier's Quest for Cultural Capital: New Light on the Original Owner of Machaut MS F-G." Forthcoming publication.

Plumley, Yolanda and Anne Stone, eds. *Codex Chantilly, Bibliothèque du château de Chantilly, Ms. 564*. Facsimile and Introduction. Collection "Épitome musical." Turnhout: Brepols, 2008.

Plumley, Yolanda, Giuliano Di Bacco and Stefano Jossa, eds. *Citation, Intertextuality and Memory in the Middle Ages and Renaissance*. Vol. I: *Text, Music and Image from Machaut to Ariosto*. Exeter: Exeter University Press, 2011.

Poirion, Daniel. *Le poète et le prince. L'évolution du lyrisme courtois de Guillaume de Machaut à Charles d'Orléans*. Paris: Presses universitaires de France, 1965.

———. *Le Roman de la Rose*. Connaissance des Lettres. Paris: Hatier, 1973.

Powell, Norman. "Fibonacci and the Gold Mean: Rabbits, Rumbas and Rondeaux." *Journal of Music Theory* 23 (1979), 227–72.

Prioult, Albert. "Un poète-voyageur: Guillaume de Machaut et la « Reise » de Jean l'Aveugle, roi de Bohême, en 1328-1329." *Les Lettres Romanes* 4 (1950), 3–29.

Randall, Lilian M. C. *Images in the Margins of Gothic Manuscripts*. Berkeley: University of California Press, 1966.

Rastall, Richard. *The Notation of Western Music. An Introduction*. London: Dent, 1983.

Raynaud-Spanke. See Spanke.

Reaney, Gilbert. "Towards a Chronology of Machaut's Musical Works." *Musica Disciplina* 21 (1967), 87–96.

———. *Guillaume de Machaut*. London: Oxford University Press, 1971.

Reichert, Georg. "Das Verhältnis zwischen musikalischer und textlicher Struktur in den Motetten Machauts." *Archiv für Musikwissenschaft* 13 (1956), 197–216.

René d'Anjou. *Le Livre du Coeur d'amour épris*. Ed. Florence Bouchet. Lettres Gothiques. Paris: Librairie Générale Française, 2003.

Ridder-Symoens, Hilde de, ed. *A History of the University in Europe. I: Universities in the Middle Ages*. Cambridge: Cambridge University Press, 1992.

Robert de Castel. "Les poésies de Robert de Castel." Ed. J. Melander. *Studia Neophilologica* 3 (1930), 17–43.

Robertson, Anne W. *Guillaume de Machaut and Reims. Context and Meaning in his Musical Works*. Cambridge: Cambridge University Press, 2002.

Rockseth, Yvonne. *Polyphonies du XIIIe Siècle: Le Ms H. 196 de la Faculté de Médecine de Montpellier*. 4 vols. Paris: l'Oiseau-Lyre, 1935, 1936, 1939.

Roesner, Edward, ed. *Le Roman de Fauvel in the Edition of Mesire Chaillou de Pesstain: A Reproduction in Facsimile of the Complete Manuscript Paris, Bibliothèque Nationale, Fonds Français 146*. Introduction by Edward H. Roesner, François Avril and Nancy Freeman Regalado. New York: Broude, 1990.

Rohloff, Ernst, ed. *Die Quellenhandschriften zum Musiktraktat des Johannes de Grocheio*. In Faksimile hrsg. nebst Übertragung des Textes und Übersetzung ins Deutsche. Leipzig: Deutscher Verlag für Musik, 1972.

Roman de Fauvel. Ed. Leo Schrade. Polyphonic Music of the Fourteenth Century, vol. I. Monaco: L'Oiseau-Lyre, 1956, rpt. 1982. See also Roesner.

Rose-Steel, Tamsyn. "French Ars Nova Motets and Their Manuscripts: Citational Play and Material Context." PhD diss. University of Exeter, 2011.

Ruffo, Kathleen Wilson. "The Illustration of Noted Compendia of Courtly Poetry in LateThirteenth-Century Northern France." PhD diss. University of Toronto, 2000.

Sachs, Klaus-Jürgen. *Der Contrapunctus im 14. und 15. Jahrhundert: Untersuchungen zum Terminus, zur Lehre und zu den Quellen*. Beihefte zum Archiv für Musikwissenschaft 13. Wiesbaden: Steiner, 1974.

———. "Die Contrapunctus-Lehre im 14. und 15. Jahrhundert." In *Die mittelalterliche Lehre von der Mehrstimmigkeit*. Ed. Hans Heinrich Eggebrecht, F. Alberto Gallo, Max Haas and Klaus-Jürgen Sachs. Geschichte der Musiktheorie 5. Darmstadt: Wissenschaftliche Buchgesellschaft, 1984. Pp. 162–256.

Saltzstein, Jennifer. *The Refrain and the Rise of the Vernacular in Medieval French Music and Poetry*. Gallica 30. Woodbridge and Rochester, NY: Boydell & Brewer, 2013.

Sanders, Ernest. "The Medieval Motet." In *Gattungen der Musik in Einzeldarstellungen. Gedenkschrift Leo Schrade*. Ed. Wulf Arlt. Bern-München: Franke, 1973. Pp. 497–559.

Scheller, Robert W. *Exemplum: Model-Book Drawings and the Practice of Artistic Transmission in the Middle Ages (ca. 900–ca. 1450)*. Trans. Michael Hoyle. Amsterdam: Amsterdam University Press, 1995.

Schmidt-Beste, Thomas. "Singing the Hickup – On Texting the Hocket." *Early Music* 32 (2013), 225–75.

Schrade, Leo, ed. *The Roman de Fauvel*. Polyphonic Music of the Fourteenth Century, vol. I. Monaco: L'Oiseau-Lyre, 1956, Repr. 1982.

———, ed. *The Works of Philippe de Vitry*. Polyphonic Music of the Fourteenth Century, vol. I. Monaco: L'Oiseau-Lyre, 1956. Rpt., with a new introduction by Edward H. Roesner, 1984.

Schwinges, Rainer C. "Student Education, Student Life." In Ridder-Symoens, ed., *A History of the University in Europe*, Chapter 7. 1992. Pp. 195–243.

Smilansky, Uri. See Plumley, Yolanda and Uri Smilansky.

Sonnemann, Günter. "Die Ditdichtung des Guillaume de Machaut." PhD diss. Göttingen: Funke, 1969.

Spanke, Hans. *G. Raynauds Bibliographie des altfranzösischen Liedes. Neu bearbeitet und ergänzt von Hans Spanke*. Erster Teil. Musicologica 1. Leiden: Brill, 1955.

Stefano, Giuseppe di. *Dictionnaire des locutions en moyen français*. Montréal: Cérès, 1991.

Stevens, John. *Words and Music in the Middle Ages: Song, Narrative, Dance and Drama, 1050–1350*. Cambridge Studies in Music. Cambridge: Cambridge University Press, 1986.

Strunk, Oliver. *Source Readings in Music History*. Rev. edn, gen. ed. Leo Treitler; vol. 2, *The Early Christian Period and the Latin Middle Ages*. Ed. James McKinnon. New York: Norton, 1998.

Sultan, Agathe. "'Lyre—cette pratique.' Texte et musique dans le motet 14 de Guillaume de Machaut." *Perspectives médiévales. Supplement au no. 28* (2002), 223–45.

———."Tombeaux de musiciens." In *La mort écrite: rites et rhétoriques du trépas au moyen âge*. Ed. Estelle Doudet. Paris: Presses Universitaires de Paris-Sorbonne, 2005. Pp. 155–71.

Thiry, Claude. *La plainte funèbre*. Typologie des sources du moyen-âge occidental. Turnhout: Brepols, 1978.

Thibaut de Champagne. *Les chansons de Thibaut de Champagne, Roi de Navarre*. Ed. Axel Wallensköld. Société des Anciens Textes Français. Paris: Champion, 1925.

Tischler, Hans, ed. *The Earliest Motets (to circa 1270): A Complete Comparative Edition*. New Haven & London: Yale University Press, 1982. 3 vols.

———, ed. *The Montpellier Codex. Part I: Critical Commentary, Fascicles 1 and 2; Part II: Fascicles 3, 4, and 5; Part III: Fascicles 6, 7, and 8; Part IV: Texts and Translations*. Recent Researches in the Music of the Middle Ages and Early Renaissance, Vols II-VIII. Madison, WI: A-R Editions, 1978.

Tobler, Adolf, ed. *Mittheilungen aus altfranzösischen Handschriften* I: *Aus der Chanson de Geste von Auberi, nach einer vaticanischen Handschrift*, Leipzig: Hirzel, 1870.

Turek, Ralph. *Analytical Anthology of Music*. New York: Knopf, 1984.

Van den Boogaard. See Boogaard, Nico van den.

Van der Werf. See Werf, Hendrik van der.

Wathey, Andrew. "The Motets of Philippe de Vitry and the Fourteenth-Century Renaissance."*Early Music History* 12 (1993), 119–50.

Weill, Isabelle. "Les « merveilles » de la cour de Flandre dans la chanson de geste d'*Auberi le Bourgoin*." In *Richesses médiévales du Nord et du Hainaut,* ed. Jean-Charles Herbin. Valenciennes: Presses universitaires de Valenciennes, 2002. Pp. 37–47.

Werf, Hendrik van der. *The Chansons of the Troubadours and Trouvères: A Study of the Melodies and Their Relation to the Poems*. Utrecht: Oosthoek, 1972.

———, ed. *Trouvères-Melodien I: Blondel de Nesle - Gautier de Dargies - Chastelain de Coucy - Conon de Béthune - Gace Brulé*. Monumenta Monodica Medii Aevi 11. Kassel [etc.]: Bärenreiter, 1977.

———, ed. *Trouvères-Melodien II: Thibaut de Navarre - Moniot d'Arras - Moniot de Paris - Colin Muset - Audefroi le Bastard - Adam de la Halle*. Monumenta Monodica Medii Aevi 12. Kassel [etc.]: Bärenreiter, 1979.

Wernli, Andreas. "La percettibilità delle strutture isoritmiche. Osservazioni sui mottetti di Guillaume de Machaut." *Studi musicali* 6 (1977), 13–27.

Wilkins, Nigel E. "A Pattern of Patronage: Machaut, Froissart and the Houses of Luxembourg and Bohemia in the Fourteenth Century." *French Studies* 37 (1983), 257–84.

———, ed. *Armes, Amours, Dames, Chevalerie: An Anthology of French Song from the Fourteenth Century*. Cambridge: New Press, 1987.

Williams, Sarah J. "The Music of Guillaume de Machaut." PhD. diss. Yale University, 1952 (UMI 6411892).

———. "An Author's Role in Fourteenth Century Book Production: Guillaume de Machaut's 'Livre ou je met toutes mes choses.'" *Romania* 90 (1969), 433–54.

Wilson, David Fenwick. *Music of the Middle Ages. An Anthology for Performance and Study*. New York: Schirmer, 1990.

———. *Music of the Middle Ages. Style and Structure*. New York: Schirmer, 1990.

Wimsatt, James I. *Chaucer and His French Contemporaries. Natural Music in the Fourteenth Century*. Toronto [etc.]: University of Toronto Press, 1993.

Winter, Patrick de. *La bibliothèque de Philippe le Hardi, Duc de Bourgogne (1364–1404). Étude sur les manuscrits à peinture d'une collection princière à l'époque du « Style Gothique International »*. Paris: Éditions du Centre National de la Recherche Scientifique, 1985.

Wolf, Johannes. *Sing- und Spielmusik aus älterer Zeit*. Leipzig: Quelle & Meyer, 1926. Rpt. as *Music of Earlier Times: Vocal and Instrumental Examples (13th Century to Bach)*. New York: Broude Bros, 1947.

———. *Handbuch der Notationskunde I: Tonschriften des Altertums und des Mittelalters; Choral- und Mensuralnotation*. Wiesbaden: Breitkopf & Härtel, 1913. Rpt. Hildesheim: Olms, 1963.

———. *Geschichte der Mensural-Notation von 1250–1460*. 3 vols. Leipzig: Breitkopf und Härtel, 1904. Rpt. Hildesheim: Olms, 1965.

Wright, Laurence. "Verbal Counterpoint in Machaut's Motet *Trop plus est belle-Biauté paree de valour-Je ne sui mie*." *Romance Studies* 7 (1986), 1–12.

Yudkin, Jeremy. *Music in Medieval Europe*. Prentice Hall History of Music Series. Upper Saddle River, NJ: Prentice-Hall, 1989.

Zayaruznaya, Anna. "'She Has a Wheel that Turns…': Crossed and Contradictory Voices in Machaut's Motets." *Early Music History* 28 (2009), 185–240.

———. "Form and Idea in the *Ars nova* Motet." PhD diss. Harvard University, 2010.

———. "Hockets as Compositional and Scribal Practice in the *ars nova* Motet—A Letter from Lady Music." *The Journal of Musicology* 30 (2013), 461–501.

———. *The Monstrous New Art. Divided Forms in the Late Medieval Motet*. Cambridge: Cambridge University Press, 2015.

Ziino, Agostino. "Isoritmia musicale e tradizione metrica mediolatina nei mottetti di Guillaume de Machaut." *Medioevo Romanzo* 5 (1978), 438–65.

Zwick, Gabriel. "Deux motets inédits de Philippe de Vitry et de Guillaume de Machaut." *Revue de musicologie* 30 (1948), 28–57.

MIDDLE ENGLISH TEXTS SERIES

The Floure and the Leafe, The Assembly of Ladies, The Isle of Ladies, edited by Derek Pearsall (1990)

Three Middle English Charlemagne Romances, edited by Alan Lupack (1990)

Six Ecclesiastical Satires, edited by James M. Dean (1991)

Heroic Women from the Old Testament in Middle English Verse, edited by Russell A. Peck (1991)

The Canterbury Tales: Fifteenth-Century Continuations and Additions, edited by John M. Bowers (1992)

Gavin Douglas, *The Palis of Honoure*, edited by David Parkinson (1992)

Wynnere and Wastoure and The Parlement of the Thre Ages, edited by Warren Ginsberg (1992)

The Shewings of Julian of Norwich, edited by Georgia Ronan Crampton (1994)

King Arthur's Death: The Middle English Stanzaic Morte Arthur and Alliterative Morte Arthure, edited by Larry D. Benson, revised by Edward E. Foster (1994)

Lancelot of the Laik and Sir Tristrem, edited by Alan Lupack (1994)

Sir Gawain: Eleven Romances and Tales, edited by Thomas Hahn (1995)

The Middle English Breton Lays, edited by Anne Laskaya and Eve Salisbury (1995)

Sir Perceval of Galles and Ywain and Gawain, edited by Mary Flowers Braswell (1995)

Four Middle English Romances: Sir Isumbras, Octavian, Sir Eglamour of Artois, Sir Tryamour, edited by Harriet Hudson (1996; second edition 2006)

The Poems of Laurence Minot, 1333–1352, edited by Richard H. Osberg (1996)

Medieval English Political Writings, edited by James M. Dean (1996)

The Book of Margery Kempe, edited by Lynn Staley (1996)

Amis and Amiloun, Robert of Cisyle, and Sir Amadace, edited by Edward E. Foster (1997; second edition 2007)

The Cloud of Unknowing, edited by Patrick J. Gallacher (1997)

Robin Hood and Other Outlaw Tales, edited by Stephen Knight and Thomas Ohlgren (1997; second edition 2000)

The Poems of Robert Henryson, edited by Robert L. Kindrick with the assistance of Kristie A. Bixby (1997)

Moral Love Songs and Laments, edited by Susanna Greer Fein (1998)

John Lydgate, *Troy Book Selections*, edited by Robert R. Edwards (1998)

Thomas Usk, *The Testament of Love*, edited by R. Allen Shoaf (1998)

Prose Merlin, edited by John Conlee (1998)

Middle English Marian Lyrics, edited by Karen Saupe (1998)

John Metham, *Amoryus and Cleopes*, edited by Stephen F. Page (1999)

Four Romances of England: King Horn, Havelok the Dane, Bevis of Hampton, Athelston, edited by Ronald B. Herzman, Graham Drake, and Eve Salisbury (1999)

The Assembly of Gods: Le Assemble de Dyeus, or Banquet of Gods and Goddesses, with the Discourse of Reason and Sensuality, edited by Jane Chance (1999)

Thomas Hoccleve, *The Regiment of Princes*, edited by Charles R. Blyth (1999)

John Capgrave, *The Life of Saint Katherine*, edited by Karen A. Winstead (1999)

John Gower, *Confessio Amantis*, Vol. 1, edited by Russell A. Peck; with Latin translations by Andrew Galloway (2000; second edition 2006); Vol. 2 (2003; second edition 2013); Vol. 3 (2004)

Richard the Redeless and Mum and the Sothsegger, edited by James M. Dean (2000)

Ancrene Wisse, edited by Robert Hasenfratz (2000)

Walter Hilton, *The Scale of Perfection*, edited by Thomas H. Bestul (2000)

John Lydgate, *The Siege of Thebes*, edited by Robert R. Edwards (2001)

Pearl, edited by Sarah Stanbury (2001)

The Trials and Joys of Marriage, edited by Eve Salisbury (2002)

Middle English Legends of Women Saints, edited by Sherry L. Reames, with the assistance of Martha G. Blalock and Wendy R. Larson (2003)

The Wallace: Selections, edited by Anne McKim (2003)

Richard Maidstone, *Concordia (The Reconciliation of Richard II with London)*, edited by David R. Carlson, with a verse translation by A. G. Rigg (2003)

Three Purgatory Poems: The Gast of Gy, Sir Owain, The Vision of Tundale, edited by Edward E. Foster (2004)

William Dunbar, *The Complete Works*, edited by John Conlee (2004)

Chaucerian Dream Visions and Complaints, edited by Dana M. Symons (2004)

Stanzaic Guy of Warwick, edited by Alison Wiggins (2004)

Saints' Lives in Middle English Collections, edited by E. Gordon Whatley, with Anne B. Thompson and Robert K. Upchurch (2004)

Siege of Jerusalem, edited by Michael Livingston (2004)

The Kingis Quair and Other Prison Poems, edited by Linne R. Mooney and Mary-Jo Arn (2005)

The Chaucerian Apocrypha: A Selection, edited by Kathleen Forni (2005)

John Gower, *The Minor Latin Works*, edited and translated by R. F. Yeager, with *In Praise of Peace*, edited by Michael Livingston (2005)

Sentimental and Humorous Romances: Floris and Blancheflour, Sir Degrevant, The Squire of Low Degree, The Tournament of Tottenham, and The Feast of Tottenham, edited by Erik Kooper (2006)

The Dicts and Sayings of the Philosophers, edited by John William Sutton (2006)

Everyman and Its Dutch Original, Elckerlijc, edited by Clifford Davidson, Martin W. Walsh, and Ton J. Broos (2007)

The N-Town Plays, edited by Douglas Sugano, with assistance by Victor I. Scherb (2007)

The Book of John Mandeville, edited by Tamarah Kohanski and C. David Benson (2007)

John Lydgate, *The Temple of Glas*, edited by J. Allan Mitchell (2007)

The Northern Homily Cycle, edited by Anne B. Thompson (2008)

Codex Ashmole 61: A Compilation of Popular Middle English Verse, edited by George Shuffelton (2008)

Chaucer and the Poems of "Ch," edited by James I. Wimsatt (revised edition 2009)

William Caxton, *The Game and Playe of the Chesse*, edited by Jenny Adams (2009)

John the Blind Audelay, *Poems and Carols*, edited by Susanna Fein (2009)

Two Moral Interludes: The Pride of Life and Wisdom, edited by David Klausner (2009)

John Lydgate, *Mummings and Entertainments*, edited by Claire Sponsler (2010)

Mankind, edited by Kathleen M. Ashley and Gerard NeCastro (2010)

The Castle of Perseverance, edited by David N. Klausner (2010)

Robert Henryson, *The Complete Works*, edited by David J. Parkinson (2010)

John Gower, *The French Balades*, edited and translated by R. F. Yeager (2011)

The Middle English Metrical Paraphrase of the Old Testament, edited by Michael Livingston (2011)

The York Corpus Christi Plays, edited by Clifford Davidson (2011)

Prik of Conscience, edited by James H. Morey (2012)

The Dialogue of Solomon and Marcolf: A Dual-Language Edition from Latin and Middle English Printed Editions, edited by Nancy Mason Bradbury and Scott Bradbury (2012)

Croxton Play of the Sacrament, edited by John T. Sebastian (2012)

Ten Bourdes, edited by Melissa M. Furrow (2013)

Lybeaus Desconus, edited by Eve Salisbury and James Weldon (2013)

The Complete Harley 2253 Manuscript, Vol. 2, edited and translated by Susanna Fein with David Raybin and Jan Ziolkowski (2014); Vol. 3 (2015); Vol. 1 (2015)

Oton de Granson Poems, edited and translated by Peter Nicholson and Joan Grenier-Winther (2015)

The King of Tars, edited by John H. Chandler (2015)

John Hardyng Chronicle, edited by James Simpson and Sarah Peverley (2015)

Richard Coer de Lyon, edited by Peter Larkin (2015)

Guillaume de Machaut, The Complete Poetry and Music, Volume 1: The Debate Poems, edited and translated by R. Barton Palmer (2016)

Lydgate's Fabula Duorum Mercatorum and Guy of Warwyk, edited by Pamela Farvolden (2016)

The Katherine Group (MS Bodley 34), edited by Emily Rebekah Huber and Elizabeth Robertson (2016)

Sir Torrent of Portingale, edited by James Wade (2017)

The Towneley Plays, edited by Garrett P. J. Epp (2017)

✒ MEDIEVAL GERMAN TEXTS IN BILINGUAL EDITIONS SERIES

Sovereignty and Salvation in the Vernacular, 1050–1150, introduction, translations, and notes by James A. Schultz (2000)

Ava's New Testament Narratives: "When the Old Law Passed Away," introduction, translation, and notes by James A. Rushing, Jr. (2003)

History as Literature: German World Chronicles of the Thirteenth Century in Verse, introduction, translation, and notes by R. Graeme Dunphy (2003)

Thomasin von Zirclaria, *Der Welsche Gast (The Italian Guest)*, translated by Marion Gibbs and Winder McConnell (2009)

Ladies, Whores, and Holy Women: A Sourcebook in Courtly, Religious, and Urban Cultures of Late Medieval Germany, introductions, translations, and notes by Ann Marie Rasmussen and Sarah Westphal-Wihl (2010)

Neidhart: Selected Songs from the Riedegg Manuscript, introduction, translation, and commentary by Kathryn Starkey and Edith Wenzel (2016)

✒ VARIA

The Study of Chivalry: Resources and Approaches, edited by Howell Chickering and Thomas H. Seiler (1988)

Studies in the Harley Manuscript: The Scribes, Contents, and Social Contexts of British Library MS Harley 2253, edited by Susanna Fein (2000)

The Liturgy of the Medieval Church, edited by Thomas J. Heffernan and E. Ann Matter (2001; second edition 2005)

Johannes de Grocheio, *Ars musice*, edited and translated by Constant J. Mews, John N. Crossley, Catherine Jeffreys, Leigh McKinnon, and Carol J. Williams (2011)

Aribo, De musica *and* Sententiae, edited and translated by T.J.H. McCarthy (2015)

Guy of Saint-Denis, Tractatus de Tonis, edited and translated by Constant J. Mews, Carol J. Williams, John N. Crossley, and Catherine Jeffreys (2017)

Typeset in 10/13 New Baskerville
and Golden Cockerel Ornaments display

Medieval Institute Publications
College of Arts and Sciences
Western Michigan University
1903 W. Michigan Avenue
Kalamazoo, MI 49008-5432
http://www.wmich.edu/medievalpublications

 WESTERN MICHIGAN UNIVERSITY